THE R

Batt

THE ROYAL NAVY AND THE

Battle of Britain

ANTHONY J. CUMMING

NAVAL INSTITUTE PRESS
Annapolis, Maryland

Naval Institute Press
291 Wood Road
Annapolis, MD 21402

Library of Congress Cataloging-in-Publication Data

Cumming, Anthony J.
  The Royal Navy and the Battle of Britain / Anthony J. Cumming.
    p. cm.
  Includes bibliographical references and index.
  ISBN 978-1-59114-160-0 (acid-free paper) 1. Britain, Battle of, Great Britain, 1940. 2. Great Britain. Royal Navy—History—World War, 1939-1945. 3. World War, 1939-1945—England—London. 4. London (England)—History—Bombardment, 1940-1941. 5. Great Britain. Royal Air Force—History—World War, 1939-1945. 6. World War, 1939-1945—Naval operations, British. I. Title.
  D760.8.L7C86 2010
  940.54'211--dc22
                              2010021996

Printed in the United States of America on acid-free paper

14 13 12 11 10   9 8 7 6 5 4 3 2
First printing

For Sarah

Contents

Acknowledgments

I n no particular order, I wish to thank a great many individuals and organizations for helping me reach this point. Mr. Richard Kennell and his staff at the Britannia Royal Naval College, Dartmouth, allowed me every access to their wonderfully comprehensive collection of naval literature and I am grateful for their invaluable encouragement throughout. Also at Dartmouth, my gratitude goes to Dr. Ian Roberts for taking time out of his busy schedule to translate a captured German Oberkommando der Wehrmacht (OKW) document. I am also indebted to Mr. Roderick Suddaby, Keeper of the Department of Documents, Imperial War Museum, London, for arranging access to documents from the estate of the late Sir Henry Tizard and for putting me in touch with Lieutenant Commander J. A. J. Dennis of Vancouver, Canada. My grateful thanks also go to Lieutenant Commander Dennis for the invaluable benefit of his wartime experiences in the Royal Navy and for our fascinating e-mail conversations. Also at the Imperial War Museum, Jane Fish of the Film and Video Archive rendered useful assistance in copying *Why We Fight: The Battle of Britain* onto DVD for my use. Annie Pinder at the Parliamentary Archives, London, made me welcome and helped me navigate around Lord Max Beaverbrook's personal papers. I must also thank the staff of the Liddell Hart Centre for Military Archives, the Ministry of Defence Naval Historical Branch, the Churchill Archives Centre, Cambridge, the British Library and their sister archive, the National Newspaper Library, not forgetting the library staff at the Universities of Plymouth and Exeter for their patient assistance on several occasions.

I was also fortunate to enjoy the hospitality of my wife's relatives, Pamela and Gordon Burridge of Sutton, who provided far better board and lodgings than I could otherwise have hoped for during my research forays. A former member of HMS *Rodney*, Mr. Ron Babb, gave valuable insights into some important operational aspects of the Home Fleet. In a similar vein, I would also like to thank Lieutenant Colonel Eric Wakeling of the Royal Engineers' Bomb Disposal Club, who took the trouble to telephone me in response to my e-mail queries regarding German maritime bombs. The rector of Dollar Academy in Scotland, Mr. John Robertson, and the Dollar archivist, Janet Carolan, kindly sent me some important material concerning Admiral Forbes and have encouraged me throughout my research. Thanks must also go Julian-André Fink of the Militärgeshichtliches Forschungsamt, Potsdam, for replying to my detailed written questions in English.

Sidney Tyas, a former Merchant Navy gunnery officer who endured several Luftwaffe bombing attacks, kindly gave me the benefit of his wartime experiences.

I am grateful for the kind and patient support of my former PhD supervisors at Plymouth, Dr. G. H. "Harry" Bennett and Professor Kevin Jefferys. Harry and Kevin went beyond the call of duty, not just in reviewing the drafts of my original thesis but also encouraging my ultimately successful application for the Julian Corbett Prize for Research in Modern Naval History. My thanks go to them and also to my mother who helped with the correction of the text. Mention must also be made of Dr. Eric Grove of the University of Salford, whom I first met at a conference in Northampton back in 2005 and with whom I have since had a number of stimulating conversations about the Royal Navy in the Battle of Britain. I would also like to express my thanks to those who heard my paper at the University of Exeter's Maritime Conference in 2006 and who contributed their constructive comments and criticism. I am, of course, indebted to the University of Plymouth for the generous scholarship covering my fees and stipend without which it is extremely unlikely the thesis, and hence this book, would have been written.

Special thanks go to my wife who has endured countless hours of World War II television documentaries and accompanied me to conferences in the UK and United States, but especially for rescuing me from the consequences of my computing blunders that have driven us to the brink of insanity on several occasions. Finally, grateful thanks must go to Adam Kane and the staff of the Naval Institute Press for their patience and support in getting this research into print. Any mistakes that may remain in the text are entirely my own responsibility.

Abbreviations

AA	anti-aircraft guns
ABC	Admiral Andrew B. Cunningham
ACAS	Assistant Chief of Air Staff
ACNS (H)	Assistant Chief of Naval Staff (Home)
ADC	Air Defence Committee
ADGB	Air Defence of Great Britain
AI	Airborne Interception
AMSO	Air Member for Supply and Organisation, Air Council
AMT	Air Member for Training, Air Council
AOC	area officer commanding (RAF)
APS	Assistant Private Secretary
A/S	anti-submarine
BBC	British Broadcasting Corporation
BBK	Papers of Lord Beaverbrook, held in Parliamentary Archives, House of Lords, London
BEF	British Expeditionary Force
BL	British Library
CAS	Chief of Staff, Air Ministry
CH	Chain Home
CHL	Chain Home Low
CIGS	Chief of Imperial General Staff, War Office
C-in-C	commander-in-chief
CMG	Companion of the Most Distinguished Order of St. Michael and St. George
DCAS	Deputy Chief of Air Staff
DFC	Distinguished Flying Cross
DFM	Distinguished Flying Medal
DNAD	Director of Naval Air Division
DNI	Director of Naval Intelligence

DOD (H)	Director of Operations Division (Home), Royal Navy
D of P	Director of Plans
DOR	Director of Operational Requirements, RAF
DPS	Director of Personal Services
DSD	Director of Staff Duties
DSO	Distinguished Service Order
GCB	Grand Cross in the Order of the Bath
GPO	General Post Office
HAC	high-angle control (naval anti-aircraft gunnery)
HMSO	His Majesty's Stationery Office
HQ	headquarters
HTT	Papers of Sir Henry Tizard, Imperial War Museum, London
IFF	Identification of Friend and Foe
IWM	Imperial War Museum
IWM EDS	Imperial War Museum, Enemy Documents Section
KCB	Knight Commander of the Order of the Bath
LAC	low-angle control (naval anti-aircraft gunnery)
LH	Papers of Captain Basil Liddell Hart, Liddell Hart Centre for Military Archives, London
MoD	Ministry of Defence
MoD NID	Ministry of Defence, Naval Historical Branch, Papers of Naval Intelligence Division
MoI	Ministry of Information
MP	member of Parliament
NCO	non-commissioned officer(s)
NID	Naval Intelligence Division
OIC	Operational Intelligence Centre
OKH	Oberkommando des Heeres (Supreme Command of the Army)
OKW	Oberkommando der Wehrmacht (Supreme Command of the Armed Forces)
OTU	operational training unit (RAF)
PA	Parliamentary Archives, House of Lords, London
par	paragraph
PC	Panzerdurchsclags Cylindrisch (armor-piercing bomb)

PM	prime minister
RAF	Royal Air Force
RDF	Radio Direction Finding (Radar)
RN	Royal Navy
ROC	Royal Observer Corps
ROSK	Papers of Captain Stephen Roskill, Churchill Archives, Cambridge
R/T	radio/telephone communication
SAP	semi-armor-piercing
SC	Sprengbombe Cylindrisch (general-purpose bomb)
SD	Sprengbombe Dickwandig (semi-armor-piercing bomb)
SFTS	Service Flying Training School(s)
S of S	Secretary of State
SRS	Stanmore Research Section
TNA ADM	Admiralty service and operational records, held at the National Archives, Kew, United Kingdom
TNA AIR	Air Ministry service and operational records, held at the National Archives
TNA CAB	War Cabinet and Cabinets, Minutes and Papers, 1905–67, held at the National Archives
TNA FO	Foreign Office, Files of Correspondence, 1906–66, held at the National Archives
TNA INF	Ministry of Information, Files of Correspondence, 1936–50, held at the National Archives
TNA PREM	Prime Minister's Office, Files of Correspondence and Papers, 1916–42, held at the National Archives
TNA STAT	Stationery Office, Files of Correspondence, 1871–1966, held at the National Archives
USAAF	United States Army Air Forces
VC	Victoria Cross
VCAS	Vice Chief of Air Staff
VCNS	Vice Chief of Naval Staff
VCNS (H)	Vice Chief of Naval Staff (Home)
VHF	very high frequency
WAC	Written Archives Centre (BBC)
W/T	wireless telegraphy

THE ROYAL NAVY AND THE

Battle of Britain

CHAPTER ONE

Introduction

We shall fight on the beaches, we shall fight on the landing grounds, we shall fight
in the fields and in the streets, we shall fight in the hills; we shall never surrender.[1]
W. S. Churchill, Speech to House of Commons, 4 June 1940

I find it difficult to believe that the South coast is in serious danger at the present time.[2]
W. S. Churchill to Commander-in-Chief (C-in-C) Home Forces,
10 July 1940

He told me . . . he, himself, [Churchill] had never believed that invasion was possible!
To which I replied to the effect that he had camouflaged it very well. He then had a go
at me. . . . However we made it up (he had perhaps had one over the odds).[3]
Admiral Charles Forbes to Godfrey Style, 6 February 1947

These statements by Winston Churchill were made just a few weeks apart in
the crisis summer of 1940 while Admiral Forbes, C-in-C Home Fleet, wrote
his comments a few years later. The first Churchill statement was designed
to raise the nation's spirit of resistance against imminent German invasion and
gain American support; the second was to downplay the invasion threat in order
to release military resources for a "colonial war" in the Middle East while the
so-called Battle of Britain (the air fighting) had barely begun. Admiral Forbes'
remarks came from a surprise meeting with Churchill at a postwar social function. It also marked the conclusion of a little publicized strategic dispute between
the former prime minister and his most important naval commander, stemming
from Forbes' refusal of Churchill's 1940 request to bring his heavy ships south
of the Wash should the enemy armada set sail. Most importantly, the second two
quotations marked Churchill's admission that even before the anticipated German attempts to control British airspace, he had not seriously expected a German
invasion in 1940. Together they suggest Churchill had practiced a subterfuge on
his own people. Needless to say, it is only the first that echoes down the ages — a

1

reminder of the nation's glorious past and a determination to resist tyranny whatever the consequences.

Indeed, Churchill's speech of 4 June 1940 represented truly noble sentiments that remain at the heart of British national identity. Myths also have value but it is not (or should not be) the historian's job to maintain them. Broadly speaking, the story of the Battle of Britain as understood by most Britons goes something like this: Because of "gutless" pre-war politicians and equally "gutless" continental allies, Great Britain stood alone against the military colossus of Nazi Germany in 1940. In accordance with his master plan for world domination, Adolf Hitler prepared to invade the British Isles with overwhelming forces but thanks only to the determination of the prime minister, Winston Churchill, and the heroic efforts of a handful of young fighter pilots he dubbed "the few," the invasion fleet never sailed. Thus the entire world, including the United States, was saved from Nazi domination. The victory of "the few" was in denying the Luftwaffe the air supremacy required to protect their invasion fleet. It also represented the triumph of modern airpower over antiquated sea power as the British fleet was helpless in the face of air attack.

Of course, some elements of this are true, but despite the efforts of revisionists, the mythology endures because the legend of the Battle of Britain remains a story close to British hearts. The historiography covering the events of 1940 is enormous and for this study preference has been given to the revisionist histories written during the last two decades. Useful for understanding the mythology of 1940 is Angus Calder's *The Myth of the Blitz*. Calder is less of a revisionist than his reputation allows, even admitting to being more laid-back about the mythology than when he first started to write about it. Sadly, he is surely mistaken in his view that "the negative effects of the myth on British societies have almost worked themselves out." However, his account of how the American press worked with British and American propagandists to develop a heroic image of the British acceptable to U.S. opinion—a tale subsequently sold back to the British public and given the validation of an American narration—is an important contribution. Phillip Knightly's *The First Casualty Is Truth: The War Correspondent as Hero and Myth Maker from the Crimea to Kosovo* has shown the official pressures placed upon journalists to toe the official line and explained the relationship between the Ministry of Information (MoI) and the foreign press during 1940.

Geopolitical concepts outlined in naval historian Paul Kennedy's classic *The Rise and Fall of British Naval Mastery* are picked up in an illuminating revisionist text dealing with Churchill's influence on military strategy—Israeli historian T. Ben-Moshe's *Churchill: Strategy and History*. Ben-Moshe claimed that Churchill once subscribed to the prevalent ideas of "sea power" from naval theorists Alfred T. Mahan and Sir Julian Corbett. Read by influential politicians such as Kaiser Wilhelm and Presidents Theodore and Franklin Roosevelt, Mahan successfully promulgated the idea before 1914 that great power status was contingent on a powerful navy, but this notion has been much criticized since. However, maritime determinist theories underpinned the concept of the "British way" of warfare: using British wealth to fund mercenaries and coalitions to fight enemies—invariably whoever was the strongest continental power—and using the navy to protect both nation and empire while imposing economic blockade upon the enemy. A powerful navy was also intrinsically linked with the prevailing nineteenth-century notion of Liberal "free-trade." Churchill broke with this from 1911, almost certainly influenced by the geopolitics exponent Halford Mackinder, who argued in 1904 that the Columbian age of maritime-state supremacy was over. Churchill's inter-war research into his ancestor Marlborough seems to have confirmed this for him, providing convenient parallels with his disastrous Gallipoli experience. Indeed, Marlborough's eighteenth-century concept of a combination of land and sea power suited both Churchill's romantic temperament and the understandable need for justification of a disastrous campaign that was to haunt the rest of his career.

Henceforth Churchill was to argue for a strong British Expeditionary Force (BEF) as the only way to help France militarily. The clashes between Churchill and the Chamberlainites in the 1930s were less over the "criminal" lack of military preparation—as argued by Cato in *Guilty Men* in 1940—than they were over whether resources should go into a powerful navy to avoid the cost of a large land army. Ironically it was convenient for Churchill to adopt the arguments of *Guilty Men* when writing up his histories after the war. Airpower complicated the arguments as the need for a powerful air force was integral both to acceptance and rejection of a continental commitment, and Churchill was clearly annoyed that his arguments for Royal Air Force (RAF) expansion were sometimes misunderstood as promoting a maritime strategy. Nevertheless, Churchill's popularity and identification with the modern concept of airpower can only have reinforced the idea that air forces would soon supersede navies. Neville Chamberlain, whose reputation has suffered as a result of Churchill's later memoirs, was heavily influenced by Basil Liddell Hart's advocacy of a maritime-based strategy, largely because of its inherent cost-effectiveness.

If Churchill proved less of a committed navalist than his Admiralty experience or self-styled "former naval person" epithet might suggest, he used this to ingratiate himself with President Franklin D. Roosevelt, a former U.S. naval secretary and a far more consistent naval enthusiast and disciple of Mahan than Churchill ever was. A useful guide to understanding Roosevelt through his relationship with the U.S. Navy is *FDR and the U.S. Navy*, edited by Edward J. Marolda. This picture widens in J. Leutze's *Bargaining for Supremacy: Anglo-American Naval Collaboration, 1937–1941*. Both publications show how the president became progressively concerned about the rise of Nazi Germany and the erosion of the traditional Royal Navy shield that for over a hundred years had protected the United States from foreign interference. It was through Anglo-American naval contacts that American resistance to German expansionism first manifested itself in a practical way. FDR's reaction to Churchill's later inept manipulation of American fears about the fate of the British fleet in the event of capitulation is well documented here.

Churchill's manipulations and outright meddling also proved detrimental to the conduct of some early military campaigns. A spirited defense of Sir Charles Morton Forbes, leader of the Home Fleet, had been mounted by James Levy in "Lost Leader: Admiral of the Fleet Sir Charles Forbes and the Second World War" (published in *The Mariner's Mirror*, the journal of the Society for Nautical Research). Levy shows that although Forbes was responsible for crippling the Kriegsmarine's surface fleet during the Norway campaign, his reputation has suffered unduly because of intelligence failures and operational interference both from Churchill and First Sea Lord Dudley Pound. These were beyond Forbes' control and neither Churchill nor Pound was disposed to listen to his sound tactical advice on matters of ship dispositions during or after the Norwegian campaign. Had the invasion of Britain been launched, Forbes' skills as a commander might have proved crucial, yet he is relatively unknown outside naval circles. Unfortunately, bearing in mind that Forbes held many key naval posts in the interwar period, Levy's article has thrown little light on his precise contribution to the development of the wartime Royal Navy.

Forbes' approximate counterpart in the Royal Air Force was Sir Hugh Dowding, a man whose name and reputation is far more widely known. Utilizing his PhD thesis on aspects of the Battle of Britain, John Ray took an insightful look explaining the "behind the scenes battle" in his book *Battle of Britain: New Perspectives*. This included the "big-wing" debate that prejudiced the RAF's survival and attacked the widely held perception that Dowding's summary dismissal was merely the outcome of a dastardly plot by "big-wing" proponents. Ray also defended Churchill for his perceived failure to protect Dowding from his critics, concluding that Dowding's faults had contributed to his dismissal. Many of these points tend to contradict the portrait of Dowding as a "tactical genius" as earlier projected by Dowding's former aide, Robert Wright, in *Dowding and the Battle of Britain* and taken up by newspaper writers during the Battle of Britain's sixtieth anniversary celebrations in 2000. One of these articles claimed Dowding's system of combining new Radio Direction Finding (RDF) technology with a complex command and control system worked as Dowding "dreamed" it would. The best monograph for understanding this specialized topic is D. Zimmermann's *Britain's Shield: Radar and the Defeat of the Luftwaffe*. This monograph analyzed the political and technical factors that lay behind the development of this technology but, perhaps subconsciously influenced by "core" histories and strong popular perceptions, it did not give the evidence highlighting the limitations of the equipment and operatives much emphasis.

If the standard of writing on twentieth-century warfare has deteriorated as a result of massive commercial demand then nowhere is this more apparent than in the literature relating to the operational history of the Battle of Britain in the air. The official story was first published during wartime by His Majesty's Stationery Office (HMSO) in the pamphlet *The Battle of Britain* and was criticized by none other than Lord Dowding for its assertion that "the fighter squadrons of the Royal Air Force . . . were indeed stronger at the end of the battle than at the beginning"; Dowding remarked that "whatever the paper return showed, the situation toward the end was extremely critical and most squadrons were fit only for operations against unescorted bombers."[4] The most inspiring study is still Wing Commander H. R. "Dizzy" Allen's controversial *Who Won the Battle of Britain?* For his critics, the nickname "Dizzy" reflected Allen's wilder ideas rather than his ability to spin a fighter. In his book, first published in 1974, Allen severely criticized the inter-war Air Staff decision-makers but was in turn savaged by Francis Mason in an influential defense journal. Nevertheless, Allen's indictments were often damning, especially those relating to RAF inflexibility and inadequate gunnery training. His charges ran contrary to statements such as that made by H. Montgomery Hyde in his book *British Air Policy between the Wars, 1918–1939*, which praised the "superb quality of the Royal Air Force."[5] Yet Allen's observations were made in considerable detail and carried special authority from a Battle of Britain ace of 66 Squadron and who later became its squadron commander. Today there is greater academic consensus that Fighter Command's position was not as disadvantageous relative to the Luftwaffe as once supposed. The weight of modern academic writing shows the Luftwaffe performed well in the circumstances and the Kriegsmarine faced massive problems in launching a successful invasion in 1940. This is best shown in Paul Addison and Jeremy Crang's *The Burning Blue*, a collection of more modern perspectives commemorating the Battle of Britain's sixtieth anniversary in 2000. Here, German writers Klaus Maier and Horst Boog argued that Germany's rapid and unexpected victories in France, Belgium, and Holland left the Wehrmacht ready for neither seaborne invasion nor airborne assault. Sebastian Cox maintained his view that the RAF was near to collapse before the Luftwaffe focused on London during September, and Richard Overy pointed out that the battle was essential for British self-esteem, vital for maintaining the wider conflict.

For an understanding of the ability of Royal Navy warships and crews to resist the attentions of the Luftwaffe, Ronald Spector's *At War at Sea: Sailors and Warfare in the Twentieth Century* is a comparatively recent publication embracing the "new methodologies." Spector used oral history to great advantage in describing the experiences and stoicism of British sailors under fire from the Luftwaffe around Crete and protected by an inadequate anti-aircraft defense—a situation with many parallels to that in UK waters during 1940. *A Sailor's Odyssey*, the memoir of Britain's most successful sailor of the period, Viscount Andrew B. Cunningham, is particularly valuable for his experience of commanding a fleet against massive and repeated air attack. Despite having been written in 1970, Vice Admiral Arthur Hezlet's *Aircraft and Sea Power* remains an influential work on operations involving the interaction of sea and airpower during World War II. Hezlet's arguments that the system of flotilla defense was probably unworkable and that the Home Fleet would have suffered more extensively in an invasion scenario than it later did at Crete are powerful and misleading arguments that will be challenged in this study. One of the best American authors is Jon Tetsuro Sumida, outspoken exponent of new methodologies and master of technical and tactical detail on matters relating to the twentieth-century Royal Navy. Sumida's 1992 article, "The Best Laid Plans: The Development of British Battle-Fleet Tactics, 1919–1942" in *The International History Review* contradicted earlier works including a radical book by Correlli Barnett, *Engage the Enemy More Closely: The Royal Navy in the Second World War*, and E. Ranson's *British Defence Policy and Appeasement between the Wars, 1919–1939*. Sumida argued powerfully that the Royal Navy's leadership was not unduly influenced by its experience at the Battle of Jutland in 1916, which supposedly led to technical stagnation and slavish adherence to the line-of-battle concept. In fact, technology and tactics were radically revised throughout the inter-war period. The primacy of the capital ship was a logical and justifiable response to the circumstances of the day, bearing in mind the power balance with competing foreign navies and the difficulty of anticipating whether the gun or the airplane would dominate future wars. Sumida blamed the strong market demand for military history for a decline in writing standards, which perpetuates the myth-making inherent in much twentieth-century military publication. Signs that some popular views are beginning to change are shown by Derek Robinson's *Invasion, 1940*, published in 2005, in which he rightly concludes the Royal Navy won the Battle of Britain. However, their "silent victory" was not likely to sufficiently motivate the United States to throw its vast industrial and military might behind Great Britain and this was why the RAF was hailed as the victor. Robinson is a good example of the fiction writer–turned–historian species but unfortunately the book lacks the authority of substantial primary source material for academic historians to take it as seriously as it deserves.

Probably the best book dealing with the German invasion plan entitled Operation Sea Lion is German historian Peter Schenk's *Invasion of England 1940*, which contains a considerable amount of technical detail relating to proposed logistics, minefields, and landing craft. Although many important German documents were destroyed, Grand Admiral Karl Doenitz defied Hitler's orders and kept intact the records of the German Naval Staff, some of which were published with a foreword by J. P. Mallman Showell as *Fuehrer Conferences on Naval Affairs, 1939–1945*. This collection covers Operation Sea Lion in the form of conference notes made by Grand Admiral Erich Raeder and Grand Admiral Doenitz. Clues to Hitler's thinking are contained together with operational details relating to the preparations. Supplementing this further are Raeder's memoirs, *My Life*. Though much criticized for its dishonesty, it also represents the viewpoint of the man with overall naval responsibility for the success of Operation Sea Lion. Admiral Kurt

Assman's membership of the 1940 German Naval Staff makes his article in the United States Naval Institute's *Proceedings*, published in 1950, an essential guide to German military thinking during 1940.

With the contributions of these and other authors in mind, I have attacked areas of the "finest hour" mythology, endeavoring to throw new light on the manipulation of events between May and October 1940. Such manipulation was made in order to convince the British public that the nation *must* continue the armed struggle against Germany and that the United States should continue its essential support. The book will help to explain why, after centuries of holding a special place in the affection of the British public, the Royal Navy lost out to the RAF as the main perceived bulwark against foreign domination. In the course of this it will be shown that the Royal Navy was actually no less effective an organization than the RAF. The British fighter pilots fought with great courage and determination but problems within the RAF's infrastructure significantly limited their impact. In particular, criticisms are made that Fighter Command was over-reliant on inadequately tested new technology and that both were less effective than generally perceived. By looking at the state of morale in the Home Fleet and examining actions in which British warships were exposed to Luftwaffe attack, it will be seen that the Royal Navy was far more robust in the face of air attack than usually assumed. The situation from "the other side of the hill," with particular regard to the true significance of the Battle of Britain and the operational difficulties of mounting an invasion, is also emphasized more than in traditional accounts. A consequence of scrutinizing the careers of Admiral Sir Charles Forbes and Air Marshal Sir Hugh Dowding should be the revision of their relative positions in Britain's pantheon of national heroes. In this connection, this study is distinctive in its inclusion of evidence showing how ineffectually academic revisionists have influenced popular writing. Extensive use has been made of primary-source evidence in British archives. Most of this evidence has been widely accessible for many years but given little emphasis because it does not sit comfortably with the popular legend. The book commences with an examination of German political, military, and strategic perspectives in order to discover the real reasons why an invasion was never launched.

CHAPTER TWO

We Can't Simply Swim Over!

Not one of the responsible persons was inclined to take a clear-cut stand against the operation. . . . Yet all felt relieved when, failing to gain air supremacy, they had a valid reason which justified calling off the operation.[1]

Vice Admiral K. Assman, German Naval Staff

The popular concept of Britain's "finest hour" rests heavily on a number of assumptions not necessarily shared by former members of Germany's wartime forces. For instance, Luftwaffe air ace Adolf Galland's most publicized allegation is that there never was a Battle of Britain as such.[2] For him, the Battle of Britain was the Battle *for* Britain—the invasion battle that was never fought. Indeed, it is not "academic" writing in its highest form likely to have the greatest impact on British perceptions. A popular biography written for British schoolchildren in a semi-comic strip format blandly asserts that "[i]f the German Army crossed the Channel by barge they would be sitting ducks for the British RAF to swoop down and bomb them,"[3] which takes no account of Bomber Command's inability to hit small targets and the fact that the initial German crossing was to be made in darkness.

Most authors have placed great emphasis on the need for German air superiority. However, a major point of contention for several Germans is that the Luftwaffe, even with air superiority, could not overcome the Royal Navy.[4] Admiral Raeder's published conference notes, his later published memoirs, Vice Admiral Kurt Assman's postwar writing, and a synthesis of captured German documents that Assman helped to prepare for the British Naval Intelligence Division indicate how the Germans really viewed the significance of air superiority. In fact, the supposed vulnerability of the British Isles to German airborne assault between 9 and 15 July 1940 was argued in 1980,[5] and given further prominence in the British press during 2000.[6] Most German figures deny such an assault could have been mounted at this time and even the British Air Ministry's evaluation of the prospects of enemy glider-borne attack in 1940 tends to bear this out.

Certainly, the attitudes of the leading German admirals maintaining that Hitler had always desired an accommodation with Great Britain are very important. Hitler's desire for a deal during 1940 is plain, for military pragmatism alone dictated the necessity. There is little point in raking over the evidence of *Mein Kampf* or the so-called *Hossbach Memorandum*, which historians have thoroughly dissected without producing overwhelming consensus as to their significance. Anti-British remarks made for public consumption or in the heat of the moment tell us very little about Hitler's fundamental attitude. A comparatively neglected German source for reexamining British assumptions is the essays of German admirals written in the aftermath of defeat at the behest of the British Naval Intelligence Division. Although somewhat hastily translated, they have the advantage of being written while the events were still relatively fresh in mind, mainly from memory and without the possible distortions arising from access to other records and editing by former colleagues. Furthermore, the admirals do not agree on everything, yet their attitudes toward Operation Sea Lion and their opinions of German intentions toward "England" are remarkably consistent. This is not to say they were untainted by "the need to produce a new narrative of defeat that Admiral Doenitz had identified in May 1945."[7] Yet such "corruption" was likely to have been less than in later memoirs, where figures convicted of war crimes had more time to provide justifications for faithfully serving a regime the world now rightly condemned as evil. Even so, the memoirs of Doenitz and Raeder on Operation Sea Lion were consistent with the views of colleagues expressed in the immediate aftermath of defeat. All of these figures preferred the West to contemplate the present "dangers" of Soviet communism rather than dwell on past German crimes, but no reasonable motive for distorting Hitler's attitudes to Britain can be divined. In addition to these sources, the National Archives holds a report from the British prewar naval attaché in Berlin revealing the powerful impact of retired Vice Admiral Wolfgang Wegener on the Fuehrer. The perceived influence of Wegener's book *Seestrategie des Weltkrieges* (The Naval Strategy of the World War), described as Hitler's "sea-gospel," is a source rarely taken into account.

The most important German perception was the importance of air supremacy to the successful implementation of the final plan. In fact, the German Naval Staff seriously doubted that air supremacy would be enough to make an invasion of England possible and hoped the Luftwaffe would fail. Suspicions over the true feelings of these officers may have contributed to Hitler's later orders to Vice Admiral Kurt Assman to investigate whether he had been deceived over the viability of Operation Sea Lion. Assman's report got the naval officers off the hook but his later reflections confirmed a sense of relief among the 1940 Naval Staff, who were thankful they did not have to put the invasion into practice. His later report for British Naval Intelligence stated that the "Naval Staff also appreciated clearly that air supremacy alone could not provide permanent security against vastly superior enemy naval forces in the crossing area."[8]

The reason that the air supremacy factor was written into Hitler's directives can be put down to the enormous operational difficulties faced by the German Naval Staff in mounting an invasion at short notice without the benefit of specialized landing equipment and sufficient warships to protect the transports. According to his memoirs it was Grand Admiral Erich Raeder who put the idea to Hitler on 21 May 1940, a date well before the French capitulation and before the evacuation from Dunkirk. The commentary in *Fuehrer Conferences* indicates that the meeting was a private one following a routine discussion with other leaders on various matters.[9] Raeder and Hitler were to discuss the navy's contingency plan for invasion drawn up in November 1939 but it appears that Raeder did most of the talking. His motive was to prepare Hitler's mind for the "impossible tasks" that invasion would entail, bearing in mind the likelihood that some "irresponsible" person would use the strikingly successful invasion of Norway as a precedent. Raeder's involvement in this campaign and subsequent Nuremberg conviction for "waging aggressive war" meant that the account of his advice to Hitler was defensive. While there is room for some skepticism regarding his motives for raising the matter, it is hard to seriously dispute the truth of this. Hitler was told the Luftwaffe would have to defeat the RAF and inflict enough damage on the British fleet to keep it away from the landing areas. Raeder emphasized the economic consequences of diverting the huge amounts of shipping required for the task and would certainly have explained the differences between landing in Norway and England. In other words the Norwegian landings involved placing troops in fast passenger liners, dashing across the docile Baltic Sea and through the Denmark Gate, evading the British fleet, and seizing lightly defended harbors using all the advantages of surprise. Hitler listened without comment and ordered no preparations be made yet.[10]

Events moved quickly from this point. The British Admiralty ordered the Dunkirk evacuation on 26 May 1940 and the *German Naval High Command War Diary* entries for 30 and 31 May paid tribute to the resistance of Anglo-French troops holding the Dunkirk perimeter. It predicted the success of the British operation in getting "a considerable part of their troops to England." Admiral Otto Schniewind had already warned the Luftwaffe that the German navy could not prevent this, presumably because the German surface fleet was seriously weakened and the remnants were still engaged around Norway where the Home Fleet was disrupting German sea communications.[11] With the French armistice request under discussion by 20 June, the question of England was bound to assume increased importance and Raeder reported to Hitler the progress of invasion preparations. This seemingly defied Hitler's earlier order not to make preparations but might be explained by clumsy drafting or imprecise translation if Raeder was only referring to contingency plans made the previous November. Raeder must have been dismayed to find that the invasion of England was now the subject for a directive. This, Raeder implied, was the result of a sudden interest by the Oberkommando der Wehrmacht (OKW), or more specifically the army—Oberkommando des Heeres (OKH).[12]

The directive of 7 July 1940 was cautious in tone, mentioning air superiority and other "necessary conditions" with no date for launching. After all, it was "still only a plan."[13] The report to Hitler on 11 July 1940 indicated agreement that invasion would be a "last resort" and economic warfare using submarines and air attacks on ports and convoys would be the best means of forcing Britain to ask for peace.[14] Faced with bullish optimism from the army representatives and no formal response from Britain to peace overtures, Hitler was clearly thinking a show of intent was now needed.

Thus far, Raeder had not quite impressed upon Hitler the impossibility of landing troops and equipment on a wide front. This became the nub of a series of acrimonious arguments regarding the landing site. With good reason, the German navy felt that only the Dover Straits could be provided with adequate sea and air defenses to cover the transports. Conversely, the German army felt landing on such a narrow front meant the British would find it too easy to concentrate their land forces in defense. The influence of the army can be observed in the next directive (no. 16) issued on 16 July 1940. This stated that S-day (D-day) was to be any time from 15 August 1940 and reflected army lobbying for a broad front from Ramsgate to an undefined point west of the Isle of Wight.[15] Two days earlier, General Franz Ritter von Halder and Field Marshal Walther von Brauchitsch had given Hitler an invasion plan that was approved after minimal scrutiny and a lengthy exposition as to why he did not want to destroy England in any military sense. With the British Empire shattered, the United States and Japan would pick up the pieces but Germany would gain nothing.[16] Hitler was actually being indecisive, but remained driven by the need to appear in complete control of all situations.

Whether Raeder completely appreciated his leader's position is unclear but it would have been irresponsible not to reacquaint Hitler with the operational problems. Raeder no doubt recalled the difficulties that Napoleon's minister of marine, Denis Decrès, experienced in having to patiently explain the situation to a skeptical (and sometimes volatile) audience with no nautical awareness. Over a century before, Decrès had told Napoleon why navies cannot be easily subordinated to mechanical timetabling independent of moon and tide and how the Channel had violent characteristics altogether different from inland waterways.

Raeder forcefully reiterated his arguments to Hitler in a memorandum sent via the Naval Staff on 19 July 1940, the day the German implicit peace offer was made before the Reichstag. This internationally reported speech by Hitler stated there was no reason why the war should continue between Germany and Great Britain but the "offer" was rejected by a BBC spokesman later that day. The operational difficulties likely to have been in the back of Hitler's mind as he made the speech were manifold. Firstly, the troops must be transported from inadequate or war-damaged harbors, installations, and adjoining canal systems. Furthermore, the army's plan involves landing on a particularly difficult part of the Channel with regard to weather, tides, and rough seas. Strongly defended harbors mean the initial waves of troops must land on beaches with complications from swells, currents, and tides. Also, the enemy can mine the coast; the position of such minefields cannot be determined day-to-day. With regard to the Kriegsmarine's air supremacy requirement, the Fuehrer had been told that German shipping has to operate in a restricted sea area and the Royal Navy will treat the situation as life-or-death and throw all their resources into combat. Weather uncertainty alone means the Luftwaffe cannot guarantee keeping the enemy fleet away. In any case, German minefields flanking the crossing zone must supplement the Luftwaffe efforts, but as minefields are not absolute barriers, the enemy may cut the supply line of the first wave. Finally, despite previous Luftwaffe success in negating enemy installations, the enemy has made long-term preparations and the lack of conventional artillery support makes German ability to disable coastal defenses doubtful.[17]

Neither Raeder nor Hitler would have known about Admiral Forbes' refusal to Churchill regarding bringing the Home Fleet south of the Wash "under any circumstances." General Hastings Ismay wrote that Churchill, from whom everyone expected apoplexy, kept his temper, spoke indulgently, and refused to believe Forbes.[18] It seems unlikely that Forbes was serious but in any case Raeder was right to be concerned about the proximity of substantial British naval forces based at Plymouth, Portsmouth, and the Nore. He was also rightly concerned about the German bases as many were still badly damaged. Zeebrugge was essentially out of action until November 1940, but Dunkirk was in service after only a "few months," with Calais and Boulogne operable from mid-September.[19] The harbors' geography was as important as their state of repair. According to General Gunther Blumentritt, who represented Field Marshal Karl von Rundstedt at Sea Lion conferences, the only harbors large enough for loading the essential panzer divisions in the short embarkation timetable were within the Antwerp area. Given the landing area along the Kent and Sussex coast, these transports, he believed, were particularly vulnerable on the long "flank-march" with the inadequate naval protection available.

Neither did Blumentritt consider the flanking minefields effective, noting that the Germans lacked "sufficient mines for viable barriers and every eight to fourteen days the mines would break away and need replacing."[20] Vice Admiral Friedrich Ruge, a former C-in-C Minesweepers West, later noted that the "flanks were poorly guarded" and could "provide only partial protection because of the strong tides and the big rise and fall," meaning the British would be able to steam over the top at high tide.[21] The main purpose of the mine barriers was to allow time for subsequent landings of troops and equipment, but as Field Marshal von Rundstedt later remarked to historian Basil Liddell Hart: "While the leading part of the forces might have landed, there was the danger that they might be cut off from supplies and reinforcements."[22] As all the naval figures knew, even if the barriers had been stronger, there was nothing that would have prevented interdicting British naval forces from steaming forward in line ahead, thus placing the burden of risk upon the leading warship in the line.

Ruge clarified the tidal current problems anticipated in the Channel by explaining the effect on the proposed barge convoys. These convoys comprised mainly unpowered craft needing tugboats that could make up to three knots in speed. Unfortunately, these were likely to meet currents of up to five knots, but assuming these could be avoided, Ruge estimated the convoys would need to travel forty or fifty miles taking a minimum of fifteen hours. As he correctly surmised, any advantage of surprise would have been lost, bearing in mind the large assortment of small craft that had been posted by the British in the Channel to watch for any unusual activity.[23] However, something was being done to offset the lack of conventional artillery supporting the operation, as pointed out by Raeder. The coastal batteries Grosser Kurfürst, Friedrich August, and Siegfried, with guns ranging from 28 cm to 38 cm, were being installed at the narrow end of the Channel to bombard Dover and contest the movement of shipping through the shallows. These would prove ineffective against shipping and were inferior to the later K5 railway guns installed in the Calais area. Ruge pointed out that the British could counter the German guns by concentrating their medium and heavy artillery in the threatened areas as well as installing their own heavy gun emplacements using guns from older warships.[24] Ultimately, this was done, although the British Winnie and Pooh batteries were even less effective for anti-shipping purposes than the German ones.

There is no reason to suppose that Hitler had the expertise to argue against Raeder's points and there is no indication that he made any serious attempt to do so. Instead he refereed the ongoing feud between the army and navy in the sort of "hands off" management style that might be used when there is uncertainty on how to proceed. Raeder's influence on Hitler was clearly discernable at the next conference on 21 July 1940. Hitler summed up the "hopelessness" of the British long-term position, but also spelled out much of what he had been told, stating that the invasion of Britain was "an exceptionally daring undertaking" not a river crossing, and it lacked the degree of surprise that had characterized the Norwegian expedition. Because of the unreliability of the weather, the operation would need to be executed by 15 September to facilitate the "essential" factor of air cooperation. In what can clearly be regarded as a further admission that the operation was not definite, he demanded that preparations be completed by early September, otherwise "other plans" would be considered.[25]

On 25 July 1940, Raeder met Hitler and senior army officers to discuss their requirements of the Kriegsmarine. The heavy gun batteries were to be ready for 15 August 1940 except for the heaviest 38-cm gun battery, which would not be ready until mid-September because of the need to construct concrete air defense shelters. Raeder needed these guns working as soon as possible in order to try and close the Straits of Dover to British shipping and provide cover for his mine-sweepers. He stressed the navy's inability to finalize its own preparations before mid-September and the gulf that still existed between the army and navy regarding the size of the invasion force and width of the landing area. The need for air supremacy was again stressed though the Luftwaffe had yet to make its major effort, contenting itself with attacking shipping while its resources were being concentrated behind the French, Dutch, and Belgian coasts. No doubt trying to dampen enthusiasm, Raeder pointed out the consequences to the economies of occupied Europe of having to commandeer and convert some three thousand miscellaneous craft, mainly from inland waterways, to meet the army's transport needs. They were still demanding 260,000 men transported—less than half their original requirement but still needing a broad front. While probably aware of the unacceptability of their proposals, the naval planners were insisting the landings should only take place around Dover but Raeder was undoubtedly hoping to bargain for something more workable.[26] He later conceded the army's demands were justifiable but he could easily prove the navy's inability to provide the necessary shipping.[27] Hitler was usually happy for subordinates to compete for his favor but the acrimony developing between his service chiefs was now becoming increasingly difficult to manage.

The naval difficulties were repeated to Hitler and the army again on 1 August 1940. The earliest date for Operation Sea Lion was recommended as 15 September 1940 although Raeder gave his personal preference as May 1941. The barge conversion program was due for completion by the end of August prior to stationing in harbors for mid-September. Shortages of merchant shipping were also reported due to mine losses in the Norwegian campaign and ice damage during the winter.[28] Skilled personnel for manning the transports were also urgently required. Minesweeping had begun but could only be carried out in earnest once air superiority had been gained, and this would be needed for two weeks. In response to a question about likely weather conditions, Hitler was told the North Sea was usually inclement around 20 September but satisfactory around the end of the month. Fog would probably be light in mid-October but heavy at the end of the month. In reality, conditions around the English coast have never been mechanically predictable and were based on Raeder's "gut-feeling" and guesswork.

The Kriegsmarine's complicated timetabling for the operation was now further justified by Raeder. First, he said, the safest time for unloading would be two hours following high tide, otherwise having to land at low tide would mean grounded vessels refloating prematurely. Conversely, landing at high tide would mean craft stuck on the beach for long periods waiting for a tide that may not refloat them. He pointed out that no point within a rising tide is useful since beached vessels will then refloat quickly, disrupting unloading. As the army required a dawn landing thirty to sixty minutes before sunrise, landing craft would have to cross in darkness. This meant that hard to maneuver transports with limited room to navigate would need the light of a rising half-moon at 2300. The best periods for this would be 20–26 August or 19–26 September, but August would be too soon. Early dawn carried the danger of interception from enemy units in the Firth of Forth and other locations, which would have left their bases the previous evening and entered the Channel unobserved by early morning. If a crossing by day had not been ruled out by these factors it would have allowed an opportunity for reconnaissance, meaning the operation could be aborted if necessary. Raeder went on to explain that good weather would be crucial, as only a calm sea would allow beaching without rock or ground damage endangering the loads. Also, heavy seas would prevent the transfer of cargo between steamers and barges. But favorable weather in the opening stages would not guarantee the same conditions for succeeding landing waves, as the intervals would be lengthy. This meant that harbors had to be taken quickly to unload cargoes otherwise no worthwhile quantities could cross for several days. Raeder also explained that the wide-front crossing from the Straits of Dover to Lyme Bay meant that Le Havre and Cherbourg transports would be running unescorted near the major British naval bases at Plymouth and Portsmouth. Attrition from the air would not stop numerous destroyers and motorboats intervening. In his view, given full operational readiness by the British, the risk to steamers off the enemy coast for thirty-six hours would be unjustifiable.[29] He wound up by highlighting the Luftwaffe's difficulty in supporting a landing in three locations. He still thought May 1941 would be the best date from an operational perspective but he continued to work toward 15 September 1940, although this would depend on the forthcoming air offensive. The directive issued through Field Marshal Wilhelm Keitel the next day overrode the navy's broad-front objection but the Naval Staff continued to object, driving General Halder to state dramatically, "I might just as well put the troops that have been landed through the sausage machine!"[30]

The navy C-in-C now tried to put Hitler on the spot by asking him to adjudicate on 13 August 1940. Again it was agreed that invasion should only be a last resort "if Britain cannot be made to sue for peace in any other way." Both men recognized the consequences of failure in terms of increased British prestige. Repelling a German invasion would stiffen British resolve and increase support from the United States. Clearly stalling for time, Hitler said he needed to talk with the army C-in-C to discuss how crucial the broad-front factor was to him. Raeder noted the British were thought to have regained much of their equilibrium on land, with estimates running at 1.5 million men under arms—including 300,000 Dunkirk veterans plus 150,000 others, all of whom had been rearmed. The last item to be discussed was the manufacturing priority of torpedoes. Higher consumption resulting from the use of Lorient as a base was hammering British merchant shipping despite a high proportion of torpedo failures.[31] Another reason for the U-boat successes, but not mentioned at the meeting, was that many potential

British escorts were tied up in anti-invasion duties instead of trade protection, but Raeder was undoubtedly concerned with building up the viability of dealing with England by "other means" in Hitler's mind.

Inevitably perhaps, Hitler had to force a compromise on his staffs by issuing a directive dated 16 August 1940 stating: "Main crossing to be on a narrow front, simultaneous landing of four to five thousand troops at Brighton by motor boats and the same number of airborne troops at Deal–Ramsgate. In addition on D-1 day, the Luftwaffe is to make a strong attack on London, which would cause the population to flee from the city and block the roads."[32]

Despite the Fuehrer's efforts, the bickering continued, mainly over whether Brighton was to be a diversionary or the principal landing point. The final plan involved dawn landings at Folkestone–Dungeness, Dungeness–Cliff's End, Bexhill–Beachy Head, and Brighton–Selsey Bill. A line from the Thames to Southampton represented the first operational objective for the army. A diversionary operation, Autumn Mist (Herbstreisse) involved the deployment of the heavy cruiser *Hipper* with three other cruisers and four transports from Norway to an area between Aberdeen and Newcastle followed by a planned withdrawal to the Kattegat. The battleship *Scheer* would also break out to the Atlantic to commerce-raid and provide a further diversion. Other diversions would also be made in the direction of Iceland.[33]

On the surface, this plan appeared to be acceptable to both services but it is more likely, however, that cooperation was achieved largely because those principally involved had already observed Hitler's lack of enthusiasm and did not expect to have to go through with it.[34] On 20 August 1940, one week before final decisions on the landing points were made, a written briefing appearing to come from Hitler's headquarters to Wirtschafts und Rüstungsamt (Department for Economy and Armament) of the OKW advised that England's defeat in 1940 could "no longer be assumed." Doubts had already been expressed at the end of July over the planned peacetime restructuring of the army, and by 2 August 1940 the "Fuehrer was now seeing things differently and that we should prepare ourselves for any conceivable political situation that might arise in 1941."[35] Herbert Doering, Hitler's Berghoff manager, has explained how the Fuehrer and his generals had penciled in lines of attack over maps of the USSR during August, and left them for Doering to clear up.[36] Operation Barbarossa was now competing with Operation Sea Lion for Hitler's attention.

According to information gained from the postwar interrogations of German military commanders by Basil Liddell Hart, the chance of a successful airborne operation diminished around the end of August. General Richard Putzier, who had temporarily replaced the wounded General Kurt Student as commander of the airborne forces, was to seize a twenty-mile zone near Folkestone and was keeping the designated fields under observation. By the end of the month these were fitted with anti-landing vertical stakes and it was presumed the fields were mined.[37] This can only have supported German Naval Staff perceptions that the British anticipated the plan. Prospects for gaining air superiority looked better now that the Luftwaffe had commenced operations against RAF airfields in earnest. However, faulty intelligence meant "the effect of the air attacks was generally over-estimated in Germany," allowing the Naval Staff "to be influenced . . . by these exaggerated hopes"—or so it was claimed.[38] It was almost impossible for Luftwaffe intelligence sources to gain an accurate picture. Fighter pilots of all nations tend to over-claim, and lacking a reliable network of agents the Germans were not as well placed as the British, who could in theory count the wrecks. There was also no way of knowing how long a bombed airfield would remain unoperational. Craters could be quickly filled with rubble and personnel re-housed in tents or boarded out with civilians. The Germans could only assess the strength of the fighter opposition each time their bombers crossed into English air space, and by the beginning of September they sensed correctly that the fighter defense was weakening.[39]

Another problem was the British Fighter Command's evasion of the German fighter sweeps. The solution, proposed by Luftwaffe General Paul Deichmann, was to throw the weight of future attacks against London. He argued that London was so important to the British they would have to commit their entire fighter resource to defend it. Deichmann later complained that when the suggestion was first mooted, Hitler would not hear of it.[40] According to Nicolaus von Below, Hitler's Luftwaffe adjutant, this was because of the risk of British retaliation against Germany.[41] This is important because so many writers blame the change of focus from bombing the British airfields to bombing London as revenge for earlier RAF attacks on Berlin, and even the radical Allen considered this to be a "fateful error of judgment," without properly analyzing the German dilemmas.[42] This nuisance bombing was an irritation but it is doubtful if the relatively slight damage inflicted on Berlin on the night of 25–26 August 1940 seriously inflamed Hitler's emotions. Hitler's tantrums were usually invoked for the purpose of political manipulation and it should not be assumed that Hitler's military decisions were irrationally based. Possibly, as the director of Naval Intelligence's synthesis of captured German documents showed, "[the bombing of Berlin] hastened the plan for reprisal attacks on London."[43] Quite possibly the minimal damage to Berlin encouraged Hitler to believe Germany was safe from effective reprisal.

If, toward the end of August, Hitler had given up hope of imminent peace with England, either by threat of or by actual invasion, then he required a political excuse for action that suited both the military situation and the political object of negating England as a hostile power. Douhet's bombing theory indicated that bombing London had the potential for forcing England to the negotiating table. It is not controversial to assert that the idea of heavy conventional bombing against civilians was then universally regarded with such terror as to make it comparable with the possibility of nuclear destruction during the Cold War era.[44] This course suggested that destruction of the RAF and mass psychosis inflicted on London's population would be enough to bring down the Churchill coalition. If these aims could be achieved, then Hitler's overriding objective would be attained. That this bombing theory subsequently proved erroneous has little bearing on what was then widely believed. Hitler knew that an unsuccessful invasion would entail the prospect of thousands of German troops drowning in the Channel or, even worse, British newsreel shots of an endless line of German prisoners being marched down Whitehall, shattering the recent myths of German invincibility and his own infallibility. It might even embolden the Soviet Union to make aggressive moves in the east. Even if an invasion succeeded, the British government and the Royal Navy could still operate from Canada and, according to Hitler's own logic, the subsequent weakening of the British Empire would assist future rivals and adversaries.

The Naval Staff believed that Luftwaffe chief Herman Goering was so confident that an air offensive of this nature would succeed that he took no interest in the plans for Sea Lion.[45] Authors such as Allen believe the Naval Staff were using Goering's ego to get themselves off the hook.[46] There is some truth in this but Goering's over-developed ego does not explain everything. It is also a mistake to underestimate Herman Goering. He had shown sufficient ability as a young man to command the elite Richthofen Jagdgeschwader I (JG1) in 1918 and though only an *oberleutnant* (lieutenant) he was effectively an acting wing commander. As a recipient of the *Pour le Mérite* (Blue Max) military order—an equivalent of the Victoria Cross—with a score of twenty-two destroyed allied aircraft he did not lack physical courage, although most accounts suggest he was unpopular with his subordinates in JG1. Goering may not have kept up to date with technological developments but he must have known the broad limitations of the Luftwaffe in dealing with the Royal Navy. He had encouraged the development of the Luftwaffe as a tactical air arm and that decision had paid off in terms of the successful land campaigns. There had been no reason for a continental air force to prepare for a major maritime role. An airman of his experience would also have appreciated the difficulties of operating in bad weather. His air fleet commanders, particularly the capable Albert Kesselring, would have told him they did not relish the prospect of facing the Home Fleet, meaning there was little option now but to attempt strategic bombing.[47] These factors make the shift in focus toward an all-out assault on London a logical decision at the time, and it can only be seen as erroneous with hindsight. Hitler now needed time for the bombing to show results and his hesitancy during September is further explained by the need to maintain the threat of invasion. Not only was this necessary to pressurize the British but to maintain face in front of his generals with whom he always had a difficult relationship.

By mid-September, there was no sign of the Luftwaffe diverting its attacks toward warships and coastal defenses or anything connected with Operation Sea Lion. Raeder noted that Hitler had gone along with Goering and both were clearly focused on forcing Britain into negotiations without risking an invasion. Raeder told Hitler on 6 September that minesweeping in the Channel had commenced but owing partly to the air situation was now behind schedule. Tactfully, he did not criticize the Luftwaffe and still described the operation as "possible" but heavily qualified this with the conditions of air supremacy and favorable weather. Significantly, this meeting appears to have given more time to discussing U-boat operations in the Atlantic, suggesting more reliance was now being placed upon a naval blockade of Britain. Another major topic was "the problem of the USA" in relation to signs of increased American support for the British, including a deal to supply fifty destroyers, an event recognized as increasing future Anglo-American co-operation.[48] The sixth of September was also the day the Luftwaffe launched its first heavy bombing raid on London. Hitler was expected to give the order for S-day (D-day) on 11 September 1940, bearing in mind ten days were needed to implement the decision. The previous day the Naval Staff reported a weakening of the RAF fighter defense and that it could be taken for granted that "the German forces have considerable fighter superiority over the English area." This was not enough for the Naval Staff, however, as they claimed RAF bombers and minelayers were still proving very active. Weather difficulties were also mentioned but most significantly it was claimed the main pre-condition for invasion had still to be achieved. In other words, "clear air superiority in the Channel area" and negation of enemy air activity in naval assembly areas. This demonstration that the Naval Staff no longer believed in Sea Lion as an ongoing operation is shown in the War Diary entry for 10 September 1940:

> It would be more in the sense of the planned preparation for operation "Sea Lion" if the Luftwaffe would now concentrate less on London and more on Portsmouth and Dover, and on the naval forces in or near the operation. . . . The Naval War Staff, however, does not consider it suitable to approach the Fuehrer now with such demands, because the Fuehrer looks upon a large-scale attack on London as possibly being decisive . . . bombardment of London might produce an attitude in the enemy which will make the "Sea Lion" operation completely unnecessary.[49]

Hitler postponed his decision until 14 September 1940. Meanwhile the RAF applied its own pressure by bombing barges moored in Ostend. The Royal Navy had also been actively bombarding minesweepers and barges, and moved capital ships from Scapa Flow to Rosyth (Firth of Forth) in obvious readiness for a descent upon the Channel. There is some dispute as to the number of barges sunk by the British during this month, arising from S. Roskill's detection of a mistranslation of German documents.[50] However, the synthesis of captured German documents by British Naval Intelligence stating that 12.5 percent of transports had been lost—12.6 percent of barges and 1.4 percent of tugs—appears reliable.

These were held to be replaceable, but not if the attrition was to continue for much longer, thus placing even more pressure on Hitler to decide.[51] The *Daily Express* of 12 September 1940 reported "strong and repeated offensive actions are being taken by our naval light forces against German shipping movements, ports, and concentrations of shipping."[52] Naval attacks had certainly been made at Calais, Ostend, Boulogne, and Cherbourg, yet the damage attributable to warships and aircraft respectively has never been ascertained. Admiral Reginald Drax's naval flotillas from the Nore broke into the invasion ports of Dunkirk, Boulogne, Calais, and Ostend and sank several invasion barges with short-range gunfire.[53] Drax's colleagues from Plymouth and Portsmouth organized many similar operations and on 11 September "every port from Holland to Cherbourg got entered and shelled." Other naval attacks continued into October, and on the eleventh Cherbourg harbor erupted into flames, with Calais harbor sustaining forty-five salvoes from the Royal Navy without the loss of a single British ship.[54] Irrespective as to whether the Royal Navy had been responsible for most of this damage, Raeder had far more reason to stress the "failure" to gain air superiority by blaming the destruction on "English bombers."[55]

At the conference on 14 September 1940, Hitler disregarded his Luftwaffe intelligence and stated that Sea Lion was "not yet practical" because air supremacy had not been obtained. If the invasion failed it would enable the British to endure the air attacks with greater fortitude. Imminent landings plus air attacks meant the "total effect would be very strong after all." No doubt relieved, Raeder agreed, though the operation could not be formally called off yet, as this would only encourage the British. The decision was again postponed, this time until 17 September 1940. By then Hitler knew the Luftwaffe had suffered heavy losses over London on 15 September 1940 without any obvious slump in civilian morale, providing him with an excuse to postpone the operation indefinitely. Finally on 19 September 1940, he ordered limited dispersal of the barges to reduce the impact of British attacks on the harbor installations. The Fuehrer was now considering "other plans."[56]

But quite apart from the German inability to launch a full-scale invasion of the British Isles in 1940, there remains the question as to whether a coup de main by parachute- and glider-borne troops around the time of the Dunkirk evacuation would have stood any realistic chance of success. The viability of an air and sea assault launched between 9 and 15 July was strongly asserted in 1980 as originally proposed by Luftwaffe General (later Field Marshal) Albert Kesselring and Field Marshal Erhard Milch.[57] Supporting these arguments and stressing British weakness at this time, a *Daily Mail* article claimed that "if control of the skies, the Channel, and the capital had been lost, defeat would have been the reality."[58] It needs to be emphasized here that airborne troops cannot carry heavy weaponry and would have required rapid reinforcement by sea.

As Vice Admiral Kurt Assman revealed after the war, other "Englishmen" had put the same arguments to him, to which he sarcastically replied "we Germans could not simply swim over." Assman, who was well qualified to answer these questions, said his questioners invariably took as "fact" there had been plans for an invasion of England since spring 1938, to which he emphatically stated no such plans had been made and the English should know from their own experience "just how long it takes to prepare for such a gigantic undertaking."[59] In fact there had been no plans until after the war started in September 1939, and these contingency plans were made on the assumption that the Germans might capture a significant stretch of the Belgian–French Channel coast. It is now generally accepted that the overwhelming success of the German offensive in May 1940 was as surprising to the German High Command as it was to the British and French.

General Admiral Otto Schniewind, responsible for the contingency plan "Case-Red" in November 1939, later co-wrote an essay for British Naval Intelligence with Admiral Karl Schuster dealing with this question of invasion immediately after Dunkirk. Their essay stated that some of the harbors necessary for loading the heavy equipment had yet to be captured. Those already captured required so much repair and clearance "as to preclude their immediate use as invasion ports." Transports and loading installations had also been successfully destroyed.[60] It is worth noting here that as late as 19 July 1940, the date of Hitler's "implicit peace offer" from the Kroll Opera House, he was sent Admiral Raeder's list of damage to these installations and adjoining canal systems.[61] Schniewind and Schuster also argued that the French army was still "sufficiently intact" to preclude the removal of sufficient troops, a point made independently by Admiral Assman a few years later.[62] Furthermore, Schniewind and Schuster argued the necessary degree of air superiority had not been attained.[63]

These objections are difficult to fault. The British were sufficiently satisfied with the harbor demolitions to justify awarding two Distinguished Service Orders, two Distinguished Service Crosses, and six Distinguished Service Medals, with eleven others mentioned in dispatches for Operations XD and XDA. This was a time when heroes were badly needed and even if the British may have been inclined to exaggerate the damage, their reports indicate the Germans would have had problems making rapid repairs. For example at Ymuiden, the facilities "rendered useless" included the power installation and machinery of the locks, the iron foundry control board and structure, and the two floating docks together with the guns and ammunition at the fort. The channel was blocked with six sunken ships, one of which jammed the gates of the South Lock. Twelve other vessels had been destroyed or scuttled in the harbor including a floating crane. The damage at Amsterdam was less clear although it should be noted the entire oil stocks at this important port had been destroyed.[64] As the French did not request an armistice until 17 June 1940, the time available to throw together a surprise operation was clearly limited. Contrary to popular British belief the French did not lack fighting spirit, and the French defenders of Lille held out so bravely, the Germans allowed them to keep their weapons for the surrender parade.[65]

Fuelling speculation as to whether an exclusively airborne operation against England would have been successful, General Kurt Student's interview with Basil Liddell Hart for the purposes of the latter's book on German decision-making revealed that Student would have recommended an airborne assault during or immediately after Dunkirk. He had not done so because he was recovering from wounds during the summer of 1940. Liddell Hart rightly considered this idea "optimistic," taking account of the small, lightly armed forces that could be carried this way.[66] According to Field Marshal von Rundstedt, the system of large-scale air supply later used in Russia was "not sufficiently developed in 1940."[67] Typical of Student's flights of fancy was his plan to invade Ulster with paratroopers in early 1941. Intended as a diversion from proposed landings in southern England in 1941, his forces were to capture airfields so that Luftwaffe units could immediately make them operational. The enormous vulnerability of sea communications required for reinforcement and heavy equipment do not appear to have figured heavily in his calculations for Ulster.[68]

Student may not have known that while he was in hospital in July there were only around 750 available transport aircraft, with 150 gliders each carrying up to eight soldiers, suggesting the delivery of no more than 1,200 glider-borne troops. Assuming six hundred Ju 52 transport aircraft each carried twenty paratroopers, theoretically some 13,000 airborne troops could have been deployed, roughly the same number later deployed in Crete. In reality the troops available were likely to have been substantially less because of the heavy casualties sustained in earlier operations and a shortage of parachute silk. Historian Peter Schenk has estimated the 7th Airborne Division, the only unit with paratroopers, to be around ten thousand strong.[69] How many of these, like Student, were still recovering from wounds received during the fierce fighting around The Hague is unclear.

While it is right to be skeptical of the perceptions of airpower in 1940, a strong defending fighter force would have been essential for deterring an attack of this nature. As the operational range of the Me 109 fighter barely reached London, an attack on Ulster or even the southeast coast of England meant the slow Ju 52 transport aircraft would have received scant protection, especially as the German Jagdstaffeln were unable to move into their new Channel bases until the French surrender. A secret British Air Ministry report on possible invasion by glider-borne forces indicated that the British had anticipated an attempt of this nature and assessed the threat. It considered such an attack might seize a bridgehead or an aerodrome near a port. However, it noted that a glider needed "to be towed to within a few miles of the coast by powered aircraft." Gliders could fly around twenty miles in still air after casting off at ten thousand feet. The British gliders used in these experiments had escaped the visual detection of the Observer Corps but RDF easily detected the slow-moving towing aircraft. Their slow approach speed indicated that it was indeed a glider formation. Surprisingly, given their wooden construction, it was asserted that "gliders can themselves be detected by

RDF." As the report suggested, glider-borne attack was vulnerable to fighter interception as it was only necessary to bring down the towing aircraft for the whole tow to be destroyed.[70] As will be seen in a later chapter, RDF was less effective than generally assumed but it is clear that without air supremacy a glider-borne attack was going to fail. The Germans may not have fully appreciated these points but the British evidence suggests caution was justified. Heavy fighter escort was clearly essential for the gliders but, as one German historian noted, after the exertions of the western campaign the Luftwaffe was exhausted, making the prospect of an immediate attack "inconceivable."

A fundamental consideration of German attitudes has to focus heavily on Adolf Hitler, who was hopeful of seeking an accommodation with Britain without necessarily eradicating her as a world power. This was one area in which Hitler was consistent, except for occasional bouts of frustration when British foreign policy announcements obstructed his aspirations. Whether or not Hitler wanted war is an ongoing controversy as Nazi expansionism can hardly be denied. But it is clear enough that Hitler did not want war with Britain in 1940. One of the earliest expressions of Hitler's foreign policy toward Britain was the Anglo-German Naval Agreement of 1935. This was heavily criticized in the book *Guilty Men* during 1940, a work setting the tone for the mythmaking of later years. The first influential publication to lay into the pre-war appeasers, *Guilty Men* was written in "a rush and a rage" by three London journalists including the well-known Michael Foot, leader of the British Labour party.[71] One of the main targets was Sir Samuel Hoare, the British foreign secretary responsible for negotiations on the British side. The essence of criticism was that Hoare encouraged the erosion of the Treaty of Versailles by overturning restrictions on German naval building with a pact enabling Germany to build up to 35 percent of British naval tonnage and up to 45 percent in submarines. Churchill publicly supported this criticism after the war, though without mentioning he had voted with the government on this issue.[72] As Hitler set aside the agreement in April 1939, it tends to be seen as an expression of hostility toward Britain and Hoare comes across as a "dupe." The German Naval Staff had a rather different view of this supposed symptom of British moral weakness.

The attitude of Admiral Herman Boehm was that the treaty represented a genuine German attempt to clear the air with England.[73] It fully recognized that England needed to maintain her position as the strongest sea power in Europe and that Germany was imposing a limit of one-third upon herself so as to reassure Britain of German intentions. An essay by Boehm blamed Hitler for a political gesture that "disappointed" the German navy by restricting battleships to a 26,000-ton displacement equipped with 28-cm guns as main armament. Having left the League of Nations in 1933 and faced with France building the *Dunkerque*-class battleships with 33-cm guns, Germany was theoretically free to build what it liked. Therefore, Boehm implied, the *Scharnhorst* and the *Gneisenau* were not built to the optimum specification. The Anglo-German Naval Agreement of 1935 demanded no counter-concessions from England and in his opinion "there never was a more generous offer made, nor more honestly meant." With regard to Hitler's later cancellation of this treaty, Boehm considered that further naval expansion was not inconsistent with Germany's position as a European power and it was only in 1938 that the possibility of war with England began to be taken into account. The "Z" plan may have been a considerable fleet expansion but this, to his mind, was still no threat to England, recalling the plan encompassed ten large battleships and battle cruisers by 1948, which still did not match England's fourteen in 1939.[74]

Vice Admiral Helmuth Heye also mentioned that a fleet of about eight "Washington standard" battleships was not expected before 1947 or 1948. Furthermore the hope of avoiding enmity was best illustrated by the fact that "the navy was forbidden until shortly before the war . . . to carry on studies and make plans in case of war with England."[75] Admiral Otto Schultze claimed Germany did not have to take account of warships under six hundred tons in this agreement, meaning she could build destroyers and E-boats to protect her vital iron-ore supply routes across the Baltic.

Admiral Schultze also mentioned the treaty was "cordially welcomed both by me and by practically the whole corps of German naval officers." Echoing Boehm, he stated that it was fully recognized that England's imperial requirements obliged her to have "a considerably stronger navy" whereas Germany, "with her central position and unprotected frontiers, based her defenses primarily on the army and the air force, relegating her navy to a secondary position." The protection of sea communications was better achieved through political understanding than through extensive naval rearmament. Therefore the treaty "conformed to the permanently expressed wish of the German national leaders."[76]

Grand Admiral Doenitz's essay laid emphasis on Germany's need to give priority to land rearmament because of her geographical position, as also argued by Schultze. The navy could not protect Germany's long unprotected land frontiers, a point later echoed by Vice Admiral Eberhard Weichold.[77] Therefore the great naval powers (Britain, Italy, Japan, and perhaps the United States) were not considered potential enemies. This was evidenced by the fact that Germany initially created a "balanced fleet" to deal with those of continental neighbors. Such a fleet might produce opportunities for an alliance with England, should the opportunity arise. If England had been a principal target, then a larger U-boat fleet would have been the logical building objective.[78]

According to Admiral Theodore Kranke, "the Fuehrer was always emphasizing the fact that war with England was politically out of the question, as there was no grounds for conflict, hence the naval treaty."[79] For Admiral Hans Meyer, "it was beyond question that Hitler never wished a quarrel with England, and that everything he ever said . . . with regard to coming to arrangements with England was seriously meant."[80]

Meyer, a former commander of the *Tirpitz*, was considered by the Department of Naval Intelligence as a "non-political" figure.[81] It was Meyer's essay that drew attention to the influence of Vice Admiral Wegener on Hitler, especially with regard to his intentions toward Norway. Wegener's 1929 monograph, *Seestrategie des Weltkrieges*, was also identified as an important influence on Hitler by the British naval attaché in Berlin, in May 1939. This analysis of the sea war of 1914–18 was written by a retired German admiral who told the Fuehrer through his book that there was no point in trying to compete with the British in terms of fleet size. Wegener made this important assertion: "The Germans were so impressed with the tactical superiority of the British fleet," he wrote, "that they did not understand that strategically the relative size of fleets plays no part." Geography, he argued, was the key. "A smaller fleet can perfectly undertake a strategic offensive."[82]

The idea of the primacy of geography as a major factor in British maritime supremacy is less firmly held now than it was then, but Wegener was certainly convinced of it. In essence, the British did not need to go on the offensive; rather it was the Germans who needed to do this, bearing in mind the slow economic strangulation of the central powers via the blockade toward the end of World War I. The concept of the "fleet-in-being" had encouraged a negative psychology apparent in the actions of both Admiral Reinhard Scheer, commander of the German High Seas Fleet, and Admiral John Jellicoe, commander of the British Grand Fleet, at this time. Wegener argued the Germans should have tried harder to capture Brest in 1914 to allow U-boats access to the Atlantic and also pressurize Denmark to open up the Belts for German shipping.[83] The importance of operating from Norway, the Kattegat, and the Atlantic coast of France were stressed. Wegener also attacked the theories of Tirpitz, the architect of the German High Seas Fleet, and claimed that neither Tirpitz nor Fisher (his opposite number) really understood strategy. Germany had assumed England would not attack her because the casualties would erode British supremacy over other European powers. Wegener said that although initially the British made mistakes, they finally geared their strategy toward their geographical advantages, by which he presumably meant protecting trade routes and strengthening the blockade of Germany rather than further extensive land campaigning. One final point is the advocacy of a unified high command, a point made because he thought German leaders would, contrary to their traditional view, see any future conflict as primarily a sea war. As the naval attaché correctly recognized, Hitler would be sympathetic to the idea of placing power in as few hands as possible, a similar notion underpinning the concept of *Fuehrerprinzip* that maximized power into his own hands.

The naval attaché did not agree the British had nothing to gain by fighting, though he accepted the idea of small fleets gaining by offensive action. But irrespective of the actual validity of Wegener's theories, the seeds of German strategy are laid bare. They help explain the lack of priority for a big fleet and the unwillingness to compete with England in terms of big-ship rivalry such as had occurred with Kaiser Wilhelm's support for naval aggrandizement—actions that had antagonized the British prior to 1914. It meant that Hitler could afford to be diplomatically generous in 1935, as a big fleet did not accord with his own priorities for resources. Geography heavily dictated where the military efforts must be directed; therefore enemy naval bases had to be captured by land power, meaning the army must take priority. Hitler did indeed make an early move toward Norway and Denmark, and the objectives for his western offensive in 1940 were the Channel ports. It must also be stated that Wegener made no mention of needing to invade England. This is not to say that Wegener was solely responsible for the direction of German strategy in 1939–40 but his influence on the German Naval Staff alone was likely to predispose Hitler in these directions.

What the admirals did regret was not the failure to gain air supremacy, but the inability to invade England in 1940. For Germany, the Battle of Britain was Operation Sea Lion, the battle that was never fought. This was because in the years prior to 1939 it had not been necessary to plan for it, and no advantage the Luftwaffe might gain over the RAF could make up for the lack of long-term naval preparation. Even if the change of Luftwaffe focus from the airfields to bombing London had been calculated to bring about a change of policy in England, there is no direct evidence stating occupation was to be part of any subsequent armistice. The Royal Navy was still the primary obstacle to invasion and "everyone connected with the operation" knew this and was relieved when the Luftwaffe seemed to have "failed." On the balance of probability Admiral Raeder had worked to insert the "get-out clause" of air supremacy in Hitler's directives concerning an operation that both men hoped would never need to be implemented. The sources show a remarkable respect for British sensibilities and an acknowledgment of the power of the British fleet. The essays by the German admirals indicate that Hitler did not regard Britain as a "natural" enemy, even if at a later stage British rearmament made it necessary to plan for the event of war with her. British naval power had been a factor in his drive for the self-sufficiency of autarky, but prior to the Ribbentrop-Molotov Pact of 1939 a naval blockade against Germany had the potential to wreck his ambitions. Hitler therefore formulated his own policy of appeasement to suit strategic requirements that found expression in a naval treaty better known as a milestone of Britain's appeasement policy.

Naturally it was political pragmatism that drove Hitler to take a cautious attitude to what he accurately perceived as British sensibilities, but there was no reason to think he had any overwhelming motive to see the downfall of Britain and her empire in 1940 or any earlier point. In theory, a potential Anglo-German peace treaty in 1940 would not have prevented Germany taking an aggressive stance toward Britain at a later date, but this did not necessarily mean the British would have been more vulnerable in the state of "armed neutrality" that must have followed such an agreement. A Nazi Europe would certainly have made an uncomfortable neighbor in the 1940s but the "inevitability" of war resuming once

Hitler's other declared expansionist aims had been achieved is something often asserted but never convincingly argued. Yet if long-standing political pragmatism had played a major part in Hitler's attitude toward "England" in 1940, any change of attitude would have had to encompass military realities. Some broad strategic and tactical difficulties have been shown to undermine German confidence but one fundamental problem had to be faced. The question at the back of German minds prior to the end of August 1940 must have been whether the comparatively recent phenomenon of "airpower" had matured to an extent that the bomber could now defeat the battleship.

CHAPTER THREE

Bombers versus Battleships

The hasty conclusion that ships are impotent in the face of air attack should not be drawn from the Battle of Crete.[1]

Viscount Andrew Cunningham

Group Captain F. W. Winterbotham of the British Secret Intelligence Service claimed in his published memoirs that, as a result of the Battle of Crete, the British finally learned that warships were incapable of surviving in the face of exposure to large numbers of land-based enemy aircraft.[2] For reasons that will become clear, it seems doubtful that this assertion—published many years after the event and entirely from memory—can really be representative of what Winterbotham actually thought at the time. His conclusion seems self-evident in the light of subsequent actions. The dramatic loss of the *Prince of Wales* and *Repulse* to Japanese naval dive- and torpedo-bombers, and the great sea battles of the Pacific where aircraft played the dominant role, have led to lazy assumptions regarding the situation in western waters. Here, the Royal Navy was facing an enemy air force that was undeniably powerful but not comparable with that of the United States or Japan. This assertion that the warship of 1940 could not stand up to mass air attack without substantial air cover remains stubbornly rooted in the public consciousness despite the comparatively recent work of academics disproving this.[3]

As mentioned previously, a former German pilot, Lieutenant Gerhard Baeker, articulated the doubts of the Luftwaffe in overcoming the Royal Navy in these circumstances through the medium of a television documentary repeated periodically on digital television channels.[4] Two authors have pointed out that prior to the loss of the *Repulse* and *Prince of Wales* there was no reason to think, even in late 1941, other British heavy ships could not operate in areas without guaranteed air cover and where there was a likelihood of heavy enemy air attack. Only three of the twelve capital ships sunk between September 1939 and November 1941 had succumbed to air attack alone and these were Italian battleships sunk at anchorage (but not permanently negated) by torpedo-bombers. One attack, on the German battleship *Bismarck*, was made by a combination of gunfire and torpedo strikes. Four ships were sunk by gunfire alone and four by torpedoes from submarines. Significantly, none sank by bombing alone, though smaller ships were more vulnerable. Twenty-eight British destroyers and five cruisers had been eliminated in this form of attack.[5]

In fact, Vice Admiral Sir Arthur Hezlet dismissed the ability of small warships to operate a flotilla defense in the English Channel in the face of Luftwaffe superiority. He also stressed the reluctance of the Home Fleet to face a single Air Corps (*Fliegerkorps*) in Norway, pointing out that the fleet would have needed to contend with five Air Corps based in France. If the Royal Navy had needed to engage in a suicide operation without air support, he argued, the result would probably have been worse than at Crete as naval forces would only have been slightly greater, whereas the enemy air force would have had roughly four times the strength it was to have at Crete. He also doubted the ability of the fleet to use the repair facilities between Portsmouth and the Humber while under air attack and asserted that Hitler did not invade "because the Luftwaffe could not defeat the Royal Air Force."[6]

What is called for is a fresh look at the *bombs versus battleships* debate as it applied to the situation in 1940. In this context "battleships" means all Royal Navy ships including their personnel, together with the anti-aircraft (AA) defense of bases providing replenishment and emergency repairs. There was far more involved with Operation Sea Lion than the question of whether German airpower was a match for British warships in 1940, but it is the fundamental assumption that British warships could not stand up to Luftwaffe attacks that needs closest examination. As Hezlet has rightly made some comparison between the Battle of Crete in 1941 and the situation in home waters during 1940, this chapter provides a more detailed analysis of the problems. While several changes may have occurred over the eight months between September 1940 and May 1941, Crete provided useful indications into the strength of naval morale at this early stage of the war as warships and crews were subjected to unprecedented attack from the air.

There is no doubt that the anti-aircraft defense of the Home Fleet and the local flotillas operating in the Channel had some limitations. However, senior naval opinion was initially satisfied with it and believed it even more important than fighter defense. That this over-confidence pervaded all levels of the Royal Navy may be doubted. Lieutenant Commander J. A. J. "Alec" Dennis thought that the anti-aircraft defense was "pathetic." While serving on the destroyer HMS *Griffin* as a junior officer, he was appalled to see how a radio-controlled Queen Bee target aircraft was able to fly straight and level through the fleet's barrage and emerge unscathed on the other side during a 1939 exercise.[7] An important reference book on naval weaponry has categorized naval anti-aircraft guns of a medium caliber to be within the range of 3 inches to 5.25 inches, firing explosive shells with timed fuses, and further supplemented by anti-ship guns to provide barrages often timed to burst at 1,500 yards. These were not very accurate but nevertheless extremely effective in closely packed formations of enemy bombers trying to make low-level bombing runs at medium and longer ranges. Also effective were the close-range guns automatically rapid-firing projectiles at less than 1,500 yards. A well-publicized handicap was the inherent limitation of the high-angle control system for controlling the medium guns, but anti-aircraft fire control was weak in all navies, with the possible exception of that used by the U.S. Navy.[8]

A detailed explanation of the working of the high-angle control system is complex, but it was competently explained in a wartime book written for a general readership. In essence fire control was managed by means of a director, which is a dummy sight usually mounted on the bridge or as high as possible. Elevation and direction positions could then be transmitted to gun layers who directed the guns onto the aircraft with the received data.[9] It was conceded that the guns did not automatically follow the directors and required the manual following of pointers for aiming, an operation difficult to accomplish while under fire. In another specialist's opinion, it was only likely to work properly with experienced personnel against slow aircraft.[10] To try and improve the fleet's air defense capability, a few older cruisers had their 6-inch guns replaced by 4-inch guns to carry out a new stop-gap role as specialist anti-aircraft ships. Inevitably this made the AA cruisers unfit for most other purposes. Consequently, a new class of cruiser was invented (the *Dido*) and this was just coming into service in 1940 with 5.25-inch guns for greater flexibility.

Largely because of inadequate gun mountings, the most vulnerable ships were the destroyers, most of which relied on World War I–vintage 4.7-inch anti-shipping guns for air defense. Being unable to elevate above 40 degrees they were vulnerable to dive-bombing attacks between 40 and 90 degrees. Luckily for some personnel, a few Hunt-class destroyers had 4-inch guns capable of high elevation. The majority of ships possessed close-range machine guns from .303 rifle caliber to 40 mm and in 1939, a situation similar to that of 1940, a typical major warship armament's effectiveness owed almost everything to the skills of the operatives and comprised "two 8-barrelled 2-pounder pom-poms and four twin Lewis guns."[11] One naval critic blamed the 40 degrees restriction on "reactionary" Admiralty attitudes that mountings permitting elevation above 40 degrees might compromise LAC (low-angle control) ship-to-ship gun performance.[12] This aside, by the mid-1930s the Admiralty needed to take account of having to fight a Japanese navy that reports indicated was already achieving gunnery accuracy well beyond anything the British could then achieve, and they were understandably reluctant to make the differential worse.[13]

Unfortunately, in 1940 all these problems were compounded by a shortage of the very effective Oerlikon 20-mm and Bofors 40-mm rapid-firing cannon for close-range defense. However, by 1937 a sub-committee of the Committee of

Imperial Defence had already considered the problem of close-range anti-aircraft gun shortages. Serving on this committee were the well- known "appeasers" Neville Chamberlain and Sir Samuel Hoare. The Admiralty had been unlucky in backing the development of an inferior gun from the British manufacturer Vickers, and while this could supposedly deliver a higher rate of fire than the available Swedish-made Bofors gun "trials had proved most unsatisfactory." Belying his popular image as a relentless cost-cutting appeaser, Neville Chamberlain argued that the financial effects of ordering the weaponry abroad were not "necessarily over-riding" and that he recognized "the essential need of obtaining a satisfactory weapon." After much discussion it was agreed that the War Office could open negotiations with Messrs. Bofors for one hundred of their guns plus ammunition together with an option for extra ammunition at a later stage. However, British close-range anti-aircraft gun development would still have to be continued, as nobody was sure that Messrs. Bofors could satisfy the demand.[14] Although not implicitly stated, hopes that British designs might lead to substantial contracts for British firms and a subsequent easing of chronic unemployment problems were bound to impinge upon the decision-making process. Unfortunately the Vickers was "slow to bear onto the target and slow in rate of fire."[15]

Although the Chamberlain government has often been blamed for complacency and penny-pinching on defense matters, they were merely following the trend prevailing since the beginning of the twentieth century. Naval technical development had become so expensive that the Admiralty had circumscribed the activities of its own research establishments, increasingly leaving this to the private sector. Despite the Anglo-German arms race prior to World War I, the naval budget was subject to severe financial restraint in order to pay for the Liberal welfare reforms from 1908. For their part, private-sector armaments firms had little commercial incentive to spend money on unprofitable military development in peacetime. Even in 1909 the Royal Navy may have been over-reliant on Vickers and Armstrong.[16] The situation had not improved much given the nation's financial state during the 1930s and it was even suggested that by 1937, Vickers was "almost a branch of the Admiralty." This critic claimed that British gun makers helped delay acquisition of more useful weapons such as the Swiss-made Oerlikon for the next two years and blamed the Admiralty for its alleged "age-old naval custom of opposing change."[17] Given these problems and the apparent over-reliance on an inadequate AA defense it might be expected that the Luftwaffe would have achieved spectacular results against Royal Navy warships in this early phase of the war. Surprisingly perhaps, this is not borne out by the evidence the Admiralty collected.

As would be expected, the Admiralty looked very closely at the effects of aircraft against shipping and prepared a report entitled *Tactical Summary of Bombing Aircraft on HM Ships and Shipping from September 1939 to February 1941*. Written in 1941, this report analyzed the experiences of the Merchant Navy and the Royal Navy during this early phase. As the authors admitted, the data had some limitations. It only included attacks where enough detail for analysis was obtainable and did not include ships damaged at anchorage, possibly because it was unclear whether the bombers were aiming at the ship or the harbor facilities. Even if the attacks were directly aimed at the ship, it could be argued that such attacks were unrepresentative as warships would be static and unlikely to be operating an anti-aircraft defense. Neither was it thought relevant to include ships refitting as these were not considered operational.[18] A "successful" attack was considered to be one in which the ship was either sunk or forced to seek extensive repairs over several weeks or months. None of this necessarily represents the situation the Royal Navy would have faced during a naval Battle of Britain, but it does say a great deal about German bombing techniques and their effectiveness in a maritime role.

For example, it is clear that the Luftwaffe's best ship-destroyer was the Ju 87 Stuka.[19] The chart in Appendix I compiled from these Admiralty data (excluding that of attacks against merchant shipping) shows clearly that dive-bombing was the most effective bombing method to use against shipping, and the best warplane for this purpose was the Stuka. However, the report does not mention that the bombing potential of this aircraft depended to some extent on whether it was the B-1 or B-2 version.

Neither does it mention that dive-bombing is subject to reasonably clear visibility and a high cloud ceiling, preferably between 10,000 feet and 15,000 feet. This was rarely a limitation in the much more predictable and fine Mediterranean theater, but in the notoriously unreliable meteorological conditions in the North Sea and English Channel, an unexpected deterioration in the weather would have negated the dive-bomber as a weapon. It is also known that the Ju 87 was slow and vulnerable to AA fire, which was fine when diving steeply against isolated smaller ships unable to elevate their guns above 40 degrees but against larger ships it meant flying through intense barrages. Even when diving, the Ju 87 was slow, seldom exceeding 200 mph, as opposed to most American and Japanese equivalents that could do this at up to 350 mph. It was usually most vulnerable to AA fire during the pullout when the dive-bomber was within a few hundred feet of the warship.[20]

However, the majority of the Luftwaffe's bombers were not Ju 87s, but twin-engine medium aircraft such as the Heinkel He III and the Dornier Do 17, which could dive-bomb but were really more suited to high-level bombing. An exception was the twin-engine Ju 88, a versatile all-round aircraft and, by 1943, a better dive-bomber than the Ju 87. However, in 1940, the Ju 88 had not reached the peak of its dive-bomber development and the limited number deployed proved much less fit for combat than the Heinkel and Dornier. Those aircraft engaging in high-level bombing achieved few successes because the altitudes of 6,000 to 19,000 feet were too high for accurate aiming. That bombs were being dropped from these altitudes indicates that the ships' long-range anti-aircraft barrage was an effective deterrent. According to witnesses, the shells exploding in front of the formation had an unnerving effect and encouraged the bombers to accelerate from 200 knots up to 250 knots as soon as they burst.[21] Had this high-altitude bombing method proved effective it seems unlikely the Germans would have abandoned the practice after May 1940. Low-level bombing runs were made at altitudes of around one thousand feet and undertaken mainly by twin-engine bombers but sometimes by Stukas on their way to, or coming back from, other targets. These were slightly more effective against destroyer/escort and trawler/auxiliary classes but unsuccessful against anything heavier. Very low-level attacks at six hundred feet or less were generally dismissed as machine-gunning runs with very little effect against warships. What was described as a "flat bombing trajectory," where the biggest target was the ship's side, made the use of bombs impractical and merely exposed the aircraft to anti-aircraft fire in exchange for a negligible chance of succeeding.[22]

As the foregoing report has indicated, dive-bombing was the most effective method for a Luftwaffe aircraft to engage a warship. According to figures held at the British Ministry of Defence, Naval Historical Branch, the Germans had 1,015 bombers and 346 dive-bombers available for operations from approximately 1 August 1940.[23] This meant the Luftwaffe had 1,361 bombers, of which only 25.4 percent were effective ship-destroyers, with the burden falling on destroyer/escort and trawler/auxiliary classes. In comparison with Crete, the Germans possessed 430 bombers of which 150 were Ju 87 Stukas, although the Ju 87s were also supplemented by a few dive-bombing twin-engine Ju 88s. These (admittedly incomplete) data contradict the indirect implication in Hezlet's book that with four times the aircraft available at Crete the Luftwaffe could be four times as effective in the Channel. It must also be remembered that the Germans needed to focus a significant proportion of their air resources on dealing with coastal fortifications and supporting their army as well as simultaneously engaging warships.

While dive-bombing was effective in good weather against the smaller warships it was still less effective than torpedo bombing. Armored decks and superstructures have to be pierced by armor-piercing or semi-armor-piercing bombs to do appreciable damage, whereas torpedoes were capable of inflicting massive damage below the waterline, and this was a significant weakness in the Luftwaffe's capability. Only the Kampfgeschwader 26 bomber wing, comprising former naval pilots, had the relevant experience, but they were substantially handicapped with the Heinkel He III, a large, slow aircraft vulnerable to AA fire when making long, slow, and straight approaches. Only slow approaches were possible because the aerial torpedo used was fragile, and in consequence only seems to have been used against merchant shipping.[24]

In the absence of efficient torpedo bombers, much would have to depend on the efficacy of the bomb. After the war, Admiral Doenitz told British Naval Intelligence that the Luftwaffe had "bombs of far too small a caliber . . . to prevent heavy ships from coming to grips with the landing force."[25] It is well established that the Germans were so short of bombs at the outbreak of war that they resorted to the desperate expedient of manufacturing bombs from concrete. In the circumstances of 1939–40, priority went to general-purpose bombs rather than the specialized types more suited for maritime operations. On the other hand, specialized bombs were unnecessary against the smaller warships. An indication of the effectiveness of bombs against warships can be obtained from the files of government scientist Sir Henry Tizard, better known for his work in the development of the Radio Direction Finding system.

Tizard's papers contained correspondence from Hugh Dowding, head of RAF Fighter Command, addressed to the Air Ministry regarding an Ordnance Board report concerning failed RAF attempts to successfully bomb German warships at anchorage on 4 September 1939. Dowding believed that earlier experiments known as "Job 74 trials" indicated that effectiveness against armor depended on the bombs detonating after contact in order for the explosion to damage the inside of the ship. He was also contesting an "expert" assertion that the semi-armor-piercing (SAP) bombs did not pre-detonate on the armor plate with the explosive fillings in use. Contrary to what had been asserted by ordnance technicians, the bombs used against the German warships had been bursting on impact as opposed to being detonated with a time-delay fuse as intended. In Dowding's opinion, those involved were "'specialists' who are too lazy to read, or too stupid to understand the reports." Much of the letter consisted of extracts from technical reports, but a number of interesting points are clear.

Quoting from the report, he drew attention to the fact that the 250-pound bombs with 0.1-second delay, dropped from 4,000 feet, hit the armored deck and rebounded before exploding. One 500-pound bomb dropped from 12,000 feet achieved much higher velocity and did more damage, but only succeeded in penetrating to the inside of the ship by striking concrete, as opposed to armor. In this case the ship's bottom was blown out. Unfortunately, the other two 500-pound bombs were ineffective, one hitting an armored deck, the other an armored hatch resulting in detonation on contact—that is, by impact rather than fuses. Quoting an enclosure to a report (numbered 0365/74/S and dated 29 November 1938) on earlier experiments, he pointed out that a 500-pound bomb with a 0.1-second fuse dropped from this altitude should rebound before exploding after hitting an armored hatch, but in this case it burst on impact. Three 250-pound bombs with a 0.3-second fuse were actually more effective despite having half the velocity and weight of the 500-pound bombs. Another 250-pound bomb but with a 0.1-second fuse penetrated one deck farther than the 500-pound bomb before rebounding three feet against 4-inch armor. The report concluded that the latter bomb might have detonated "owing to the sensitivity of the filling, rather than its lack of armour-piercing qualities," suggesting that the casing was probably satisfactory.

Dowding also doubted that fuse delays of 0.2 and 0.3 seconds would work properly for a semi-armor-piercing bomb. A bomb with a 0.1-second fuse delay dropped from 12,000 feet "not stopped by armour" burst in the bottom of the ship, but one with a longer fuse went straight through the bottom and exploded far below. Dowding argued the longer fuses for non-armor-piercing 250-pound bombs existed because there was no expectation of piercing the armor and it was considered more effective to allow the bomb to bounce around before detonating. It is not very clear from this letter why allowing the bomb to bounce was considered to be more effective than direct detonation onto decks and superstructures but the implication is that a ricocheting bomb might drop down an open hatch or explode in the sea immediately next to the hull where water compression would exacerbate the explosive effects. In effect, this would result in what the Admiralty defined as a "near-miss," something capable of inflicting heavy damage because of the vulnerability of brittle cast-iron machine components.[26] The long delay was only acceptable, Dowding argued, if it were known the longer-fused bomb would not penetrate the armor but if it did, then the full effect could be wasted because the bomb would explode too far beneath the ship. Finally Dowding ridiculed what he termed an "American idea" that bomb-blast effects can decisively damage a heavy ship, and quoted trials that took place ten years before showing that 1,200-pound light-case bombs only did localized damage. Finally, Dowding quoted another paper (0365/74/S, dated 29 November 1938), which further confirmed that the semi-armor-piercing bomb was "weight-for-weight" more effective for these purposes than the general-purpose instantaneously fused bomb. Dowding was understandably annoyed that results of the expensive tests he was involved with during his earlier career appeared to have been lost and had been forgotten by the Air Ministry. Consequently "we now have no means by which we can sink a German Battleship."[27]

Dowding's ridicule of an "American idea" is probably rooted in the experiments of U.S. general William Mitchell to sink warships by bombing during the 1920s. Mitchell had worked with British bomber advocate Sir Hugh Trenchard (no friend of Dowding) toward the end of World War I and ultimately became chief of the Air Service Army Group. His well-publicized experiment to sink a series of warships by bombing was exactly the sort of showbiz stunt that would have irritated the introverted, dispassionate scientist that made up much of Dowding's character. In one test, a 2,000-pound bomb sunk the obsolete battleship *Alabama* with a center hit.[28] The experiments were rightly criticized by the U.S. military for their artificiality, even though the ships had been sunk. After all, the warships had not been conducting an anti-aircraft defense or taking avoiding action. Also importantly, they possessed heavy armor only for the purpose of deflecting shells from the side rather than bombs from the vertical, suggesting that non-armor piercing bombs would have been sufficient in these instances. Mitchell subsequently made himself a nuisance to those in authority and, as many colorful characters do, alienated those who may have responded to a more tactful approach. But to the public his showmanship made him a hero and ensured his place as one of the prophets of airpower. Such was Mitchell's status that Hollywood immortalized him with the release of Otto Preminger's well-known feature film *The Court Martial of Billy Mitchell* (1955). If any film has underlined the ascendency of the airplane over the warship in the minds of the Anglo-American public, this was surely it.

Dowding's evidence indicates that bombs used against the armored ships of World War II needed to be at least semi-armor-piercing with a stronger steel casing to allow penetration, and fused for 0.1 seconds if 500 pounds. They also had to be dropped from an appropriate height (the report implied 12,000 feet) to achieve the desired velocity. As already indicated by Admiralty data, high-level bombing—though achieving the necessary velocity—was generally ineffective because the bomb-aimer had to cope with factors including the smallness of the target, the fact it was invariably moving, and the drift created by wind. What the Ordnance Board said about Dowding's comments is not known, but his remarks seem justified, bearing in mind the RAF never showed much expertise in sinking warships by conventional bombing until 1944 against *Tirpitz*, and this was only achieved using bombs of immense power.[29] It might also be remarked that the British experience may not have mirrored exactly that of the Germans but is still a reasonable indication of the problems that had to be faced. An anonymous "Serving Officer in the Naval Air Arm" informed a general readership around 1942 that fuse settings varied from several days to hundredths of a second but against ships would usually be a tenth of a second.[30]

British experts studied unexploded German bombs and the tactical summary referred to earlier statements that these were of various types and fuse settings. The summary tends to confirm much of what Dowding had said earlier about the greater effectiveness of bombs with slightly delayed fuse settings. Bombs that penetrated deeply into a warship or those that exploded in the water as very near misses would do much more damage than those going through and bursting well below the ship or those that simply exploded upon impact.[31] The report indicated that German bombs varied in size from about 50 kilograms to 600 kilograms, though the latter only represented 2 percent of reports. The majority of the bombs reported (70 percent) were up to about 100 kilograms (no more than 250 pounds), and 73 percent of these were fused for delay, suggesting the Germans had some appreciation of the importance of timed fuses.[32] Needless to say, "bombs reported" is not necessarily an indication of actual bombs available, and whether the men under fire could really be relied upon to have accurately counted the type and size of the bombs falling upon them seems unlikely. But it does provide some evidence of Doenitz's assertion that the bombs were far too small against heavy ships. That a few large bombs were reported in this Admiralty analysis can perhaps be put down to the report covering the period up to February 1941, moving outside the danger period for invasion that ended in late October 1940. Armor-piercing

1000-kilogram bombs were used against the modern British carrier *Illustrious* on 10 January 1941 without sinking her, suggesting the larger bombs were only just coming into service (at least on any scale) by the end of 1940 and would not have been a factor in a large-scale Channel battle.[33]

Dowding's letter tells us that the matter of obtaining an effective bomb for use against armored warships is more complex than weight alone, and this issue was one the Germans may have also found confusing. In the milieu of competing priorities before the war, there would have been no reason for Germany to devote significant resources to acquiring enough bombs of a maritime specification. German diplomatic efforts, however incompetently executed, were intended to avoid war with Britain, the only major maritime nation likely to be offended.

Germany did eventually develop effective bombs against warships. These were semi-armor-piercing bombs designated Sprengbombe Dickwandig (SD) of 500 kilograms (1,100 pounds), 1,000 kilograms (2,200 pounds), and 1,400 kilograms (3,090 pounds), but there is doubt as to when they were introduced.[34] Another source mentions reports of a heavy armor-piercing Panzerdurchsclags Cylindrisch (PC) of 1,400 kilograms (3,200 pounds) used against shipping and heavily protected targets, some of which fell on the Bristol area. Indications are that this size of PC bomb was not used until 1942.[35] The latter type may have been developed because of the disappointing attack on *Illustrious* using lighter PC 1,000-kilogram bombs in January 1941, as described earlier. In his book *The First and the Last*, Adolf Galland stated that during the attacks on London that commenced in September 1940, German aircraft bomb loads varied between 2,500 pounds and 4,500 pounds and comprised individual bomb weights of between 150 pounds to 1,250 pounds "and very rarely 2,500 lb high explosive bombs."[36] As a fighter pilot, he obviously obtained these data from a source outside his personal experience, but it does tend to confirm what has been said about the lack of large bombs. The main bomb for the Ju 87 could be as small as 250 kilograms (551 pounds) and could be augmented by four wing-mounted general purpose Sprengbombe Cylindrisch (SC) 50-kilogram (110-pound) bombs. Given that bombs were, of necessity, externally mounted, the opportunity to make last-minute adjustments to fuse settings according to the type of target presenting itself did not exist for the Ju 87 crew.

From approximately mid-1940 onwards, it was the Ju 87 B-2 that carried the SD 1,000-kilogram bomb, and from February 1940 a deflection fork designed around this bomb had been under test at Rechlin.[37] The testing appears to have taken some time. The Ju 87 B-2 was fitted with a more powerful engine (Jumo 211D) to lift 1,000-kilogram bomb loads, but few of these aircraft were available in 1940. Twenty-nine B-2s were ordered in June 1940 to be produced between July and September 1940. Another 100 were ordered for production between July and October 1940, with a final order of 98 sometime afterwards. During 1940, the Ju 87 B-1 gradually began to be brought up to B-2 standards by installing the

Jumo 211D motor as aircraft were' repaired in the workshop for battle damage. Despite this, probably no more than half of all Ju 87s could deliver this more powerful bomb load by September 1940. Only 230 B-2s were produced up to the summer of 1941 and an unspecified number were destined for the Italian Regia Aeronautica (Royal Air Force) during 1940.[38]

The merits of his bombs aside, a major consideration for the Luftwaffe pilot had to be hitting a vulnerable part of the enemy warship. It must be remembered that the first wave of German shipping was to cross at night, meaning that the problems of scoring hits on warships were greatly exacerbated anyway. As far as the heavy ships were concerned, retired naval architect John Harper Narbeth and Admiral Sir Reginald Bacon revealed some common weak points even before the war had ended. The points where bombs may have caused severe damage were: the lightly armored stern, where there was a possibility of damaging the screws or shafts; the funnel, where there was a possibility of destroying the boiler uptakes; the control top nerve center of the ship; the operating mechanism of the turrets at their bases; and the relatively thinly armored bow.[39] All of these were fairly small targets that were difficult to hit. With all the limitations of AA fire, all warships had to rely on their passive defensive characteristics.

As the smaller ships were most vulnerable to air attack it was especially important for these vessels to dodge the bombs being aimed at them. British destroyers proved adept at this. Commander J. A. J. "Alec" Dennis was serving on the destroyer HMS *Griffin* while she was on lone patrol in the Channel on 6 July 1940. *Griffin* was attacked by thirty-six twin-engine Dornier Do 17 medium-bombers arranged in four formations of nine each. Swinging around at a speed of thirty knots, *Griffin* dodged bombs from the first three formations but was shaken by near-misses from the fourth. The ship then went into harbor to repair a few minor leaks but went hunting U-boats very soon afterwards.[40] Perhaps *Griffin* was lucky, but such incidents can also be seen as a tribute to the skill of these British sailors and further evidence of the ineffectuality of high-level bombing against supposedly vulnerable destroyers. In my interview with Ron Babb, who served on a Class 1 Hunt-class destroyer in 1941, he also confirmed the reliance of small ships on evasion, maintaining he had survived many German aircraft attacks.[41] Rear Admiral L. H. K. "Turtle" Hamilton wrote to Admiral Charles Forbes from the cruiser HMS *Aurora* in May 1940 and told him that *Aurora* had been subjected to a combination of continuous dive- and high-level bombing for thirty-six consecutive hours. He continued: "From my experience, I think that provided one has sea room and independence of manoeuvre in a ship of this size, one is most unlikely to be hit."[42]

The captains of even larger ships recognized the necessity of dodging. On 26 September 1939, three Heinkel He III medium bombers attacked the aircraft carrier *Ark Royal* in the North Sea. *Ark Royal*'s gunnery officer (later Rear Admiral)

T. V. Briggs held a clear view from the top platform deck mounted on the bridge. His account stated that the cloud base was 6,000 feet with visibility from three to five miles. The first bomber made a shallow dive from 5,000 feet along a 3,000-yard line on the port quarter. A "huge bomb" was dropped at 1,500 feet as the captain pulled sharply to starboard. This caused the bomb to narrowly miss and as the aircraft passed over at 150 feet the AA batteries opened fire but failed to shoot it down because the sharp maneuver had disrupted the tracking. The second Heinkel then attracted fire from four eight-barreled pom-poms and four .50-caliber machine guns as it passed over at 100 feet. This "terrific barrage" caused the pilot to lose his nerve and drop the load prematurely. Almost immediately the third Heinkel machine-gunned the flight deck without effect. Briggs recorded that many lessons were learned on this occasion—for example, the substitution of "cease-fire gongs" for voice pipes, and headphones to aid rapid transmission of orders. However, the main problem was associated with the rapid evasion of the ship because it threw out the HAC (high-angle control) system for anti-aircraft defense.

This was the reason why the *Air Defence Instructions, 1939* did not permit fast avoiding action against dive-bombers. However, because of experiences such as the one detailed above, some commanding officers felt this action was appropriate when steaming at twenty knots at the start of the attack.[43] Even at this early stage of the war, the matter became so controversial that it was referred to the director of the Naval Air Division in October 1939. In reply, the deputy director (later Vice Admiral) G. M. B. Langley pointed out that ship displacement was small during "time of fall" yet high-speed avoiding action might cause the pilot to change his aim in the dive, but he thought this was difficult for a pilot to accomplish. He stated that trials evidence had proved the ineffectiveness of low-speed avoidance but conceded to a probability that high-speed avoiding action would increase bombing error—everything depended on the speed and maneuverability of the ship and the ability of the enemy pilot. Reinforcing the official view, he then gave his opinion that it should not be done at the cost of throwing out the AA fire.

However, other types of maneuvering were considered acceptable. These included "changing course to bring the guns to bear and to produce a high relative wind across the direction of attack."[44] Bearing in mind the Royal Navy's dive-bombers would soon have the distinction of being the first aircraft of the war to sink a heavy ship (*Konigsberg*), Langley's opinion was not to be lightly discarded. Supporting this further, the director of Naval Ordnance expressed his disquiet about avoiding action "with the use of a large wheel" at high speed as it would handicap the long- and close-range AA defenses. There was still a grudging acknowledgment of the AA deficiencies by the statement that "ideal" long- and close-range weapons systems would not become available until 1942–43, and until then the only improvements attainable were likely to "come from practice."[45]

Sidney Tyas, gunnery officer of the SS *Southgate* in 1942–43, was in general agreement with the above official views but acknowledged that his merchant ship was perhaps less maneuverable than naval destroyers, and that the vessels of 1940 were less well equipped with Oerlikon cannon. When "dodging" was necessary, he preferred the method of spinning 90 degrees back to the dive-bomber in order to make the pilot overshoot.[46] Despite these objections, captains were going to depend heavily on the ability of their ships to dodge for some time to come. Commander Dennis has suggested that one of the reasons the new destroyer HMS *Gurkha* was sunk by air attack in the Norway campaign was because her captain was a "gunnery officer" who believed in the efficacy of the AA system and deliberately chose to keep a "steady gun platform without weaving."[47] *Gurkha* had "detached from screen to improve arc of fire" and had also lost the protection of mutual covering fire from the other warships.[48]

Bearing in mind the limitations of the AA defense and the heavy reliance on "dodging" it becomes clear that morale would have been crucial in any Channel battle. This was as true for the heavy ships of the Home Fleet as it would have been for the local flotillas bearing the initial brunt of Operation Sea Lion. At this stage, it is perhaps worth reflecting on what "morale" actually is. We are told "it is an imprecise term." Carl von Clausewitz divided morale into two components of "mood" and "spirit," the first being transient and liable to change in relatively short periods depending largely on the state of the soldier's physical comforts. On the other hand, "spirit" is needed to maintain cohesion under extreme conditions, including "murderous fire." The latter can be created by ceaseless military activity "warmed by the sun of victory." More recent research indicates that Western armies create and maintain morale by attending to a variety of factors including a belief in the cause, effective training, leadership, a sense of honor, and good logistics. Logistics in this sense means the provision of comforts, food, postal services, and the fostering of self-worth. It is particularly important for the Western soldier to feel part of the substitute family represented by his mates, who rely on mutual support. This research also shows this sort of commitment can temporarily hold off the mental breakdown liable to occur when soldiers are placed under extreme stress for prolonged periods.[49] This bears some relationship to what psychologists call "attachment theory" in an attempt to explain human behavior within a framework of social interaction.

It is often when the fleet is at anchorage for long periods that morale is susceptible to steady and potentially disastrous erosion. The revolt of the lower decks in the German High Seas Fleet and the crucial participation of Kronstadt's naval garrison in the Russian Revolution of 1917 testify to the corrosive effects resulting from long periods of inactivity, which predispose men to defy the orders of incumbent authority. The Admiralty had recent experience of dealing with discontent among the fleet during the Invergordon Mutiny of 1931. Equally relevant were the naval mutinies of 1797, during a war with France and a serious invasion crisis. All of these situations indicate a failure of "spirit."

Admiral Forbes identified one potential problem of morale at the beginning of the war. This related to the youth of junior ratings without combat experience, even to the extent of "not [having] even heard a gun fire before."[50] Forbes claimed that in HMS *Rodney* alone, 374 ratings were less than nineteen years of age. Addressing this issue, the director of Naval Intelligence noted that some 22,000 ordinary seamen and boy seamen had entered the fleet over three years, marking a period of rapid expansion. These youthful sailors amounted to 50 percent of all active seamen, and he considered that in the circumstances the high proportion of young men in all active service ships was not surprising.[51] Whether Forbes was concerned about potential fighting efficiency or simply expressing a paternalistic noblesse oblige is difficult to ascertain, but "youth" was not necessarily a disadvantage. The advantage of "youth" for those individuals committed to a cause can be an inability to envisage the fatal consequences of engaging in battle. Members of the Hitler Youth fought with extreme tenacity in the fierce Normandy battles of 1944 despite an average age of sixteen, though it seems likely the factor of "youth" may work best if coupled with that of an intense ideological drive and training.

But it was the relative lack of action for the Home Fleet that caused the greatest concern. Despite the failure of the hunter-killer experiment intended to remove the U-boat threat from the Channel with mixed groups of heavy ships, there were no major actions to participate in. Apart from the sinking of *Graf Spee* and the expedition across the North Sea to test equipment against the Luftwaffe, there was not much action for the men beyond routine patrolling and escort work. Ron Babb of HMS *Rodney* reflected upon some frustration belowdecks that the enemy was not being engaged. Nevertheless, this was not seen as a significant problem of morale or a symptom of "no confidence" in the leadership of Admiral Forbes. The men were kept busy practicing drills and getting used to the equipment.

In 1940, the Royal Navy took the view that morale was primarily the concern of each individual ship's commanding officer; however, Admiralty files do reveal some wider concerns over morale at the end of 1939. The director of Personal Services (DPS) commented on "very real and widespread resentment" among the men and their families that much of their work was not being adequately publicized. The DPS discounted the idea of mutiny as "absurd," but noted how disheartening it was for the men to see other services receive "inspired publicity" while "they themselves and their arduous work are the main bulwark of the country" and were largely ignored. Interestingly, it was the lower deck that felt this the most and the ratings did not understand why it was not feasible for the navy to have the type of regular radio broadcast on the lines of "our observer attached to the Army/RAF" enjoyed by the personnel of the other services.[52] The file was passed to the desk of Admiral J. H. Godfrey, director of Naval Intelligence, who obtained an interview with Fredrick Ogilvie, director general of the BBC. A discussion ensued on the lines of reducing the depressing frequency of broadcasting shipping losses and giving the navy a higher profile. On the latter item, some substantial progress seems to have been made. The BBC commentator, Bernard Stubbs, had already increased his output on naval matters, and possibilities of broadcasts from battleships or shore canteens were discussed. A proposed system of accrediting newsreels and photographers to naval commands was also being considered.[53] This was all considered "satisfactory" and the file closed. However, the navy was never going to match the RAF for inspired publicity in 1940.

Morale was first put to the test during the Norwegian campaign in the spring of 1940. On 5 May 1940, the commanding officer of the AA cruiser HMS *Curacoa* reported that his Royal Navy Volunteer Reserve ratings manning the guns were "very much shaken after the first bomb salvo of near misses but after a few encouraging remarks, their behavior was all that could be desired."[54] Ron Babb in the engine room of the battleship HMS *Rodney* heard the Ju 87 Stuka sirens through the air ventilation system but as an engine room artificer, occupied with a great many jobs, found he was not overly concerned. While some of his colleagues working deep in the ship worried about having to get out of the bowels of the ship in an emergency, he could not recall anyone breaking down over it. Expressing confidence in the ship's ability to fight the enemy, he rated *Rodney*'s gunnery and construction highly, pointing out that it was *Rodney*'s guns that later "did in the *Bismarck*." This is surprising considering *Rodney* was a modernized but fundamentally old battleship built under the terms of the Washington Naval Agreement of 1921–22, which imposed severe tonnage limits on capital ships. When questioned further about morale in the Home Fleet during 1940, Babb asserted that it was high throughout the fleet and denied that it ever fell in the face of bad news. Because he took part in rugby matches and had conversations with other ships' crews at the Scapa Flow base, he was able to state the prevailing attitude was one of "give us six months and we'll knock 'em to kingdom come!"[55]

Writing to Admiral Forbes from HMS *Aurora* during the Norway campaign, Admiral Hamilton praised his men. On 27 May they had done fifty-one consecutive days "under weigh [*sic*] with no leave or let up to the sailors." He allowed there had been a moment when the men got "a little jumpy over the bombing" but this was only at the end of thirty-six hours of constant air attack. Hamilton confirmed that it was the men between decks that got the most jumpy but even they eventually reached a point where exhaustion enabled them to sleep through a raid. One petty officer did go to the Sick Bay but threats to "disrate him and put him in cells, and if necessary . . . shoot him" kept him at his post. An unfortunate Chinese crew attempting to abandon their merchant ship was also dissuaded with violent threats. What particularly impressed Hamilton was the "alertness and awareness of the destroyers attached to me," suggesting that morale was also high in the ships most vulnerable to air attack. A feature of the Norway campaign was the greater need for constant alertness among the crew, as the Luftwaffe could shield their approaching aircraft with the mountainous terrain and reduce the available warning time to a minimum. As the report of *Curacoa* observed, "In the fjords, everything is to the bomb-aimers advantage," also a reference to the constricted room for defensive ship maneuvers.[56] It seems, then, that those crewmen most susceptible to mental breakdowns were often less directly involved in the fighting, and because they could not see what was occurring had to contend with their destructive imaginations. But in any case the option of fleeing was hardly a feasible one. Where the captain wanted to go the sailors had to go too.

The most severe test for the Royal Navy in the early phases of World War II must have been at the Battle of Crete in May 1941. It must be stated that the circumstances of this battle could not have exactly mirrored that of 1940. The equipment was similar but not quite identical and the geographical and meteorological conditions somewhat different. As in Sea Lion, the navy needed to operate within close range of numerous enemy bombers in order to frustrate enemy land forces arriving by sea. Crete is an island approximately 160 miles long and with considerable mountainous terrain. The Royal Navy had to enter the Axis-"controlled" Aegean because Crete's harbors, bays, and airfields were located in the north and facing the Wehrmacht waiting on the Greek mainland. Unfortunately, the warships also had the disadvantages of operating nearly 450 miles away from the main naval base at Alexandria. A related problem was that RAF fighters lacked adequate range to operate over Crete from North Africa for long periods. The Fleet Air Arm could not compensate adequately for this deficiency as they only had a few low-performance fighters operating from a single aircraft carrier. Consequently, the air defense burden from repeated and sustained attacks fell on the ability of the captains to dodge the bombs and upon the skills of their AA gunners. As in 1940, there were still not enough guns and the destroyers' AA mountings were still generally incapable of high-angle elevation. This meant that a great deal still depended on the gunners' ability to stand up to murderous fire and their skills in sighting through a primitive "spiderweb" sight.[57] It did not help that many sailors were already tired from recent operations such as evacuating the army from Greece and from having to escort convoys to Malta. So great was the strain among the sailors that Admiral Andrew B. Cunningham (known as "ABC"), the C-in-C of the Mediterranean Fleet, was driven to warn the First Sea Lord about the pressures on his officers and ratings "particularly in the anti-aircraft cruisers and destroyers. . . . Never a trip to sea without being bombed."[58] On 20 May 1941, and as German paratroopers dropped over Crete, the Mediterranean Fleet attempted to prevent the enemy from landing seaborne reinforcements. The fleet was organized into four surface "forces," A, B, C, and D. As the battle progressed, these groups would change their components but the ships would usually operate together, rather than as individual units. One consequence of operating so far from base was a shortage of AA ammunition, amounting to an approximate 25 percent shortfall in most warships.[59]

Alec Dennis was serving in the destroyer *Griffin*, which was part of Force B with her sister ship *Greyhound* and the cruisers *Gloucester* and *Fiji*. He has vividly described how Force B came under heavy air attack during 21 May. Twenty Ju 87s carried out the first attack, coming down in "groups of three, one after the other, dividing their attention among all four ships. It was a classic attack, technically interesting, physically terrifying and, actually, ineffectual." Dennis went on to explain how all the bombs missed as they weaved around at full speed with the cruisers throwing up large amounts of flak. The AA fire was equally ineffectual. "We pooped off with our 3-inch museum piece, and our 0.5-inch machine guns did their best with their antedeluvian [*sic*] control system," he was to write. With ironic humor he continued, "They deserved better luck as one could see holes appearing in the aircraft, but little bullets like that weren't much use unless they hit the pilot in a painful place."[60]

Force B then sailed west to rendezvous with battleships beyond Kithea but soon after the first attack the same Ju 87s struck, again without success. Only the night before, Admiral Sir Irvine Glennie's Force D had destroyed an invasion convoy of twenty-five vessels of fishing boats (caiques) and coasters carrying troops, artillery, anti-aircraft guns, anti-tank guns, and a few tanks. Then on 22 May, Rear Admiral Edward Leigh Stuart King's Force C forced another invasion convoy of forty caiques back to Greece. If Force C had not come under massive air attack it seems likely it would have totally destroyed this convoy. Irritated at this lost opportunity and what he must have considered a bad error of judgment on the part of King, Cunningham was to write that the safest place for King's ships would have been in the middle of the enemy convoy.[61] Sadly, King may not have been the best person to command Force C, as he had difficulty maintaining a calm demeanor in a crisis. Commander Sir Godfrey Style wrote to the official historian after the war and told him that when there were problems on the bridge "ELSK would come in and push one out of the way."[62] These mistakes ended King's seagoing career.[63] For all that, these contributions by the navy ought to have won the Battle of Crete for the British. The Germans had intended to transport light tanks once sea communications were secured, but in the event this was not achieved until German airborne forces decided the issue by the capture of Maleme airfield.

The capture of Maleme and the subsequent British retreat left the Royal Navy to carry out an evacuation of British and Commonwealth troops under fire. Inevitably, evacuation piled further pressure onto the naval forces and the ships coming under air attack were now overloaded, a factor hindering the defense. Dennis wrote later: "Johnny [Lee-Barber] avoided all nine [Stukas] with great skill, turning as far as possible into the dive at 30 knots. . . . With all the extra weight on board, this meant a sickening roll over at each turn, and one wondered . . . whether we might turn over anyhow."[64] The fleet now took a serious pounding but the navy had done everything it had been called upon to do. Cunningham was later to write:

"That the fleet suffered disastrously in this encounter with the unhampered German Air Force is evident," he conceded "but it has to be remembered on the credit side that the Navy's duty was achieved and no enemy warship or transport succeeded in reaching Crete or intervening in the battle during these critical days."[65]

The Mediterranean Fleet did do its duty in dire circumstances because the sailors' morale was strong enough to endure this trauma, and because the ships had sufficient defense capabilities to survive hours of constant air attack. The ships that went down did not do so easily. The light cruiser *Naiad* sustained an estimated 108 hits over two hours, having dodged over thirty-six near-misses in one ten-minute period. The cruiser *Fiji* endured over thirteen hours of air attack before being hit by a bomb in the forward boiler room. Another strike half an hour later caused the captain to order, "Abandon ship!" Many other ships endured heavy and sustained punishment including the destroyer HMS *Kipling*, which staggered through an astonishing eighty-three attacks within a few hours. Another destroyer, HMS *Kandahar*, was commended by Cunningham for her part in rescuing survivors from *Greyhound* and *Fiji* while enduring heavy machine-gunning and bombing; he also noted that she had undergone twenty-two separate air attacks over some four and three-quarter hours.[66] Dennis condemned the initial splitting away of *Greyhound* to sink a caique as "a serious mistake." He claimed that her fate could have been foretold by any of the men at the scene, and on trying to rejoin the other ships *Greyhound* was sunk by eight Ju 87s. The subsequent need to rescue survivors led to the splitting away of *Fiji*, which in turn was sunk. Shortly afterwards, the same fate befell *Gloucester*. These ships had been detached singly and therefore sustained unnecessary casualties and damage. *Gloucester* and *Fiji* were both low on ammunition, and in the case of the latter had been down to practice-ammunition (solid shot). Ruefully noting that *Griffin* was the last survivor of Force B, he wrote: "[T]he lesson of it all, which should have been known already, was: stick together."[67]

Unsurprisingly, some mental breakdowns occurred in the wake of air attacks unprecedented in naval history. Today, psychologists recognize that the human endocrine system helps the response to emergency situations by flooding the body with adrenaline in preparation for the "fight-or-flight" syndrome. When this occurs, some fifteen bodily changes occur. This response works better in the short term, and if it occurs repeatedly or for longer periods the body will continue to pump hormones into the system. In the longer term the body will consume more resources that it can produce, meaning that the victim can no longer perform normally. In time, a loss of perspective will occur where the body will adopt an extreme reaction to even minor stress, having lost the ability to differentiate. Thus life-stressors are cumulative.[68] Delayed and recurring stress reactions to life-threatening events are now categorized as post-traumatic stress disorder. Even if combatants are taken out of the combat area, they may continue to behave as if they are still under fire. This is most likely to happen if there is any prospect of returning to combat.

In the case of the *Leander*-class light cruiser HMS *Ajax*, the toll of mental breakdowns seemed high. Out of a crew of eight hundred men, approximately thirty breakdowns were reported, a worrying enough statistic but hardly representing a mass mental breakdown.[69] Unfortunately for them, Cunningham was determined to force all damaged ships and battle-weary personnel back into combat. *Ajax* had a distinguished war record and the crew had already been recognized for their part in the sinking of the German battleship *Graf Spee* in 1939. It was therefore not surprising that much resentment was felt when Cunningham told them they had been "a little peppered but this is no time for men and ships to be loafing around the harbor."[70] In fact, the vessel had been hit by a 1,000-pound bomb and seriously damaged. Considering that Cunningham was directing operations from the safety of Alexandria, his handling of the situation was clumsy and tactless. On the other hand, if the way Admiral Hamilton of the *Aurora* dealt with men attempting to opt out was indicative of the military culture in the 1940s, then Cunningham's action was not that unusual. His task was to ensure that "fight" was going to win over "flight," and ruthless determination was necessary if the army was going to be rescued from Crete. He was still sufficiently worried about the mental state of his sailors to signal his concern to the First Sea Lord on 30 May 1940. Cunningham was not oblivious to their suffering, but in his opinion other ships were being forced to endure even more than *Ajax*, which had, he believed, been in harbor for ten out of the previous sixty days. This situation was compared with the AA cruiser *Dido*, which he claimed had only one day in harbor during the previous twenty-one days. As other warships were in a similar state, he was surprised to find the only real signs of mental breakdowns were in *Ajax*.[71]

This ruthless drive and determination allowed 17,000 troops to be rescued in under five days, and Cunningham was undoubtedly correct in stating that abandoning the troops would mean "our naval tradition would never survive such an action."[72] The C-in-C was also right about not drawing the hasty conclusion that ships could not stand up to air attack. As he pointed out, not just the HAC system, but no existing AA defense system could have dealt with heavy and repeated air attacks made from several directions at the same time. Experience had already shown that ships needed to cluster together for mutual support in the face of such attack. Therefore it was not just hindsight that allowed Cunningham to state it was a mistake for units to have been detached from the main formation of Force C to rescue *Greyhound*'s stricken crew, instead of sending the whole force in support.[73] Dennis and his comrades on *Griffin*, with previous experience of attack from the air, were correct in stating that this was a lesson that should have been learned before King's force had been decimated. As a result, the Mediterranean Fleet had suffered unnecessarily. The balance sheet showed that the Axis sank three cruisers and six destroyers, and heavily damaged thirteen ships including the sole aircraft carrier. The Italian Regia Aeronautica sank at least one of those destroyers, the *Juno*, on 20 May 1941. Tragically, some 1,800 personnel were killed in action.

The damage limited the Royal Navy's ability to operate in the Mediterranean for some time but the setback was temporary. Against all of this, the Luftwaffe sustained the significant loss of around 147 aircraft, mainly to the Mediterranean Fleet's AA defense, and 73 "from other operational causes," representing over 25 percent of their aircraft deployed.[74] The Battle of Crete had been lost but it cannot be denied that the Royal Navy had given the army its full support. It achieved its objectives and did so without massive psychological casualties.

Hezlet suggested that in the event of German air superiority in the Channel and North Sea, it would not have been possible for the Royal Navy to use their local bases. As the Ju 87 B-1 had a limited operational range of 490 miles, this particular warplane operating from the Calais area could not fly north of the Wash and return to France. However, bases between Portsmouth and the Wash would have been within range.[75] It is also known that the Luftwaffe had a small number of extended-range Ju 87R aircraft that would have had to operate without fighter escort against northern bases. Bases closer to the landing area would at least have had the benefit of a ground-based AA system with barrage balloons to protect the warships. In 1940, the only local base forced into temporary closure after dive-bombing attacks was Dover, but it must be remembered that the town and harbor were also under long-range artillery bombardment.

The vulnerability of ships in port was examined in December 1939 by R. M. Ellis, the director of Naval Air Division (DNAD), on behalf of the Chamber of Shipping. As he could only rely on the Spanish civil war experience, Ellis was contemptuous of the skills of the Italian Regia Aeronautica, stating "their average distance error against stationary targets might be estimated at 300 yards from an assumed height of release of 1000 feet." In what appears to be an arbitrary calculation, he quantified their accuracy at "an unremarkable 0.025% per bomb" on their attacks on ports. While Ellis was prepared to recognize the superior skills of the Luftwaffe, he thought that the AA defense of British ports should compensate for their bigger bombs and loads. A hitting figure of 10 percent against a large merchant ship and 5 to 10 percent for dive-bombing was suggested, but disturbing high-level bombers with AA fire and erecting barrage balloons to deter dive-bombers should reduce the figures to the level of the Italian air force. Even taking into account the undisputed fact that docks crowded with larger ships were bigger targets, he was still inclined to think the rate would be less than 1 percent per bomb, "though DNAD has no information on this point."[76] Limited and arbitrary as this was, being based on an earlier conflict between different combatants, it does challenge Hezlet's sweeping assertion about the "impossibility" of not being able to use the bases between the Humber and Portsmouth. Hezlet is also partly contradicted by his own statement relating to the "phony war" period that "the bombers of both sides had very little success against the fleets, either at sea or in harbor," qualified by an admission that neither side had tried very hard and that the ships endeavored to keep out of the way.[77]

However, there was one problem that Ellis may not have considered. Rear Admiral Bruce Austin Fraser forwarded a report to the Admiralty on 26 July 1940, complaining about the over-centralization of fighter and AA defenses. He described an incident where an AA Bofors unit failed to fire at a German seaplane landing close to the RDF station at Bawdsey. This was because the procedure required permission from Fighter Command at Uxbridge and the unit could not obtain a clear telephone line, resulting in the seaplane escaping without hindrance. While this incident begged the question as to whether the commanders of AA units ought to be allowed to use their initiative, it also highlighted a problem with the organizational structure relating to early warning against attacks by enemy aircraft. Supporting Fraser's arguments, Admiral Drax, C-in-C Nore, wanted RDF stations to alert AA units directly before the enemy aircraft came into sight. As will be seen in Chapter 5, the built-in delay in passing enemy aircraft information gleaned through RDF and the Royal Observer Corps via the filter room at Fighter Command HQ was too long for some critics. Some delays were inevitable because of the need to differentiate between enemy and friendly aircraft movements before alerting all units. As far as he was concerned, Drax thought it preferable to risk shooting down a friendly aircraft than permit an enemy aircraft to destroy a cruiser or destroyer with a mine.[78] However, the problem was not quite as serious as this situation implied. Fraser indicated in a separate report that when the circumstances of "maximum air warfare" developed, large formations of enemy aircraft were going to be more readily identifiable than single aircraft. Clearly, an invasion situation would have formed part of this "maximum air warfare" scenario, and in these circumstances there would be far less reason for hesitation.[79] Drax and Fraser could have made some reference to paragraph 14 of the *Recognition Instructions* (2nd edition, July 1939), which stated that "friendly aircraft should avoid naval anchorages." Arguably, this placed the entire responsibility on friendly aircraft for the consequences of "friendly fire."[80]

However, it was the RAF's attacks upon the invasion barges moored in Dunkirk harbor during September 1940 that provides the best example as to how ineffective bombing could be. The British prime minister was unimpressed when he wrote: "What struck me about these photographs was the apparent inability of the bombers to hit these very large masses of barges." He continued, "I should have thought that sticks of explosive bombs thrown along these oblongs would have wrought havoc, and it is very disappointing to see that they have all remained intact and in order with just a few damaged at the entrance."[81] An RAF aerial photograph corresponding to Churchill's description, showing the limited damage inflicted on barges and installations at Dunkirk, was published in the Air Ministry's official account of Bomber Command operations during the war.[82] Why the Air Ministry released this as an example of effective bombing is a mystery.

With all this in mind, both Winterbotham's assertion that after Crete ships could no longer survive against large numbers of land-based aircraft and Hezlet's claim that "it was now proved beyond any doubt that command of the sea could not be regained by ships alone" must be re-assessed.[83] "Command" is a difficult word because it implies absolute control and while the Royal Navy had overwhelming British naval superiority during the Norwegian campaign, it did not prevent the Germans transporting their army to Norway in a surprise move that caught the Allies off guard. Two years later, German air superiority allowed for temporary Axis naval superiority in the Aegean, but only in terms of inflicting "crippling" (but not fatal) losses. It did not prevent the interdiction of German seaborne reinforcements that only got through after the land battle had been decided with the capture of Maleme airfield. Neither did it prevent the Royal Navy evacuating the majority of British and Commonwealth forces. In fact, warships could successfully operate against large numbers of land-based aircraft, though at a cost. In reality, neither navies nor air forces can be strong everywhere and therefore sweeping assertions referring to command of the sea are meaningless.

On balance, the Germans did better around Crete than they were likely to have done in British waters a few months before. In the Aegean, the Luftwaffe had reliable weather for dive-bombing and better bombs, bearing in mind most Ju 87s could now carry the 1,000-kilogram SD and PC bombs. As previously mentioned, only a few months prior to Crete Ju 87s from Stukageschwader I and II severely damaged the aircraft carrier *Illustrious* with 1,000-kilogram PC bombs, scoring six direct hits and three near misses.[84] While the failure to sink *Illustrious* disappointed the German aircrews, it indicated the Luftwaffe had improved its antimaritime capability. During the evacuation, the British ships were heavily loaded, a factor making the smaller ships more sluggish to maneuver. Also, Cunningham's men went into battle already tired and stressed by recent operations, something likely to have limited their overall effectiveness. Mistakes made in the heat of the battle also contributed to the heavy losses, and despite operational experience around Norway suggesting that ships needed to keep together for mutual support, this dictum was ignored during the *Greyhound* incident. Rear Admiral King's failure to press home the attack against the second convoy meant a potentially damaging blow to the enemy was not made, and his force consequently suffered the full effects of air attack. Furthermore, the shortage of AA ammunition contributed to the difficulties experienced by the Mediterranean Fleet, and easy replenishment of stocks would not have been possible because the fleet was operating far from its naval base. Despite Hezlet's assertion about the alleged inability to use bases between the Humber and Portsmouth for emergency repair and replenishment during Sea Lion, the evidence suggests that, unlike at Crete, warships could use bases (except Dover) for these purposes. Finally, at Crete, only one carrier was available. Had the RAF been unable to operate in the Channel during an invasion, the Admiralty could use all of its seven carriers and approximately 130 low-performance fighters.[85] These Fairey Fulmars would have suffered heavily against German fighters but they would also have disrupted many Ju 87 attacks.

There is no guarantee that Admiral Forbes and the various flotilla commanders would have avoided mistakes, but we do know from Forbes' correspondence with Admiral Hamilton that he was told about the importance of ships keeping together. A desperate Channel battle would have been a bloody affair and strong morale was essential for survival, but all the indications show that naval personnel would have vigorously stood up to the constant air attacks. Bearing in mind the crucial importance of defending the homeland, this vigorous naval determination and "back-to-the-wall" spirit pervading all levels of British society boded well for British victory. The evidence indicates that German bombers were not necessarily a match for British warships in 1940. While the circumstances of the naval Battle-of-Britain-that-never-was still hold a number of imponderable factors, what can be stated categorically is that the ships and men of the Royal Navy in home waters represented a formidable obstacle to the most determined invasion attempt. Whether the RAF existed as a similarly effective force will be examined next.

CHAPTER FOUR

Who Won the Battle of Britain?

So whoever won the Battle of Britain, surely the Luftwaffe did not lose it.[1]

Wing Commander H. R. Allen, DFC

The testimony from wartime German admirals has already indicated German planners were privately content to let the supposed failure to win air superiority over England postpone and ultimately cancel the invasion attempt. Also, owing to training and equipment deficiencies, Luftwaffe intervention against the Royal Navy in support of the Kriegsmarine was unlikely to have gained "command" of the Channel. Though air superiority was not the dominant operational factor assumed in core histories, attention must be given to Wing Commander Allen's statement that the Luftwaffe *did* gain sufficient air superiority over Kent and Sussex for an invasion, an assertion criticizing the effectiveness of Fighter Command. If Hitler had proceeded, Admiral Forbes would have had a "great opportunity."[2] A second "Trafalgar"—involving the dramatic submerging of vast quantities of German men and materiel beneath the waves, together with the surrender of thousands of troops cut off from supply—would have created opportunities for an advantageous peace treaty from a desperate Hitler. Sadly, the fascinating question as to how the British might have exploited these opportunities belongs within the realm of counterfactual history. In the event, Forbes' "opportunity" of a truly decisive victory at sea was shrouded by the perceived victory in the air that Churchill was later to call the Battle of Britain. Ironically, Churchill's initial reference to the Battle of Britain in his speech to the House of Commons on 18 June 1940 referred to the resistance of the entire nation, with a cutting reference to "some people" forgetting that "we have a Navy."[3]

Hubert Raymond Allen was a Spitfire pilot of 11 Group, serving as a pilot officer of 66 Squadron during the Battle of Britain at Kenley, where he later became the squadron commander. Allen's book, *Who Won the Battle of Britain?*, came out in 1974, representing a scathing indictment of the Air Staff from someone on the "sharp end" of their policies. Historians have given it scant attention, possibly

51

because of an emotive review from F. K. Mason in a prominent defense journal and Allen's unfortunate tendency to over-state his case.[4] This was still no excuse for historians to ignore all of his allegations but unfortunately, the timing was not right. When the paperback edition was issued in 1976, H. Montgomery Hyde's *British Air Policy between the Wars, 1918–1939* was also published, praising the "superb quality of the RAF" and claiming that the "RAF exhibited the highest qualities in training, organisation, skill, and morale, amply proved in the Battle of Britain."[5] Maybe, as Allen suggested, the myths endured because the pilots who wrote about the conflict were not trained historians, and the main Battle of Britain historians lacked flying combat experience and thus could not understand the intimate details. The latter group, including Basil Liddell Hart, was forced to rely on the accounts of operational participants who, in Allen's words, may have "wanted to put the best possible light on their performance, and this led to factual misinterpretations."[6]

Even surviving German airmen found it difficult to criticize their RAF counterparts. Since the end of World War II, the Germans have been told this was an unambiguous defeat for the Luftwaffe, with commentators linking the failure to destroy Fighter Command with the failure to invade and to the ultimate German defeat in World War II.[7] Even in a bad cause, failure has to be justified and lauding an opponent's virtues can be an effective way of explaining away one's own shortcomings. Luftwaffe air ace Adolf Galland became friendly with British airmen such as Douglas Bader after the war, with Bader even writing the foreword to Galland's book, *The First and the Last*. Galland was understandably concerned to explain the failings of the Luftwaffe during the battle by praising the quality of the RAF, stressing the military incompetence of the Nazi leadership and what Galland considered to be the unjustified demands of his less glamorous bomber colleagues. He tactfully refrained from pushing his oft-quoted opinion that there never was a Battle of Britain so Germany could not have lost it.[8]

The extent to which "comradeship of the air" might distort the expressed opinions of former British and German airmen is not conducive to measurement, yet it is surely a force transcending national boundaries, making former Luftwaffe personnel acceptable in today's world. For Germans sensing the importance of the battle to the British psyche, it can be conveniently forgotten that the Luftwaffe was the arm of the Wehrmacht most imbued with the spirit of discredited National Socialism. It has been difficult for Luftwaffe veterans to win the acceptance of their former enemies. In 1968, Battle of Britain Association members turned down a proposal for German ex-fighter pilots to meet their old enemies at Bader's old Duxford base. It was turned down ninety-five to five following speeches that it was too soon and would be offensive to the widows and orphans whose men were "murdered" in 1940. Passions have since cooled and individual friendships forged. Undoubtedly, many have followed Galland's line that the air war was a "fair war" and without politics.[9] The situation also allowed the British to bask in confirmation from their former enemies that the Battle of Britain represented a British moral triumph, and the Luftwaffe personnel to believe their discreditable political leadership automatically doomed their own Herculean efforts to failure. Thus a certain unspoken consensus has arisen in which both groups can, to paraphrase Allen, "put the best possible light on their actions." All this aside, it still seems mean-spirited to make implied criticism of "the few," given their genuine sacrifices and the many popular presentations giving the unavoidable impression that for a few weeks it was only the men of Fighter Command maintaining an active resistance.

Naturally this ignores the little-publicized fact that while the air battle raged over southern England, German U-boats and surface raiders were in the process of sinking 243 British merchant vessels, representing a higher loss of life in the crucial but unglamorous cause of keeping the Atlantic supply lines open.[10] Churchill, in correspondence with President Roosevelt and in his *History of the Second World War*, chose to express the supply situation for 1940 in impersonal terms of tonnage and ships lost, rather than human casualties.[11] Even Churchill admitted that he was "even more anxious about this battle [of the Atlantic] than I had been about the glorious air fight called the Battle of Britain."[12] Naturally, he did not say this publicly at the time. As will be discussed in a later chapter, Churchill's praise of "the few" made much better propaganda because the inhabitants of southern England (including foreign journalists) could see for themselves the drama unfolding over their rooftops, while the merchant ships were largely invisible to their gaze. But Churchill was also an incurable romantic and, as his daughter-in-law revealed on television, he had a natural empathy for young people and wanted to pay his tribute.[13]

But despite the undoubted heroism of "the few," the actual operational weakness of Fighter Command must now be shown, particularly how the pilot shortage (especially of experienced pilots) linked to the inadequacy of training became the ultimate limiting factor. Also, a detailed examination of the eight-gun fighter's weapon system, tactics, and other aspects of combat effectiveness must be undertaken in order to reveal how the effectiveness of Fighter Command personnel was handicapped.

The pilot shortage shocked Churchill even before the air campaigns had begun. Writing to Secretary of State for Air Archibald Sinclair, on 3 June 1940, he expressed the War Cabinet's distress that the Air Ministry was running short of pilots and these were now "the limiting factor." Claiming this was the first time this "admission of failure" had been made, he stated that only a few months before they were told about seven thousand pilots existed, some with considerable flying experience, who did not have machines to fly. Many of these were said to have more flying experience than some of the German airmen now being captured. Churchill was now asking, "How then therefore is this new shortage to be explained?"[14] The prime minister did not reproduce the reply in his *History of the*

Second World War, and Sinclair was unable to achieve any significant improvement in time for the battle. Sinclair had only been secretary of state for three weeks at the time of this memorandum but the most likely explanation was that that many of these fighter pilots were civilians, or trained in bombers or transports and requiring extensive conversion training. Most were probably too old or otherwise unfit for the extreme physical exertions of fighter combat. In fairness to the Air Staff, the prime minister was almost certainly regretting his earlier provision of fighters and pilots to France in a vain effort to keep it in the fight, and this was the real cause of his anger.

Churchill and the cabinet may have allowed themselves to be misled about pilot numbers back in September 1939, but as a pre-war member of parliament (MP) with a reputation for agitating about air strength and later as a member of the War Cabinet, Churchill must have known about Dowding's protests over the reduction of his home defense fighter squadrons below the level previously set by the Air Council—fifty-two squadrons. Dowding's twenty-eight-paragraph letter to the Air Ministry, dated 16 September 1939, reminded them that on 3 September he had the equivalent of only thirty-four squadrons. In August he had been asked to reassure the country by radio broadcast that this was still enough to deter an attack on Britain and that "in a comparatively short space of time his [the enemy's] attacks would be brought to a standstill." Having understood an all-out effort was being made to expand home defense, he was appalled to discover his establishment was to be reduced to twenty-six or twenty-seven squadrons within a few months in order to bolster a commitment to France.[15] This letter was couched in terms of aircraft and squadrons rather than pilots, and Dowding's worst fears were not realized, but it does show that Churchill should have understood the consequences of sending more resources abroad.

A "continental commitment" had been vociferously advocated by Churchill throughout much of the 1930s as the best defense against Germany, and even now, a change of course went against the grain. Five days after he became prime minister, Churchill came under intense pressure from a desperate French government for Dowding's strength to be reduced further. Nevertheless, his decisions to send yet more aircraft and pilots abroad defied expert advice and strong opposition from Dowding, though the latter resented what he saw as a lack of support from Cyril Newall, the chief of Air Staff. Emotions were running high on all sides and Dowding was vulnerable to political accusations of allowing the fighter strength to ebb away. Not one to weigh the strength of pragmatic considerations over emotionally charged appeals, Churchill disregarded Dowding's carefully prepared statistical evidence at a cabinet meeting on 15 May 1940, with the result that four more fighter squadrons were to be put through the mincing machine.[16]

Newall's initial "failure" to give Dowding adequate support was doubtless rooted in the difficulty of countering Churchill's steamroller personality. However, Newall must have been in a dilemma. A note written by him on 9 May, the day before the German attack in the west, reveals that the Air Staff were under pressure from John Dill, then chief of the Imperial General Staff. The note suggests that Dill was pressing for Bomber Command to be used tactically against any German columns that might advance into Holland or Belgium. All previous assumptions had been made on the basis of strategic efforts against the industrialized Ruhr area, described as "Germany's most vital spot." The note reveals the Air Staff view "that to employ the heavy bomber force in this new role—except as a last resort . . . would not only be ineffective but disastrous."[17] The long-standing bomber orientation of the Air Staff made it difficult to contemplate risks to what they considered Britain's main war-winning asset, but Churchill's dislike of Dill limited his influence. At the later cabinet meeting, Newall must have thought that if he argued in support of Churchill then he would alienate a difficult subordinate, and he would find it hard to argue that medium and heavy bombers could not operate tactically if he had contributed to decisions removing the availability of fighter escorts. On the other hand, if he supported Dowding, not only would Churchill's displeasure be incurred but the focus of support for France might eventually turn in favor of sending in the bomber force with no fighter escort whatsoever. Finally, Newall did lend some belated support for Dowding: Bomber Command was not ordered to use their heavy bombers tactically, and the subsequent massacre of the Fairey Battle light bomber force in a tactical role must have confirmed their fears.

Wishing to "cover his back" and probably to save face with junior colleagues, Dowding famously iterated his advice to the Air Ministry on 16 May 1940, the original of which now hangs on the library wall at the RAF College, Cranwell. He reminded the Air Council that it was they who had estimated the minimum strength for home defense as fifty-two squadrons and that he was now down to the equivalent of thirty-six squadrons. Furthermore, he now needed to know what the revised minimum strength was to be set at, and then receive an assurance this would be adhered to. In no uncertain terms, he urged that Allied commanders on the Continent be told that no further aerial reinforcements would be sent irrespective of the situation abroad. Providing that adequate fighter forces were retained, home forces suitably organized, and the fleet remained in being, then the nation could carry on single-handed, for some time "if not indefinitely." He rounded off by starkly warning of "complete and irredeemable defeat" if forces earmarked for home defense continued to be drained in order to "remedy the situation in France."[18]

Unrepentant, Churchill issued a demand for a further six squadrons, the spirit of which was denied by the Air Staff by keeping the squadrons based in England and allowing the aircraft to stop in France long enough for rearming and refueling only.[19] An unsigned draft memorandum, dated "about 24 May 1940," written possibly by Newall and later filed in *Second World War: Fighter Control and Interception 1952*, must ultimately have found its way to Churchill, perhaps in revised form, prompting his scathing memo of 3 June 1940. In paragraphs five and six of this unsigned draft memorandum, it was stated that between 10 May (the day Churchill came to power) and 24 May (approximately), nearly two hundred fighter pilots were lost, in other words a "fifth of our most highly trained fighter pilots." So devastating was this loss of trained personnel that the "number of pilots available per squadron was now little more than adequate to man the available aircraft. More serious is the loss of a considerable proportion of trained leaders." While many of the aircraft had been replaced, "there remains a grave deficiency in pilots."[20] Of course, Churchill was not directly responsible for the units already in France on 10 May, and it is not possible to ascribe a specific number of pilot losses linked to the above decisions but they must have been significant. If the battle was won by a narrow margin, as is usually claimed, then Churchill's "generosity" must have significantly imperiled the effectiveness of Fighter Command. The sense of guilt he must have experienced certainly explains the anger expressed in his missive to Sinclair and partly explains his subsequent gratitude to "the few," ironically a group he helped diminish in number.

Fortunately for the RAF, the measures taken by the Baldwin and Chamberlain administrations during the 1930s, combined with the later efforts of Lord Beaverbrook at the Ministry of Aircraft Production, allowed for adequate fighter aircraft availability when the critical time came. However, it was a near thing as the Air Ministry's plans had rested on the reasonable (but wrong) assumption that the Messerschmitt Me 109E fighter would not appear in British airspace owing to its short fuel range and therefore saw no need to give priority for single-engine fighters over more heavily armed twin-engine fighters. Furthermore, the Air Ministry had been let down by the industrialist Lord Nuffield, who was slow to produce Spitfires from his expensive new factory at Castle Bromwich.[21]

However, fighter production was only one prerequisite for survival, as the Luftwaffe discovered in 1945, with plenty of new aircraft hidden in forests and under autobahn bridges yet with few trained pilots to fly them. For the Germans in 1944–45, the problem was rooted in a shortage of aviation fuel that starved the training schools of the means to conduct training programs. With no enemy bombers pounding petroleum installations in the period prior to the Battle of Britain, RAF training establishments had less excuse for the inability to maintain a supply of well-trained pilots capable of filling the ranks of the fallen. However, like other organizations within the armed services, the RAF training organization suffered from problems resulting from the rapid expansion of the 1930s. It would be easy to blame the Baldwin and Chamberlain administrations for not bankrolling the perceived needs of the RAF, but the plans for air expansion involved astronomical expenditure. A minute by the chancellor of the exchequer in 1937 stated: "If that scheme is approved without reservation the Air Ministry will need to expend in the five years to 1942 a sum which exceeds by nearly £350 millions the amount which could be allotted to it out of the total five years expenditure of £1,650 millions for all Defence Services (including Civil Defence)."[22]

It needs to be understood that defense spending as a whole had risen from £100 million in 1933 to over £700 million in 1939, rising by approximately 40 percent per annum from 1935. It had also opened up a yawning balance-of-payments gap from £18 million in 1936 to £250 million in 1939, because most raw materials required for rearmament had to be imported. Historian Clive Ponting believed the government "got it right" in 1934 by setting their rearmament program to peak in 1939. If it climaxed before war broke out, the services would be armed with obsolete equipment. On the other hand, if rearmament had peaked later, they would not have had enough equipment.[23] The post-Munich decision to expand Fighter Command by 30 percent prompted the chancellor's warning that it was "so costly as to raise serious doubts whether it can be financed beyond 1939–40 without the greatest danger to the country's stability."[24] Serious deficiencies still remained in 1939 but given the country's economic predicament and an acknowledgment that resources are always finite, the Royal Air Force had secured more of these resources than the nation could afford and probably more than it had any right to expect in the circumstances. It cannot be denied that the Royal Navy had received more funding than the RAF and the British army between the wars, but given the expensive infrastructure of dockyards and the fact that a maritime strategy was still the foundation of British defense, this was only right. As will be seen, both the Royal Navy and crucial areas of the air defense would have derived considerable benefit from the money spent on the perceived need for strategic bombers.

The Air Ministry plan had been to train 5,800 pilots per year, rising to 11,000 by 1942, but in the event, this proved inadequate.[25] That pilot shortage became the ultimate limiting factor is hard to dispute, but nobody on either the British or German side seriously viewed the likelihood of the Luftwaffe operating from bases in northern France before the sudden collapse of that country in May 1940. Dowding told the historian Basil Liddell Hart in 1943 that "our greatest danger lay in the failure of the training organization to stand the strain."[26] Another writer claimed the training schools continued to work at peacetime levels after the war had begun and Dowding's pleas to the Air Staff went unheeded.[27] The truth was a little more complex. Shortly after the battle commenced in earnest, the Air Council met to discuss increasing the output of pilots. In a note dated 6 August 1940, the main limiting factor was identified as "deficiencies of advanced trainer type aircraft." The solution was seen as using operational-type aircraft to supplement existing trainer types, reducing the length of courses in Group II schools from fourteen to twelve weeks, and reorganizing the training so that more time was spent at Operational Training Units (OTUs) at the expense of Service Flying Training Schools (SFTS). These necessitated additional OTUs, some of which might be based abroad. It was envisaged the proposals would increase the weekly output of trained pilots from 124 to 204 over a period of "some months." Incredibly, given the crisis in home defense by this date, the emphasis in the note was on the training of bomber pilots with no specific reference to fighter pilots or the grave situation currently facing Fighter Command.[28]

The Air Historical Branch Narrative of the Ministry of Defence represents the starting point for any student of the air battles. This shows that in August 1940, the training schools could only deliver 260 trained fighter pilots to partly fill the gaps caused by the 304 killed or wounded. In the critical period of 24 August to 6 September, 103 pilots were killed or missing, with 128 seriously wounded, meaning 231 pilots would not be available to resist an invasion, had one come after 6 September. This meant that from not quite one thousand pilots making up his fighting strength, Dowding was losing 120 pilots per week.[29] Another Air Ministry table shows the total killed on operations between 22 August and 11 September 1940 to have been 127, which seems reasonably consistent with the above figures.[30] Clearly this was not a situation that could be sustained for long without a major impact on efficiency, and it was noted that fresh squadrons rotated into the main battle area suffered more heavily than tired but experienced ones. Squadrons now averaged only 10 operational pilots per unit out of an establishment of 26, though in the all-important 11 Group the operational pilots averaged 19.[31]

Even if the entire casualty list could have been fully offset by the influx of new pilots, a "rookie," or non-operational, pilot can hardly have been much use to his squadron in view of the fact that the training course had recently been cut from one month to two weeks. Before the war it had been twelve months. In terms of practical experience, a new Spitfire pilot could (and undoubtedly did) enter combat with a mere ten hours' solo flying experience and without ever having fired his guns.[32] Of course, even a well-trained "rookie" would have been a short-term liability to his flight leader, but one that was only half-trained was a menace to his own side. Whatever efforts were made to enforce radio/telephone (R/T) discipline at OTUs, excitable new pilots were notorious for jamming up airways with unnecessary verbiage, thus preventing warnings and interfering with directions from the ground.[33] In an interview conducted by Nigel Lewis, Battle of Britain ace Peter Brothers maintained it was the pilots who went into combat after a few hours' training that suffered the worst attrition rate. "The new boys were the poor chaps who got the chop." Brothers also made the telling observation that "of the 20 pilots in the pre-war 32 Squadron, not one was killed."[34]

On 23 October, toward the end of the battle, a training conference was held at Fighter Command HQ, chaired by Dowding's aide, Air Vice Marshal Douglas Evill. The background was Dowding's decision of 8 September to discontinue his system of rotating squadrons in and out of the 11 Group's area in favor of feeding squadrons in Groups 11, 12, and 10 with individual pilots. The so-called "stabilisation system" was an operational expedient intended to last only until the OTUs could provide enough pilots to meet the wastage problem. By mid-September, 11 Group's squadrons had been reduced to less than 16 per unit on average, but the situation now improved to 19 per unit. At one stage Fighter Command was receiving four-fifths of SFTS output, overloading OTUs that were forced to accommodate eighty to ninety pupils to be turned out at the end of a fortnight "as best they can." Consequently 120 replacement pilots per week needed to be brought up to operational standard in mainly "C"-class squadrons located in quieter backstop areas. This meant that on 23 October there were 440 non-operational pilots, representing one-third of all Fighter Command pilots. This implied that the twenty "C"-class squadrons with approximately 16 non-operational pilots each were virtually non-operational units. At this date, 11 Group had about 19 operational pilots per squadron, despite an aspiration to bring them up to 25 operational pilots, or perhaps 22 with a few non-operational pilots to train. This suggests that in terms of operational pilots, a "typical" 11 Group Squadron would have been no stronger at the end of October than in the "critical period" of 24 August to 6 September 1940.

The solution was seen as increasing the number of OTUs and making changes to the syllabus.[35] Nevertheless, a picture emerges of an organization that had enough pilots overall, but not enough of whom were fit enough to engage the enemy. The "stabilisation system" was unpopular with squadrons generally, many of which lost the operational pilots they had just trained. In Dowding's words, "The stabilisation of squadrons in the line and the creation of class 'C' squadrons was a desperate expedient forced upon me by the heavy losses."[36] But internal correspondence within the Air Ministry shows it was not until the end of November 1940 that Fighter Command's new C-in-C felt the organization had recovered sufficiently to discontinue the stabilization system, and even then a significant factor was the lighter scale of enemy daylight attack.[37]

Yet it may be misleading to suggest the performance of Fighter Command was primarily determined by the ability of the training schools to churn out a sufficient number of adequately trained pilots. The Luftwaffe disposed of the fledglings presented to them quickly enough but perhaps, as Allen suggests, it was the diminishing pool of experience as the conflict progressed that became the true limiting factor. That 231 pilots were killed or seriously wounded between 24 August and 7 September was bad enough, but the real significance lies in the fact that these figures included approximately 50 of 11 Group's experienced flight leaders.[38] As the casualty rate mounted, there were fewer experienced flight leaders for the fledgling pilot to turn to. Veteran fighter pilot P. B. "Laddie" Lucas, representing what were clearly the views of himself and Douglas Bader, wrote that: "Subject to height (which was critical), there was not a lot to choose between the Hurricane I, the Spitfire I, and the Messerschmitt 109E *in actual combat*." According to these officers "pilot quality counted for much—much more than most would credit."[39]

The "critical period" was marked by Luftwaffe attacks on Fighter Command airfields and sector stations, of which the latter were by far the most important. German tactics were to use large formations of bombers closely escorted by Messerschmitt Me 109E fighters weaving around their charges with engines throttled back. This airborne battering ram proved difficult to stop. To begin with, the close-escort policy reduced the effectiveness of the German fighters, but as more fighters became available from Air Fleet III to serve with Kesselring's Air Fleet II, a high-altitude escort layer was added to the formations, giving the initiative back to the Luftwaffe's fighter arm. The majority of German fighter pilots were very experienced, in some cases from serving in the Spanish civil war. A memorandum from Keith Park, area officer commanding (AOC) 11 Group, to Dowding on 12 September remarked that these tactics meant raids "on several occasions . . . barged through our first and second screen of fighters and reached their objectives by sheer weight of numbers."[40]

RDF aside, the main advantage possessed by the defending eight-gun fighters was the tighter turning circle essential in the classic dogfight. The advantages conferred by this were now negated as German fighters could swoop in at high speed, open fire with their superior firepower, and climb back faster than their opponents could follow. The top-cover Messerschmitts could often launch their attacks from the altitude and direction best suiting the attacker. When the Spitfires, whose job it became to engage the top layer, reached the level at which the Messerschmitts were operating, they remained at a disadvantage because the German aircraft performed better at the higher altitudes. As RAF aces Johnnie Johnson and Laddie Lucas put it, "tight-turns did not win air battles, as tight-turns are more of a defensive than an offensive tactic." They went on to state that only superior height could save a fighter from the "bounce" and that the Messerschmitt Me 109E was "decidedly superior" at the higher altitudes where many fights occurred.[41] With the Luftwaffe now holding the tactical advantage, enabling the full exploitation of their equipment, it was only pilot quality that might have redressed the balance. Sadly, this was a fast deteriorating asset for the British. In the circumstances, an adverse effect on pilot morale might be expected. This is not something susceptible to measurement but if the views of three experienced combatants during the "critical phase" are typical then it is hard to see how the circumstances permitted any of these men to function at optimum performance. Group Captain Peter Townsend admitted that the enemy were now "wearing us down; we were weary beyond caring, our nerves taughtened to breaking-point."[42] The normally ebullient Al Deere, reflecting on the fact that only four pilots originally with him since the battle started were left, remarked that the prospects of victory "could only get worse, progressively worse."[43] Even the imperturbable South African ace "Sailor" Malan was said to have "burst into tears" at this time.[44]

One of the most serious shortcomings in the new pilot's training lay in the inability to use his guns effectively. The pre-war pilot may have had a sounder grounding in most aspects of flying training, but the financial constraints referred to earlier would severely restrict his access to target ranges, practice ammunition, and towing aircraft. Later it would be the pressure to produce trained pilots within a short space of time that would be blamed for neglecting what should have been an essential part of the syllabus.[45] In November 1939, Dowding responded to a complaint that the "shooting has gone off" in a letter to Sir Henry Tizard, chief scientific advisor to the chief of Air Staff. On the basis of two combat reports, he pointed out that inexperienced pilots tended to fire their guns in short bursts. Each time the guns fired, the recoil forced the aircraft's nose downwards and bullets were wasted until the line of sight was realigned on the target. The displacement of the pilot's aim would then cause him to cease firing, meaning that the fighter would never get the chance of firing a steady burst of fire into the enemy bomber.[46] Bearing in mind that eight-gun fighters of the RAF could fire continuously for only fourteen seconds, a desire to conserve ammunition was understandable. Furthermore, the lack of round-counters made it impossible to monitor ammunition expenditure in combat.[47] Undoubtedly, firing "short bursts" was good advice for 1914–18, when gun stoppages due to over-heating from extended firing were commonplace. Aircraft dynamics were also different, but by 1940 the weaponry was more reliable. At this early stage of the war, Dowding believed some 300 strikes were necessary to bring down a Heinkel He III medium bomber, largely because of their "extremely efficient self-sealing [fuel] tanks."[48] If correct, then even more strikes would have been needed to bring down a machine such as this in the Battle of Britain, when they carried more armor plating. Indeed, Allen emphasizes Group Captain Peter Townsend's failure to bring down a German bomber with 220 strikes. This was no fault of Townsend. In fact, it represented good marksmanship, but it was a number probably not achievable by the average pilot.[49] According to Dowding's post-battle dispatch, the Germans adopted more armor plate to protect the crew and vulnerable parts of the aircraft as the Battle of Britain progressed, suggesting the chance of a "rookie" downing a bomber with a short burst was negligible.

The inspector general's visit to Sutton Bridge OTU on 3 May 1940 revealed the problems faced by establishments in bringing gunnery trainees up to standard. Gunnery practice for visiting units consisted of firing at 4 x 20–inch target drogues from the beam. The training was limited by the serviceable state of the four Henley towing aircraft. A spares shortage limited these to one or two aircraft at a time. Air Chief Marshal Ludlow Hewitt, a former C-in-C of Bomber Command with a special interest in gunnery, was skeptical of the OTUs claim that the targets "get shot to bits at once" even though "the target is very big and was being towed very slowly." Ludlow Hewitt also criticized the small twenty-five-yard firing ranges and noted that the other Fighter Command OTU at Aston Down needed a 400-yard range to "enable fighter aircraft to fire their fixed guns at various ranges on the ground." He was also critical of Sutton Bridge's location, stating that the "air defence restrictions there are most hampering to every form of training," though it is unclear exactly what he meant by this.[50]

A further limiting factor for the marksman must have been the quality of the armament carried. After all, the guns represented the final point of contact between the attackers and defenders without which everything else counted for little. Armament also had a fundamental effect upon tactics. Dowding had the problems spelled out to him again in a letter from the RAF Staff College at Andover, dated 3 October 1940, toward the end of the battle. This quoted the opinion of an anonymous "test pilot who was attached to a Squadron and bagged four Huns." He asserted that the existing armament was good for destroying enemy fighters but "is rapidly becoming obsolete for use against enemy formations," and went on to describe the heavy rear armor German bombers were carrying together with rear-mounted cannon and cross-fire. "The armament of eight .303 guns is therefore insufficient, both in range and penetrating power for effective attack in these formations." Also interesting was the recommendation that fighters be re-classified as "Dogfighters" whose role would be to engage enemy fighters, and "Destroyers," equipped with frontal armor and with a minimum of four Hispano cannon to take on the lower-flying bombers. Both types would operate in close cooperation.

It was already too late. The large-scale daylight battles were over by October, and in any case Keith Park, AOC 11 Group, had used these tactics as far as he could by using the Spitfires against the escorts and the slower but slightly more effectively armed Hurricanes against the bombers whenever circumstances permitted.[51] The anonymous author was undoubtedly correct in his analysis, as the Luftwaffe later proved by blowing apart the early American Flying Fortress attacks over Germany with the heavily armed Messerschmitt Me 110 "Destroyers" that had earlier proved so disappointing in fighter-to-fighter combats in the Battle of Britain. With hindsight, it might be said that the Air Ministry should have pushed for earlier delivery of the Bristol Beaufighter, a twin-engine fighter aircraft that was only available in small numbers during the battle but had been in development since late 1938.[52] Oddly enough, before 1940, the Air Ministry had allegedly shown more interest in the Beaufighter than the Spitfire because of the former's heavier cannon firepower.[53]

One of Allen's more dramatic assertions is that the Air Ministry should have fitted American Colt .50-caliber machine guns instead of the Browning .303, the latter being a scaled-down version of the former (though much modified) and made under license in Birmingham. In view of the foregoing evidence, the inadequacy of the .303 cannot be denied, and Allen quoted figures to support his contention that the Colt .50 (Mk II) batteries would have been fifteen times more effective than the Browning.[54] A review of Allen's work by one distinguished historian deplored the "unnecessary ('computerised') lengths" in proving the superiority of the .50 bullet to the .303 fired from a Spitfire or Hurricane. However, this armament comparison ought not to be summarily dismissed.[55]

The inconsistency in Allen's data with that of L. Deighton related to the Browning. Allen quoted the Browning .303 muzzle velocity at 2,240 feet per second, while Deighton allowed a higher 2,660 feet per second, explainable by differences in ammunition used. Allen also allowed a rate of fire of 1,350 rounds per minute, as opposed to Deighton's slower 1,200 rounds per minute. Deighton did not specify which mark of Browning he referred to, and unfortunately neither author has specifically attributed his sources. However, even if Deighton's figures are preferred, there is still a substantial advantage in favor of the Colt.

The Air Ministry could have opted for this in 1933 but after trials with other products, including Vickers, the Air Ministry decided that the advantages of the Colt in terms of range and hitting power were outweighed by the lighter weight and faster cyclic rate of the .303 Browning.[56] Overheating problems in earlier versions of the Colt may have influenced the decision but these problems were overcome during the 1930s.[57] According to the notes of Air Marshal Sir Ralph Sorley, controller of Research and Development, the Colt .50 had developed little. He went on to say that "[although] it possessed a better hitting power, the rate of fire was slow and it was a heavy item of installed weight and ammunition." Sorley conceded "the 5-inch gun, although attractive from the point of view of hitting power," had another problem. It "did not lend itself to the rapid build-up of lethal density within the limits of weight which could be allowed for such a fighter at such a time."[58] What Sorley meant by "rapid build-up of lethal density" was the ability to deliver maximum destruction within the two seconds it was thought possible for a pilot to keep an enemy within his sights. He went on to admit defensively that the whole question of an appropriate gun was "something of a nightmare during 1933–34."[59]

If Allen's somewhat dramatic figures are accepted, then any idea of the Browning .303 outperforming the Colt .50 appears ludicrous, but the term "within the limits of weight" is a crucial one because aircraft were quite different in the early 1930s. The gull-wing Spitfire prototype of 1933 bore little resemblance to that of 1940, and was built around the inadequate Goshawk II engine demanded by the Air Ministry in an earlier specification. This gave a top speed of only around 238 mph. The armament specification was still only four machine guns, and the period was prior to the full development of 100-octane aviation fuel and the variable pitch propeller that significantly boosted the performance of British fighters in time for the battle. Furthermore, the speed margin between fighters and bombers was much narrower in 1933.[60] Heavier guns would therefore slow a fighter down, and make it less responsive. The Colt .50 Mk II weighed 29 kg as opposed to 9.9 kg for a Browning Mk II.[61] Assuming the Browning Mk VII was a similar weight to the Mk II, Sorley was in a genuine dilemma.

Sorley's notes inevitably reflected the Air Ministry's thinking in terms of fighter versus fighter World War I dogfights, where snap shots with short bursts at fragile but fast maneuvering targets were the norm. One does not have to be a pilot to realize that twin-engine bombers did not generally move in this way. Bombers needed to keep together in tight formations for mutual defense, and any sharp maneuvering of a heavy bomb-laden aircraft would jeopardize mutual safety by upsetting the defensive cross fire. This is similar to the problems created by naval fire-control systems used for AA defense. With fighters attacking from above, the problem related to fast overtaking speeds giving little time for aiming and firing. The problem with a two-second burst is that if eight guns deliver 2,400 rounds over fourteen seconds, my calculations suggest no more than 343 rounds can be fired in that time. If one takes Dowding's standard (or guesstimate) of three hundred hits against an unarmored bomber to bring it down, then a very high standard of marksmanship would have been required. This needed improving as the Germans progressively adopted armor protection.

The Air Ministry's decision was correct at the time given that every air force in the world was predominately equipped with flimsy wood and fabric biplanes. Furthermore, the designers of the Spitfire had difficulty fitting the Browning to this machine once the Air Ministry decided to increase the specification to eight guns in 1935. This meant the wing had to be completely redesigned as a result of the new armament specification. Therefore, if the new wing had been designed around the Colt, the distinctive thin elliptical wings would not have been developed, with a likely adverse effect on aircraft performance. Had the decision been made to use Colts after the elliptical wings had been produced, it would have involved fitting large "blisters" to the wing, a modification inevitably affecting speed and maneuverability as happened when cannon were fitted. However, drastic modifications were less necessary for the Hurricane. As it transpired, the Spitfire was most effective in a fighter versus fighter role, where the advantages of hitting power were clearly less crucial given the relative fragility of fighters to bombers. None of this is covered in Allen's critique, lending substance to the complaint about his "bland ignorance of aircraft design." The need for economy linked to the availability of World War I surplus .303 ammunition has also been raised and this was also mentioned by Sorley; however, it seems doubtful if this was other than a subsidiary factor.[62]

By 1933 the Air Ministry might have anticipated that other powers would soon be following the British with their own sturdy metal monoplane fighters and bombers. By keeping the Hurricane's armament under review, the development of tactics referred to by the Staff College letter might have been introduced at an earlier stage of the battle. Armored protection of vital parts in some aircraft was even carried out in World War I. Quoting a letter from the Imperial War Museum, Allen attributed the original introduction of the .50 to circumstances that partly blamed the death in air combat of former President Theodore Roosevelt's son, Quentin, on the inability of his twin .303 machine guns to penetrate the armor of his adversary.[63]

One official publication stated that it was only in 1935—when armor was becoming more widely adopted and fighter designs sufficiently robust to take the recoil of larger guns—that attention began to be paid to developing these weapons. The Air Staff took a strong pro-cannon line, and one can only conclude this prevented any further serious consideration being given to installing the .50 Colt until the war began.[64] This does not necessarily mean the Air Staff lacked reservations about cannon installations in fighter wings. It has been suggested those reservations were overridden by Lord Beaverbrook, minister for aircraft production in 1940, "as completely as only he knew how."[65] It would still be wrong to blame Beaverbrook for not adopting the Colt. By the time Beaverbrook came on to the scene, it was too late. The emphasis needed to be on aircraft numbers now the battle was about to begin.

The correspondence between Dowding and Tizard in November 1939 throws some light on this matter as it considered the possibility of higher caliber guns offsetting the armor-plating defense capability of the German planes. Tizard opened with comment on recent fighter combats, which he did not think very satisfactory. He raised the possibility of pilots standing off "too much" and firing at too long a range. Tizard suggested that ranges of up to four hundred yards and down to one hundred yards would result in the "bomber . . . dead every time." He had also been looking at the problem of penetrating armor plate and mentioned an "American Browning of (? .55 inch)," presumably the Colt .50 referred to by Allen. Tizard was told the muzzle velocity of the larger weapon was 2,800 feet per second, and plenty were available. He thought very high muzzle velocity (presumably over 2,800) was counterproductive in that the bullet tended to break up on impact. Although there was a difference of opinion about this gun's use in fighters, "everyone" was keen on developing it. He ended by asking Dowding if he was prepared to accept this gun.[66]

In paragraph twelve of his reply, Dowding claimed that a .50 Vickers had been tried but tests proved it could not penetrate aircraft armor plate. Dowding's information in paragraph thirteen, which he admitted was "probably quite unreliable," is that the muzzle velocity of both the Vickers and the "Browning" .50 is 2,450 feet per second. While some clash of evidence can be seen on the effectiveness of a .50-caliber weapon, perhaps explainable by types of ammunition used, it is interesting to observe Dowding's characteristic rant in paragraph fourteen about "'Scientists,' 'Experts,' and 'Practical men,' all arguing about a point which can quite easily be settled by practical experiment." Dowding's contention was that the ordnance institutions at Woolwich and Farnborough preferred to defend their positions "at all costs" rather than resort to a reasonable method of resolving differences.[67] Even allowing for the streak of paranoia in Dowding's personality it is an interesting commentary on the difficulties of trying to push through technological improvements. Such entrenched stances can be found in most organizations to some extent, but it does suggest that the inherent dissention among the technical advisors may have influenced the quality of the original decision to install the Browning. Later on Tizard was claiming "everyone" was for developing the .50 and there were plenty available. Whether "everyone" referred to members of the Air Defence Committee or the technicians at Farnborough and Woolwich is unclear. Sadly, for the fighter pilots of the RAF this last chance to partially re-equip with more effective weaponry in time for the Battle of Britain was lost.

As can be seen from Allen's table, the muzzle velocity quoted by him is 2,900 feet per second, which is reasonably close to Tizard's figure.[68] It must be stated here that his figures are purely theoretical, though he does observe that the Colt .50 was the weapon used by the United States Army Air Forces (USAAF) in the formidable Mustang fighter, generally attributed with achieving air supremacy against the Luftwaffe over Germany in 1944.[69] Dowding on the other hand seems to have based his conclusions on memories of actual practical tests (presumably the trials held in 1933) but it must be remembered he did not have complete faith in his source. It seems that Tizard had correctly identified this problem prior to the Battle of Britain and saw the Colt as a potential remedy. Sadly, neither man was confident of his facts and if they had looked into this matter more thoroughly, perhaps something better than the unsatisfactory Hispano 20-mm cannon would have been found. The Hispano saw experimental service in small numbers during the latter stages of the battle but proved so unreliable that RAF pilots using these asked to revert to the Browning. Ironically, the Hispano was one of the weapons rejected in 1933 because of insecure mountings. Dowding gave some belated acknowledgment to the .50-caliber genre in his post-battle dispatch when he mentioned arrangements for it to be fitted in the Spitfire universal wing "if the production of cannons is insufficient for requirements."[70] He seemed to favor cannon over further machine-gun development, and tests at Farnborough during 1940 seemingly confirmed that cannon would be better. Whether the Colt .50 was tested alongside the cannon in this later round of testing is unknown but in any case it was probably too late to help the fighter pilot in the Battle of Britain.[71]

Dowding had considered the possibility of enemy aircraft adopting armor protection by 1938 at least. He advised Air Vice Marshal William Sholto Douglas that the eight-gun fighter was "at present a very effective and deadly weapon" but recognized that protective devices might "make it comparatively ineffective in the future." He agreed with Sholto Douglas that a new type of air cannon was needed for the future but expressed a sarcastic opinion that the Woolwich Arsenal would probably take seven years to develop it. In his view, the situation was not helped by a "fixed-idea" in the Air Ministry that such a weapon would entail the concurrent development of sophisticated long-range sighting apparatus, something unnecessarily delaying implementation of the weaponry.[72] The Air Ministry would not have been completely wrong about the need for a sophisticated sight. Those used by pilots in the battle were essentially the same primitive ring design as in World War I and this was probably a factor in their poor gunnery performance. In the very long term, cannon would indeed supersede machine guns but it was by no means obvious at this stage, bearing in mind the lesser number of strikes obtainable from slower cannon shells. While it was reasonable to think of the cannon as a long-term solution, indications are that Dowding would have done better to adopt the Colts as a medium-term solution to the problem of piercing German armor. As may be gathered from the tone of his correspondence, Dowding seemed to have had difficulty dealing with "experts" in the ordnance field.

Nevertheless, a caveat has to be added to this. It has been claimed the system of operational requirements was not one in which the commander-in-chief's views could always be represented to the technical departments of the Air Ministry through a single channel. There existed "the absence of anything that might be described as a strictly concerted progression of ideas." Technical demands from the squadrons to the Directorate of Operational Requirements through to the Ministry of Aircraft Production were made in a multiplicity of ways. Senior staff such as the director of Operational Requirements (DOR) had enormous scope for making and interpreting requirements, and staff would often act on their own initiative. In such a chaotic environment and lacking a proper system of evaluating requirements, there was no guarantee that Dowding's opinions on fighter development and armament would receive prominence. The "uncertainties and vacillations which occasionally marked the Air Staff policy" go some way to explain the impatient and intemperate language adopted by Dowding in his correspondence.[73]

Because the Spitfire's wings were thin, its eight machine guns were spread out along the wings. This made a reasonable concentration of fire impossible without harmonizing them to converge at a fixed point ahead of the aircraft. Deighton advises that during the battle the Spitfire's Brownings were set to converge 650 yards ahead, although other sources indicate a range of 400 yards was used. Both ranges were too long. With regard to the 650-yard harmonization, one anonymous pilot from 54 Squadron was quoted as claiming, "All this guarantees is a few hits by the indifferent shot; the good shot on the other hand is penalized." Unfortunately, the number of "indifferent" shots was probably quite high and it has already been shown that the OTUs were desperately short of resources. Gunnery instructor George Unwin believed many fighter pilots during the early part of the war lacked the ability to calculate the distance to the target. His first flight commander taught him that if a "Wellington"-size bomber exactly filled the ring sight, the range was 400 yards, but if it was just outside the twin engines, it had closed to 200 yards. Although this was both simple and effective, Unwin believed the method was never applied universally throughout the service.[74]

Allen claimed that it was only as a result of camera-gun analysis over Dieppe in 1942 that the RAF realized their pilots could not shoot. No confirmation of this could be found at the National Archives. However Dowding's successor, Air Marshal Sholto Douglas, was recorded in late 1941 as being "very concerned about the standard of air gunnery in Squadrons and anxious that more gunnery training should be given to pilots prior to joining their Squadrons." Stating it was "imperative" standards be improved, he noted that pilots at OTUs fired their guns only two or three times per week. Furthermore there was a serious shortage of towing aircraft and this "would exist in the near future." If this was the situation at the end of 1941, when the OTUs had the opportunity to re-organize and "get their act together," the standard of 1940 must have been very low and the leadership slow to realize the magnitude of the problem.[75]

Dowding's correspondence with Tizard suggests that an exceptionally brave pilot who closed in to near point-blank range, either to increase penetration or to overcome the limitations of his gunnery training, would have been exposed to return fire from the bomber's gunners for no commensurate advantage if his machine had the official harmonization. He told Tizard in 1939 "that my policy of long-range firing has nothing to do with the safety of the fighter pilot, who is (at the moment) very safe from return fire."[76] Some pilots ignored the "regulation on 650 yard harmonization" and Sailor Malan had his armaments officer re-harmonize them at 250 yards.[77] It has been claimed that as a result of the air battles over Dunkirk "more than one squadron learnt to harmonise its guns at 250 yards instead of 400 yards and to forget about textbook tactics."[78] How many squadrons actually did so is not known, yet if Allen is to be believed—and he should have known—no general edict to do this was issued. Even sympathetic writers have commented on the apparent "lack of effort" in promulgating the lessons learned at the front line to the fresh squadrons waiting their turn to move into the major combat zones.[79] Although no specific instructions on this subject could be located in the Fighter Command Tactical Memoranda file at the National Archives, it is clear that machinery for issuing these from a central point did not exist until June. A memorandum registering concern about the growing amount of correspondence on the subject of tactics, "which if allowed to accumulate, may well defeat its own object," was sent to the Air Ministry at the end of June. It noted the tendency of Groups to circulate their own notes and that "War Tactics" were considering issuing their own notes. In future, it was considered that correspondence would be coordinated at the Air Fighting Development Unit, bringing together both Fighter Command and Air Ministry War Tactics.[80] While it was desirable not to submerge pilots in mountains of potentially conflicting papers from different sources, it seems strange that the need for lessons learned the hard way should not have been consolidated in a single set of technical memoranda long before this. Arguably, the relative inaction of the "phony war" may only have provided limited opportunity to test out the gunnery issues with which this section deals, but the well-known failure of fighter squadrons to adopt the more effective flying formations used by the Luftwaffe in the opening stages of the battle, despite earlier demonstrations of effectiveness in the Spanish civil war and the Polish campaign, suggests an unwillingness to temper theory with practice. It also tends to support the assertion regarding the lack of a concerted progression of ideas mentioned earlier. A failure to disseminate "best-practice" is surely a major flaw in any organization.

It may have been that Dowding was opposed to changing his long-standing ideas about gunnery. His memorandum circulated to the Group Commands in

October 1939 attempted to draw conclusions from the handful of engagements with German aircraft over Rosyth and the North Sea. The first conclusion he drew was "there is nothing much wrong with the harmonisation of the guns of an 8-gun Fighter at the ranges for which this harmonisation has been designed." Without defining "close-range firing" he wished to discourage the practice, as the cones would not have a chance to open out. The tone is complacent and dubiously suggests the German air force had a general fear of the eight-gun fighter. But bearing in mind the target audience, it must be supposed that he was trying to build the confidence of his men in their machines.[81] It must be conceded that Dowding acknowledged the conclusions were "tentative" but it does suggest that he was slow to acknowledge the problem in assessing an optimum range for gun harmonization and was awry in his estimates.

A memorandum from the Air Ministry's Air Tactics Directorate supported Dowding's views on harmonization but caviled over his discouragement of close-range firing on the stated grounds of the cones' failure to open out. They considered this point to be fallacious and in practice "a minor point," as a "well-handled" fighter should have inflicted sufficient damage before closing to such short ranges. However it must be emphasized that the Air Tactics view was based on an assumption that Dowding meant ranges of less than one hundred yards. It also noted that a "fighter pilot closing on an enemy bomber whilst firing is unlikely to break away until he is forced to do so to avoid collision."[82] It is obvious that a pilot's decision as to when to open and close firing would have largely depended on his closing speed, which in turn would have been governed by the angle of approach he was able to take.

Although this correspondence seems to lump the Spitfire and Hurricane together as if they had the same characteristics, it should be noted that differences in wing design meant differing configurations for the installation of their Brownings. As described, the Spitfire's widely spaced guns converged in a single cone of fire. The Hurricane on the other hand had a much thicker wing enabling a closely grouped battery of four guns to deliver a "shotgun" effect, which with the other battery fired two cones of shot ahead of the aircraft. This has been universally acknowledged as a more effective configuration against more robust bomber types. Fortunately, there were more Hurricanes than Spitfires but even the Hurricane was outgunned by the Messerschmitt Me 109E, which could open up with cannon fire well beyond the range of the .303.[83] The German fighter could also deliver eighteen pounds of firepower as opposed to its British contemporary's equivalent of thirteen pounds from a three-second burst.[84] From this, one can only draw the conclusion that Dowding's policy of long-range firing against bombers was one likely to have damaged the effectiveness of the defense.

Unfortunately, "getting in close" was not an easy thing to accomplish, especially if circumstances forced the pilot to approach from the rear of his target where the bomber's slipstream could easily upturn a small pursuing aircraft.

Furthermore, the German air gunners had often been trained to a high standard, a factor helping to offset the bomber's weapon inferiority to the firepower of an eight-gun fighter. It would therefore take "nerve" and flying ability to accomplish close shooting. A 1988 survey in which one hundred Battle of Britain veterans gave opinions on the quality of German air gunners came up with interesting results. Forty considered it excellent or good, with thirty-two rating it average and thirty classing it poor. Pilot Officer Donald Stones, DFC, thought it varied greatly according to the individual unit. He gave an example of his squadron's "badly thought-out and executed attack" on 29 September 1940 against nine Heinkel He III bombers of a specialist unit, which led to the loss of three Hurricanes as a result of the bombers' disciplined and concentrated cross fire facilitated by the pilot's perfect formation flying.[85]

Yet being prepared to "get in close" marked out the more successful pilots. The *MoD Narrative* also mentioned the success of pilots prepared to risk collision but also to avoid the German gunners and rear armor protection by attacking formations head-on. Dowding did not approve of this either but doubtless out of desperation was forced to endorse the tactic by 25 August.[86] But getting in close was no guarantee of success in all situations and head-on attacks were not the answer. Dowding's opposition was partly justified by Flight Lieutenant Dr. Alfred Price's research indicating that fighter attacks never once succeeded in breaking up a high-flying German bombing formation. Aircraft would only leave formations and lag behind after suffering damage or mechanical failure, which often meant being overcome by a swarm of British fighters. Therefore, for a bomber to leave a formation when under attack would have been "foolhardy in the extreme." Price blamed over-hyped accounts for establishing this myth.[87] But even if German formations were not broken up like this, firing at close ranges was still the best way of overcoming the shortcomings in the eight-gun fighter weapons system.

Three "foreign" units had entered the fray during July to offset the pilot shortage, and both Allen and Deighton have remarked on the comparative success of foreign pilots serving in the RAF and trained in other air forces. Since they had flown lower-performance aircraft with even less effective armament prior to serving in the RAF, not only was it natural for them to fire from comparatively short ranges but in the case of Czechs and Poles, a burning hatred of the enemy made them relatively oblivious of risk. The main debate about using these personnel centered on the issue of either integrating them into British squadrons or forming the men into their own units. Once again, seemingly inappropriate consideration of the bomber situation was given, this time at the Expansion and Re-equipment Policy Committee meeting of 3 August 1940. If more fighter squadrons were formed, it would be seen as "necessarily reducing our strength in bombers" unless pilot establishments to these units were reduced from twenty-five down to twenty-one or twenty-three. Fortunately, this consideration did not prevent the formation of three more Polish and one more Czech squadron.[88]

Naturally, one should not draw definitive conclusions from the apparent success of these foreign pilots bearing in mind the small sample presented. Considering what has already been said about the deficiency in RAF pilot training, some tentative conclusions can still be drawn. The highest scoring ace in the Battle of Britain was the Czech Sergeant Pilot J. Frantisek, DFM, with seventeen kills attributed. A Polish pilot, Flying Officer W. Urbanowicz, DFC, scored fourteen (some say fifteen). Allen argues that only seventeen pilots claimed more than ten aerial victories between 10 July and 31 October, the official Battle of Britain dates. Considering mid-European pilots made up only 184 out of 2,749 participants, the comparative success of these foreign-trained airmen seems to illustrate the bankruptcy of RAF training methods and fighter tactics.[89] Of course, this is a small sample and the source is necessarily unofficial, but it is generally accepted that mid-Europeans were effective pilots who tended to disregard personal safety and fired at point-blank range. George Douglas Blackwood, commander of 310 (Czechoslovak) Squadron, remarked: "Then I saw how Czechoslovakian airmen can fight. There was no need for commands by radio, they dashed at Germans without abashment," he wrote admiringly. "Excepting the fact that I have been shot down . . . I was absolutely content with the result of the first encounter."[90] A Polish air historian has claimed that during the course of the war, statistics showed that Polish pilots destroyed 10.5 aircraft for each death as opposed to 4.9 kills per death for the RAF as a whole, thus suggesting they were not unduly reckless. Polish pilots represented 5 percent of the RAF's participants but still accounted for 7.5 percent of German aircraft destroyed (including those downed by AA and balloons). During the Battle of Britain, 303 Squadron had shot down three times the average RAF score but with only one-third of the casualty rate.[91] His sources have not been specifically referenced. However, there appears no alternative evidence in publication to disprove these assertions.

The seventeen top scorers were responsible for 221 aircraft destroyed, out of 1,200 Luftwaffe aircraft destroyed or damaged (less 15 percent repairable) between 10 July and 15 September, meaning that this minority destroyed around a quarter of the overall total. Leaving aside the method of "half-scoring," whereby any number of aircraft could attack an enemy bomber and each be credited with a half, a mere 15 percent of pilots could claim a "whole" aircraft, of which—based on random sampling—only 12 percent scored two and 7 percent over four whole German aircraft.[92] The problems with this analysis are the unavoidably poor quality evidence, the small sampling, and the absence of referencing. The case remains technically unproved. However, it is an indication that the average RAF pilot was somewhat less effective than generally assumed. At least one writer sympathetic to the RAF has conceded that "most pilots never shot anything down," with less than 900 of some 2,330 pilots of Fighter Command claiming (though not necessarily achieving) victories between July and November.[93] Unfortunately, the writers trying to address these issues have not revealed their sources and they do not quite tally with each other. Even so, a glance at the overall statistics for the air campaign indicates that, through no fault of his own, the average RAF fighter pilot was not very effective. Indeed, when one considers the difficulties described in this chapter, it would be surprising if he were.

Source statistics for aircraft destroyed disagree (see Appendix II) and if estimated losses of Bomber and Coastal Commands are added, the aircraft exchange rate is approximately three to two in favor of the RAF instead of the two to one more usually quoted. The casualty ratio favoring the RAF also plummets from nearly five to one to less than two to one if all commands are vectored into the calculation. A common view that the British bomber force was "not part of the battle as such" ought to be disregarded if one accepts (as most British authors do) that the bombing of Berlin caused a crucial change of focus from the airfields to London.[94] Whichever view one takes, the rate of attrition was disappointing for a defending force operating with all the advantages of fighting over home territory. Bearing in mind that some of these German aircraft had been destroyed by the AA ground defense, including guns and balloons, and many British aircraft were bombed on the runways, the RAF pilots and aircrew probably did not destroy many more German aircraft than the Luftwaffe destroyed of the RAF.

In many respects, Allen's version of the battle has not been taken into account by other historians and remains starkly at odds with populist accounts. Some historians have moved closer toward Allen's version of events though they balk at using him as a source. Sebastian Cox, head of the Ministry of Defence's (MoD) Air Historical Branch, RAF, has described Fighter Command as being "on the ropes" during this period, but neither Cox nor any other modern-day writer has gone as far as claiming that Fighter Command's 11 Group was a "defeated force" by September 1940. The most important of Allen's assertions is that the Luftwaffe did achieve the necessary degree of air superiority for Operation Sea Lion and that the RAF was a far less efficient organization than generally supposed. Insofar as the air dimension was operationally relevant it has been seen how ineffective Fighter Command was during September and beyond. As described in a previous chapter, it is well known that prior to 15 September, Luftwaffe intelligence was telling Goering and Hitler that Fighter Command had been virtually destroyed.

The crisis in Fighter Command during the critical period of 24 August to 6 September was extreme but the re-emergence in strength of the RAF over London on 15 September is usually taken as evidence of recovery. As described previously, the result of the air fights on this day provided the excuse needed by German military and political figures to postpone the invasion without anyone having to admit to a loss of nerve over the prospects of success. Superficially it would seem that Fighter Command did exceptionally well, shooting down fifty-six in exchange for twenty-seven aircraft (although the newspapers inflated the former figure outrageously), but what impressed itself particularly on the German airmen was the number of RAF fighters aloft. It may have been the case that most actual fighting was being done by experienced veterans while many more relatively untrained, inexperienced pilots or even non-operational pilots made a show of strength on the periphery of the combat. Some accounts have described Hurricanes and Spitfires nearly colliding with each other, some flying through friendly AA fire in "eagerness to get at their prey,"[95] something which might alternatively be seen as evidence of poor pilot skills or of too many defending aircraft in one place. One view concedes the relative ineffectiveness of most pilots but also stresses the "simple presence of a Hurricane or Spitfire," the "demoralizing effect on the enemy," and the "courage that was needed to simply maintain yourself in the air."[96] But maintaining an impression of strength—however hard—does not compare with the actuality of being strong. Luftwaffe intelligence may have been awry in the overall number of RAF fighters remaining but in terms of the only ones that really counted—that is, those flown by thoroughly trained and experienced pilots who knew how to shoot—they may not have been far off the mark in stating the RAF could not muster more than around one hundred fighters in any operation. Adolf Galland, commanding Jagdgeschwader 26, was disparaging about the effectiveness of Luftwaffe intelligence on this point, but his own perception of the strength of the opposition was also flawed. In 1945 the senior narrator, Air Historical Branch, queried Galland's assertion that "anything from two hundred to three hundred [British fighters] might be found." The narrator claimed instead that even with the squadrons that engaged from 12 Group, there were rarely more than three hundred available fighters in the whole southeast and "it would be surprising if Galland ever saw all of them in the air at once."[97]

The air battles of 15 September would also herald a further demonstration of Fighter Command impotence. The subsequent re-evaluation of tactics that was forced on the Luftwaffe regained the initiative for Germany, and bombing by night continued until Hitler began his assault on the Soviet Union. For the rest of 1940, thousands of tons of bombs fell on British cities with Fighter Command unable to prevent it, and the balance of modern writing is that the failure to make an adequate response contributed to the dismissal of its two most prominent leaders. Later on, it proved convenient for Dowding and others to differentiate between the Battle of Britain—otherwise known as the air battle that prevented invasion—and the night blitz—the campaign to bomb Britain into a negotiated peace (or surrender as most commentators prefer to view it). To ensure this was understood Dowding told Liddell Hart, arguably the leading military historian of his day, that the Battle of Britain was a day fight to gain command of the air, while the night bombing was a "sideline with an entirely different object."[98] The second stage was technically a failure for the Germans in that it did not secure their overriding political objective, but their failure had little to do with Fighter Command.

If any individual RAF commander could claim to be the victor of the Battle of Britain it was surely Keith Park, the officer commanding 11 Group. Yet even he was disappointed by the performance of his units at this climactic moment. Writing on the events of 15 September 1940 he stated he "was far from impressed with the performance of 11 Group." He reasoned that with 1,600 potential targets, and three hundred defending fighters in the air, his pilots should have shot down many more than 56, bearing in mind all the advantages of fighting over home territory and being close to base.[99] Needless to say, this opinion of Parks was unpopular with the pilots, yet 11 Group "failed" largely because the damage inflicted on Fighter Command during the earlier periods had drained too many experienced pilots away. Even Dowding, who wished to emphasize the way his organization had stood up to the strain, contradicted the assertion made by the authors of the best-selling official HMSO (His Majesty's Stationery Office) pamphlet *The Battle of Britain* that "the fighter squadrons of the Royal Air Force . . . were indeed stronger at the end of the battle than at the beginning." Dowding pointed out that whatever the paper return showed, the situation toward the end was extremely critical and most squadrons were "fit only for operations against unescorted bombers. The remainder were battling against heavy odds."[100]

At this point, Dowding might also have mentioned the damage incurred to Fighter Command's supporting infrastructure during this period. The system had been heavily damaged, though not put out of action. Many of Fighter Command's airfields had been heavily bombed but it was not the cratered runways that really mattered. Some airfields were also vital sector stations, meaning vital communications centers were no longer functioning properly. Park wrote to Dowding on 22 September 1940. His views expressed below have the virtue of raw immediacy, being written within a fortnight of the "critical period" coming to an end. "Contrary to general belief and official reports, the enemy's bombing attacks by day did extensive damage to five of our forward aerodromes and also to six of our seven Sector stations." Park continued, "The damage to forward aerodromes was so severe that Manston and Lympne were on several occasions quite unfit for operating fighters."[101] Because there were only limited financial resources to support Fighter Command's infrastructure, the buildings containing the technical equipment and personnel were in flimsy surface constructions rather than in underground installations where logically they ought to have been placed. Worse perhaps, no real effort had been made to protect their vulnerable power and communications cables. Consequently, Kenley and Biggin Hill were transferred to emergency facilities that were far less well equipped. Park remarked that the "Emergency Operations Rooms were not only too small to house the essential personnel" but lacked enough General Post Office (GPO) telephone landlines to "enable normal operations of three squadrons per Sector."[102] Only the respite offered by the Luftwaffe in switching to other targets enabled a complete reorganization of the sector station system.[103] The sector stations were the final point in the command system, containing operations rooms fed by data from Group level. As Cox pointed out, if the sector operations room was a "smoking ruin" or the telephone line was bombed, then pilots at the dispersal point could not be scrambled to meet the incoming raids. Unsurprisingly, Park wrote that the damage to the command and control infrastructure between 28 August and 5 September was to seriously affect the tactical handling of the squadrons.[104] All of these problems were "seriously felt for about a week in the handling of squadrons by day to meet the enemy's massed attacks."[105] Experienced flight leaders were losing confidence and other problems would be seriously felt for some time to come. The number of operational pilots in 11 Group's squadrons had not improved by early October and was only slightly better by the end of December.[106] The ability of pilots to shoot accurately would not significantly improve until 1942, a damning indictment of any training organization. Although there were days when the Luftwaffe sustained heavy losses, an admittedly simplistic comparison of losses shows the battle of attrition did not favor the RAF to any great extent. Shortly after the main day fighting had ended, Park and Dowding were sacked, hardly representing recognition of a job well done.

For several reasons, the Luftwaffe did not lose the air battles even if they failed to achieve the overriding objective of forcing Britain into negotiations. First, the Luftwaffe had seized the initiative from Fighter Command from 24 August and demonstrated their air superiority by day until approximately the middle of September. Second, having realized that air superiority alone could not ensure the success of Operation Sea Lion, Hitler and Goering finally geared their strategy toward applying political pressure by targeting civilians. Even then, the Luftwaffe showed its ability to bomb targets at night with minimal Fighter Command interference for the rest of 1940. Third, if subsequent campaigns by air forces of other nations to break civilian morale with heavier bomb loads and more sophisticated technology have invariably failed, then it is hard to blame the supposed shortcomings of the Luftwaffe for the failure to force a political solution in favor of Germany. Surprisingly then, it is the Luftwaffe that emerges as the more effective organization during the summer of 1940. However, as the air campaigns known as the Battle of Britain were inconclusive, neither the RAF nor the Luftwaffe can be said to have won them. Before final judgment can be given as to who (or what) won the wider Battle *for* Britain, a fuller appreciation of Fighter Command's leadership and "command and control" is required as part of the explanation as to why Fighter Command did not win it.

CHAPTER FIVE

My System May Not Be Perfect

Where would we have been if Stuffy had lost the battle?[1]

Squadron Leader "Ginger" Lacey

Dowding should go.[2]

Air Marshal Sir John Salmond to Lord Trenchard, 25 September 1940

Hugh Caswell Tremenheere Dowding (1st Baron Dowding, 1882–1970) has attracted considerable sympathy from almost all of the pilots' memoirs published since the air battles of 1940. Robert Wright's biography, published with Dowding's cooperation in 1969, effectively broke the C-in-C's silence on the circumstances of his summary dismissal and established the legend that he was sacked through the machinations of RAF rivals, including "big-wing" proponents Trafford Leigh-Mallory and William Sholto Douglas. Shortly afterwards, A. J. P. Taylor further supported this in a letter to the *Times* implying that the politicians had let the C-in-C down.[3] This period also saw a sympathetic portrayal by Laurence Olivier in the feature film *Battle of Britain* that held itself up as an objective account of the operation, which like the earlier film *The Longest Day* (covering D-day, 1944) viewed events from both sides of the Channel.

Dowding's death in 1970 spawned at least one eulogistic newspaper article hinting at tactical dissension within his command without allowing for any flaws in his leadership and attributing the "victory" in large part to "Dowding's outstanding qualities as a commander."[4] Nevertheless, an article in the *Times* hinted at his difficult personality, noting that he was not an easy man.[5] By 1988, sympathy for him culminated in the unveiling of his statue in St. Clement Danes, London, by the Queen Mother. Typifying the tone of the battle's sixtieth anniversary celebrations in 2000, a British *Daily Express* article praised the leadership of RAF Fighter Command to the point of hyperbole and claimed that the radar chain Dowding helped to create "worked as he dreamed it would."[6] This "martyr" image was maintained in a television presentation to mark the sixty-fifth Battle of

Britain Day in 2005.[7] No evaluation of Fighter Command's organization can be complete without considering whether the reputation of its leader and his command and control system has been exaggerated, and if so, why?

Like many World War II officers in senior appointments, Dowding had served in World War I, first as a squadron commander, later in charge of a wing. After quarrelling with Sir Hugh Trenchard, head of the Royal Flying Corps, over unduly forcing his pilots into offensive action, Dowding was posted to a training command.[8] Trenchard was a difficult character and a potentially dangerous enemy because of his influence on the development of British military aviation during the interwar period. Fortunately, they reconciled but it was a portent of the poor relations Dowding would later have with key figures. In 1930 he became a member of the Air Council, serving as air member for supply and research. Later he became air member for research and development and along with the other members has to be viewed as jointly responsible for the successes and failures of technical development at that time. Taking over the leadership of Fighter Command in 1936, his arguments increasingly revolved around using fighter aircraft as a deterrent to enemy action. Dowding's logic was helped by the fact that monoplane fighters were now much faster than the earlier biplanes. One reason the Air Staff had not placed much faith in fighters was because of the marginal speed differential between biplane fighters and bombers. Such reasoning would not endear him further to Lord Trenchard, whose bomber theories dominated Air Staff thinking until Sir Thomas Inskip, minister for the co-ordination of defence, forced a change of priority in the matter of increased fighter production during December 1937.

Although constrained by having to work within the framework laid down by the Air Staff, his personal responsibility for overseeing the technical development of aircraft and other equipment must have been considerable. It would be easy to follow Allen and criticize Dowding and the Air Council for the design disappointments of the 1930s that failed to meet the demands of 1940. Aircraft such as the Hampden bomber and the Fairey Battle light bomber were disappointing in the event, but Mason is correct to point out that military aviation development in Britain was comparable with most other countries at that time.[9] Dowding's work bringing the eight-gun fighters into service is well known and doubtless it was his idea to invite tenders from the private sector, to capitalize on the technical achievements arising from the British victory in the Schneider Trophy air races of 1931.[10] Even here it must be remembered that the Spitfire's and Hurricane's births owed more to the willingness of Messrs. Vickers and Hawker to finance and develop their own designs rather than to their ability to adhere to the official operational requirements of design specification F7/30. As Allen pointed out, the later specification F5/34 was written with these partly developed aircraft in mind, and theoretically the object of design specifications is for the users to dictate what the manufacturers will produce, not the other way around.[11] However, Allen made a little too much of this. By the time F5/34 was written, the Air Ministry's representatives were working closely with the aircraft designers and Squadron Leader Sorley was the main driving force behind the eight-gun concept. This does not quite explain why the Air Ministry did not lead the way toward fighter monoplane development more proactively, but it was a period of rapid technological change and it can be argued that a truly collaborative approach was now being taken.[12] Perhaps a firmer lead and closer monitoring by the Air Ministry would have resulted in more Spitfires entering operational service before and during the air campaigns of 1940. The industrialist Lord Nuffield had promised the government that he would manufacture sixty Spitfires a week from his new Castle Bromwich works in Birmingham once it was completed. Unfortunately, Nuffield "proved a disastrous organizer," having "lost his grip," and by March 1940, had spent £7 million without producing a single aircraft.[13]

One influential study of RDF praised Dowding for supporting the Bawdsey scientists' development of RDF, especially after test failures during 1936–37, but not without admitting to some errors of judgment that "pale in comparison to his central role in developing the Dowding system."[14] However, the so-called Dowding system was not entirely original, though the use of RDF for early warning was truly innovative. An early-warning system had been put in place during World War I because successful German raids on London in the summer of 1917 provoked widespread rioting, leading to Lieutenant General Jan Christian Smuts' examination of the air organization. This culminated in the appointment of Brigadier General E. B. Ashmore, who organized information gathering and dissemination through a central command structure bearing many resemblances to Dowding's system. Signals traffic was analyzed for volume and content and a dedicated telephone communications system installed. Twenty-five regional sub-control rooms used large-scale maps with counters to represent aircraft. Plots would then be read to a "teller" in the central control room in Whitehall. Within the central control room stood a large table map, surrounded by plotters with headphones who moved around colored counters. The activity could be viewed from a gallery behind the plotters. Having assessed the information, a central control room could then pass it back to the sub-control rooms for action. A primitive form of radio-telephone (R/T) communication also linked the aircraft to ground control.

The system was never fully tested because the Germans decided it was more profitable to concentrate resources on tactical bombing in France. At this stage, all information gathering was dependent on high-flying aircraft on standing patrols, lightships, and ground observers, as there was no effective long-range early-warning device.[15] The system soon became reasonably efficient, and on 19 May 1918, it helped eliminate six night-flying German bombers, more than the advanced system of 1940 proved able to achieve.[16] However, these early bombers flew more slowly over longer approaches than their later Luftwaffe equivalents, meaning less warning time was needed. Postwar continuity was aided by Ashmore's membership in the Romer Committee of 1924, resulting in the formation of Sir John Salmond's Air Defence of Great Britain (ADGB), responsible for all home air forces. ADGB took responsibility for homeland defense against air attack until the formation of Fighter Command and Bomber Command in 1936.[17] The system Dowding helped create was ingenious, but lacking from most accounts is the observation that he was able to develop it from a partially tested earlier model.

The system used in 1940 included both the RDF system and the Royal Observer Corps (ROC). Two chains of RDF stations known as Chain Home (CH) and Chain Home Low (CHL) on (or near) the coast were directly connected by telephone landline to filter rooms in several locations. CH represented the main line of defense, with CHL existing to counter low-level raiders attempting to creep under the screens of the CH operators. Aircraft detected over the sea were to be plotted and their numbers and height estimated prior to passing this to the relevant filter room. These aircraft would then be plotted on the filter room table where the staff would identify friendly, hostile, and doubtful aircraft. With each aircraft formation duly labeled, the information would be disseminated via a multiphone to the command operations room (Fighter Command HQ, Stanmore) and the group operations room, together with the sector operations room. This would then be displayed on the operations rooms' tables at all of these establishments. Coastal observer corps centers would also receive the information in order to track the course of the raid after it crossed the coast. Observer corps intelligence centers would plot on their own center tables, with information telephoned from their inland web of observer corps posts situated approximately eight miles apart. Friendly aircraft would then be filtered out by these intelligence centers and the refined data forwarded to command, group, and sector operations rooms where it would be integrated with any other information held there.

The command operations room at Fighter Command HQ could now retain an overall view of the nationwide situation. Fighter Command HQ could then issue air raid warnings and maintain liaison with the Admiralty and Home Office. The positions of convoys would also be plotted with information from naval liaison officers. Another tier contained six group operations rooms where the area officer commanding controlled the squadrons under his command. He would then use this information to instruct sector commanders to intercept specific raids. Gun liaison officers also had gun operations rooms within the group operations rooms. At the sector operations room, the sector commander would control three squadrons for the purpose of accomplishing the interception. Each sector had satellite airfields where aircraft could be dispersed if necessary.[18]

Average times for information processing were given in official documents. As soon as an incoming raid from northeastern France was detected at the RDF station, it would take twenty seconds to plot on the filter room table. Placing a directional arrow added a further five seconds and plotting at the operations rooms a further thirty seconds, resulting in fifty-five seconds for the raid information to appear in visual form at the operations rooms. It took a significantly slower one minute and forty-five seconds (approximately) for Royal Observer Corps information to be processed. This was presumably due to the difficulties of visually discriminating between friend and foe and the need for information to pass through the intelligence center before sending it on to the operations rooms. The delay between the appearance of a plot on the operations table and the takeoff of defending fighters shows that if the aircraft were in a state of "readiness," the delay would be six and a half minutes. If the fighters were only at "available," the time would increase to sixteen and a half minutes.[19] It seems unlikely that these official figures had been independently corroborated or were precise. Takeoff time would be limited by runway congestion with two squadrons sometimes sharing the same facilities. Aircraft cannot always be at "readiness" as refueling and rearming were time-consuming, with some units achieving a faster turnaround than others. As these times were probably worked out before the air fighting reached its peak, no account seems to have been taken of the exhaustion of ground personnel responsible for refueling and rearming. The timing would have been less crucial had it been possible to use the system to its maximum potential. Now that the Germans were operating from airfields in northern France, enemy aircraft were operating from bases well within the range of RDF. The similarities of the systems used in both wars are obvious, from the use of operations rooms and plotters to coordinate aircraft and AA guns to the use of what would now be called "no-fly" zones, in which any aircraft found was assumed to be hostile. Even the 1940 system had to place heavy reliance on primitive ground observation, as once German aircraft had crossed the coast they could no longer be tracked by RDF. In clear weather the ROC was proficient at this, but in bad weather with bombers concealed by cloud there was little they could do.

The system had many problems, the most contentious being response times. For Allen, the filter room had "some importance, but it is doubtful whether this exceeded its operational limitations. . . . The Filter Room, in fact, never functioned effectively in 1940."[20] Allen considered the filtering process meant a built-in delay of some four minutes within the system. He explained this by stating that the indicator plaque showing the raid on the operations table might be showing the enemy aircraft twenty miles from its precise location if the raid was moving at 300 mph, meaning that intercepting aircraft were often guided to an incorrect position. His experience as a pilot and commander told him that the average pilot had problems spotting aircraft at two miles. This was a particular problem when operating at high altitudes because the pilots lacked a frame of reference. Furthermore, the information on altitude was frequently inaccurate. If it came from the ROC in cloudless conditions, it was reasonably accurate, but with the CH (Chain Home) it was much less reliable. Indeed, with reference to his flying logbook, he claimed that "only on 50 percent of occasions did my squadron achieve an interception after the order was given."[21] What was needed and later adopted (but not in time for the battle) was a second chain of stations sited farther inland to maintain the tracking of enemy incursions. Large raids would also flood the screens with light, meaning little useful information could be deduced about the incoming raid. Allen suggested that Dowding might not have placed such reliance on the system if he had appreciated the magnitude of these problems beforehand. The only caveat that should be added to his comments is that during the large daylight battles, a typical raid was far more likely to be moving at the slower speed of approximately 175 mph.[22] What he referred to here must have been the later "gadfly" fighter-bomber attack phase, designed to wear down the nerves of the civilian population during the day while much greater physical damage was done by the heavier bombers at night. Even so, at 175 mph, an error of some thirteen miles seems reasonable.

The *MoD Narrative* states that September to December 1939 was a quiet period for Fighter Command, but some fifty-one enemy aircraft had been engaged, with thirteen confirmed destroyed. It conceded that the filtering process was "still giving much trouble," which it implied was solved by using a radar officer as a dedicated filtering supervisor.[23] This was an inadequate description of the problem. Dowding's correspondence with the Air Ministry in January 1940 reveals the C-in-C's annoyance with what he saw as criticism from ill-informed individuals. The C-in-C objected to a note written by Assistant Chief of Air Staff Air Marshal Philip Joubert containing "certain inaccuracies of fact," indicating that to his mind Joubert "was imperfectly acquainted with all aspects of the problem."[24] Joubert had been appointed by Chief of Air Staff Newall "to investigate the RDF chain from the point of view of service control," because of Joubert's interest in the command system and his previous responsibilities under the old ADGB organization.[25] The note was intended to form the basis of discussion on RDF policy in Newall's room at the Air Ministry on 12 January, though as Newall had no time to study it beforehand, discussion was made on general lines. The meeting alleged that some interceptions had been missed following delays within the filter room. Dowding admitted there had been delays in order to avoid "nugatory flights" but did not believe this had resulted in any missed interceptions. Newall accepted this but wanted delays reduced and an experiment conducted in devolving filtering from HQ to Group. Without fully explaining his objections, Dowding opposed this as "thoroughly unsound and would lead to a grave loss of efficiency." He had already ordered adequate minor procedural adjustments, with the "first arrow" (or plaque) immediately "told" (relayed) to groups and sectors with an identity (friend or foe) allocated when established. He was seemingly trying to establish the principle that his three and a half years of developing the system should make him the sole arbiter of organizational practicalities, while the Air Staff should confine themselves to improving the equipment.[26] Unfortunately for Dowding the committee system of waging war was not one in which any single officer could be allowed the complete autonomy many clearly desired and, as will be seen in a later chapter, Admiral Forbes also had his freedom of action severely circumscribed by staff officers and politicians.

The note that Dowding referred to above could not be positively identified beyond all doubt at the National Archives, but a separate file contains an unsigned, undated note headed "Present Filtering Organisation." The statement "in the few months of comparative inactivity which may yet remain to us" seems to place it in early 1940. It makes some criticism of the filtering system, implying "missed interceptions," and does not mention decentralization as a remedy. The note claimed that since the filter room had been located at Fighter Command HQ there had been a decrease in filtering efficiency and an overlap of function between non-commissioned officer (NCO) filterers and filter-officers, resulting in duplicate requests for information. The author stressed this was "not meant to be an indictment of anyone or any system" and that problems were to be expected as a result of the expansion of the RDF chain. However, despite the improvement in instrument quality the operators now had "much less average ability than they formerly possessed." The recommendations were that the filter room should drop the operational functions it had recently acquired and that "it should be staffed with competent personnel."[27]

Another letter from Dowding dated 31 January 1940 seems to have been prompted by his earlier failure to explain why he opposed the decentralization experiment. Paragraph six explained that sometimes groups delegated tactical control to sectors, and a raid appearing on the table over one hundred miles away may make several alterations in course, making it seem that several targets would be attacked. Each sector might then scramble formations unnecessarily. Dowding also emphasized the cost of relocating new filter rooms in underground locations. All of this was reasonable, but however unenviable his predicament, paragraph eleven would have angered the Air Staff: "My contention is that [members of] the Air Council have the right to tell me what to do but should not insist on telling me how to do it so long as I retain their confidence."[28] This had the desired effect insofar as the Air Council backed down and did not raise the matter again for several months. It was a question of "back him or sack him," but inevitably the problem re-emerged after the main day battles had ended. So acrimonious did relations become that Dowding involved the prime minister. Despite the earlier problem in their relationship, and doubtless because Dowding was then the only commander of 1940 who had delivered something that could be projected as a victory, Churchill pressed Sinclair to investigate.[29]

An Air Ministry draft reply to Churchill, prepared by Joubert during October 1940, revealed that the Air Ministry was "unconvinced of the rightness of the C-in-C's views . . . but decided not to press him further at that time." As the Luftwaffe's night offensive from September highlighted interception problems relating to insufficient warning against higher flying raids, "The question of decentralisation of filtering very naturally was reconsidered." The only real advantage of filtering at Fighter Command HQ was the presence of liaison officers from other commands, though only until Identification of Friend and Foe (IFF) apparatus became widely available in operational aircraft. Consequently the Committee on Night Air Defence chaired by Sir John Salmond recommended "the operation of filtering should be transferred from Fighter Command [HQ] to Group Headquarters *in order to reduce delay.*" As far as Joubert was concerned, it was a matter of either retaining a system giving "the simplest dissemination of air raid warnings and one which at a moderate expense . . . gives us a vital addition to the time . . . to attempt to intercept the enemy." With IFF devices widely available soon there was no reason why decentralization should not be made. The Air Staff was concerned about the likelihood of the Luftwaffe resuming "intense operations" by day the following spring, with 2,000 to 2,500 aircraft aloft simultaneously, and this could only result in "impossible congestion" if the filtering was not relocated soon. Supporting the case for change was a claim that decentralization of filtering had already been carried out in the more far-flung groups with no "ill-effects" but with many advantages, including the "savings in the cost of land lines." The benefits would mean that tracking of raids would be "told" simultaneously from groups to Fighter Command HQ and sector operations rooms.[30] However, some members of the Air Staff were dubious about Joubert's claim that the time saved was between thirty seconds to several minutes depending on the scale of enemy activity, and had the draft edited accordingly.[31]

On 8 October, Dowding wrote to the War Cabinet referring to a meeting in the Central War Room on the seventh. Sir John Salmond's report had been discussed where Dowding stated he only agreed to some of the proposals under pressure. His main objection was to the proposal that "filtering should be transferred . . . to Group headquarters in order to reduce delay." The C-in-C explained that the principle of filtering was to process the information from RDF stations in order to weed out individual plots unsuitable for display on operations tables. He complained that much of his time had been consumed resisting this proposal when first made and was surprised it had been more recently "disinterred" by this committee. In paragraph eight he explained that he advised the Air Ministry on 27 September 1940 that he thought the matter had been closed. Nothing had changed except for the increased night attacks and filtering was not particularly relevant to this. Finally, he asked that he "may be spared the necessity of discussing the question afresh." Only at paragraph nine did he finally get around to explaining his objections. Until IFF was fitted to all operational aircraft the proposal was not feasible and even then, the filtering could not be done on the operations table itself but in separate filter rooms. These rooms required excavation and construction, representing wasted resources and actually reducing efficiency. As the chief of Air Staff (CAS) was determined to go ahead once the IFF devices were installed, Dowding had his objections placed on record in the minutes. These stated that delegation would not improve night interception. Sectors already acted on direct information from RDF stations in relation to interceptions over the sea, but as far as land interceptions were concerned the information went to sectors from Fighter

Command HQ via groups. Delegation would therefore mean a "very small saving of time" against which there would be a greater time-lag in sending information to Fighter Command "with resultant further delay in the issue of air raid warnings."

These objections must have been confusing to members of the War Cabinet, who may not have understood the precise details. Despite his pre-war membership of the Air Defence Committee, Churchill may not have quite grasped the intricacies of the system either. Bearing in mind it was the prime minister who had instructed Dowding to make his case on paper, his order may have been a stalling maneuver. As illustrated by the pilot-shortage affair, Churchill was not partial to long and involved paper-based arguments or messy details and Dowding's arguments were not particularly clear. He was partly right about the irrelevance to night interception in the sense that it was not enough to place interceptors across the course of the incoming raiders. If the average pilot had problems seeing aircraft at distances of more than two miles in daylight then this was going to be much reduced at night, meaning bombers could usually slip past fighters scrambled by ground control especially as altitude estimates were frequently inaccurate. However, as Luftwaffe bombers were now flying at high altitude to avoid the London AA defenses, the defending fighters were going to need more climbing time to reach the height of the attackers.

Dowding's minute to Churchill, dated 24 October 1940, revealed that he received a personal minute (No. 225) from the prime minister, dated 23 October 1940, containing information of a personal nature that he promised not to reveal. The major bone of contention remained in accepting the "undoubted fact" that time would be saved by filtering at group headquarters. In paragraph eleven he stated that if the Luftwaffe came over at full strength simultaneously, then the saturation point would occur throughout the system anyway. By double-banking operations room controllers the filter staff would not otherwise be overloaded beyond the point at which groups could respond, though this "solution" does beg the question as to how efficiently the staff could have worked in noisy and over-crowded conditions. Paragraphs fourteen to eighteen give brief scenarios, with reference to a diagram no longer available for inspection. As RDF stations were often inaccurate in assessing the direction of raids, "cross-cuts" could be made by using stations situated in 12 Group to plot aircraft moving within 11 Group's sea-area. A decentralized system would have eliminated this "cross-check." At this point he might also have mentioned the need for two stations to report on the altitude of enemy raids when this was in doubt. The second example suggests that if a raid flew along the sea boundary of 11 and 12 Groups, both groups might allocate a raid number and scramble their fighters. Alternatively neither might allocate a number—meaning consultation would be required between the groups in order to decide who should respond. At present, he claimed, there was no confusion as Fighter Command HQ would allocate a raid number and decide which group should respond.

Some members of the Air Staff did not see the advantage of cutting out a step in the process, since the filtering task had to be done somewhere. The advantage in the reform proposals was that additional filter rooms would handle "less total information," thus reducing the possibility of the system being saturated with information.[32] The majority of raids was also occurring within just one group, making a centralized control of warnings unnecessary in most instances; however the Luftwaffe had frequently sowed confusion in the system by sending bombers to fly up and down the French coast in order to flood RDF screens. If groups lost control of the situation, then Fighter Command HQ would have to sort out the confusion, and organizing a response would be even more time consuming. Unfortunately the onus of making his technical explanations clear to the uninitiated was on Dowding.

Dowding also used this opportunity to throw darts at the Air Staff, especially Joubert, whom he accused of "dumping the problem" of how to discriminate between friendly and enemy aircraft on his shoulders. With some justification, the Salmond committee was accused of reaching conclusions with "phenomenal rapidity and without any adequate examination of this particular problem." Admitting the "system which I have devised may not be perfect," he lashed out at "people who did not understand it as a whole" for making "disruptive incursions." He concluded by stating bitterly, "My main grievance, however, is the matter of the expenditure of my time in arguing with the Air Staff every intimate detail of my organization." His final plea to Churchill was that "a Commander-in-Chief should be left to manage his own affairs if the general result is satisfactory. I have expended not less than 50 hours of my time in this controversy."[33]

The fact that Churchill was corresponding with Dowding on a personal and confidential level suggests that he was broadly sympathetic to the C-in-C's plight. In fact John Colville's diary (the prime minister's private secretary) mentioned that Churchill held a high opinion of Dowding's abilities during the Battle of Britain, even describing his paper on Airborne Interception (AI) as "masterly" in the entry for 21 September 1940.[34] The note may even have given the C-in-C an unjustified feeling that the prime minister would support him irrespective of criticism. But Churchill's long record of meddling in military affairs indicated he was unsympathetic to C-in-Cs managing their own affairs. Furthermore, even if Dowding's performance up to mid-September was "satisfactory," German night bombing was proceeding with minimal interference, and so the "general result" was by no means satisfactory for Churchill politically. In addition, it must have been dawning on Churchill by now that Dowding's relationships with colleagues were unsatisfactory.

Dowding may have had some justification defending centralized filtering in the context of the night blitz, and the arguments that have gradually emerged from his correspondence revolve around the undoubted difficulties of responding to the changing directions of enemy raids. He was also probably right about the

Salmond committee, who only involved Dowding on the last day and after the committee had written most of its recommendations. It had only taken three days to complete its task, and as Salmond disliked him he may have allowed personal factors to influence his judgment.[35] Dowding knew that the only long-term solution to night interceptions lay in AI (night fighters carrying their own radar) but this did not excuse him from cooperating with attempts to find interim solutions. Pressures to reduce response times stemmed from the fact that even slow bombers could move substantially off-track in the time between the first positioning of the arrow on the table and the moment of anticipated interception. He was so closely involved with AI he could not tolerate arguments diverting attention away from the "real" solution. Added to his hypersensitivity to personal criticism and a desire to "talk up" an RDF system that was now linked to his reputation, this sort of "meddling" was exasperating to him, and he lost the ability to communicate with colleagues and laymen effectively.

However, the Air Staff was not hounding Dowding without reason. Having backed away from confrontation at the beginning of the year they only returned to it at the end of the main day battles when "response times" were becoming a genuine matter for concern. Neither could it really be said he was unduly distracted from controlling the battle, as minute-to-minute control had been delegated to the group AOCs, mainly Park, but also Leigh-Mallory and Sir Quintin Brand. If anything, it is remarkable how relatively free Dowding was to concentrate on those matters that interested him. As the acknowledged technical expert, it was only Joubert who had enough overall technical knowledge of the air defense systems to seriously put him on the spot, and this may provide some explanation for Dowding's disdainful remarks. His apparent inability to make clear, unambiguous explanations of the problems pertaining to the RDF chain might also be explained by a subconscious desire to conceal the shortcomings from politicians, as he clearly wished to be remembered for his role in introducing it.

The inadequacies of the training system did not extend merely to fighter pilots or their colleagues in the filter room but also to RDF operators and mechanics, and this can be seen as part of the wider problem relating to the rapid pre-war expansion of the RAF. Joubert's note—mentioned in relation to filtering problems—referred to RDF operators having much less ability than before, and this allegation is supported by other documents.[36] In October 1939, J. A. J. Tester, officer commanding at the RDF School in Bawdsey, sent the Air Ministry his proposals for expanding the school to meet the increased demand for personnel. He claimed the "operators at present leave the school with little or no idea of the following points, which are considered essential." These were then listed as: "(1) The RF [radio frequency] type of receiver, (2) The Anti-Jamming Devices, (3) Multiple Raids, (4) IFF, (5) Plotting and filtering, [and] (6) Counting." RDF stations were left to finish off the training of operators, a situation that was clearly unsatisfactory. The school lacked a "complete dummy RDF system for training purposes," and a detailed list of equipment requirements was enclosed. Mechanic's training was described as in a "lamentable state of affairs" because there was not enough equipment to train on. This meant that trainees graduated with a good theoretical but a poor practical knowledge when engaging with "(1) Any transmitter; (2) Any receiver, with the exception of the mobile one; (3) Any work culminating in the equipment actually going 'on the air;' (4) Phasing; (5) Stand-by power equipment; [and] (6) GM [presumably either General Maintenance or Geometric Mean]." It may have been quicker to state what tasks the graduates were capable of actually doing. Again the solutions were seen largely in terms of more equipment.[37] The school was probably exaggerating problems to obtain resources, but there was other evidence to show the training system was not going to stand up to the strain.

Just days before the Luftwaffe launched the intensive Adlerangriff (Eagle Attack) phase, E. C. Williams of the Stanmore Research Section (SRS) at Fighter Command HQ criticized the declining standards of RDF operators. In 1940, SRS was responsible for investigating the RDF chain's performance. He explained that SRS continuously reviewed standards and found this "is lower than it ever has been." Williams held this as directly attributable to shortening the Radio School Course, sending "completely untrained personnel to the Chain" and employing "totally unsuited personnel." Personnel were being trained by "half-trained" operators, and Williams alleged that the question of recruiting the wrong people had "probably never been tackled courageously." The Radio School Course should not have been shortened to a fortnight, as even the original course was not long enough and training needed to be carried out longer at the RDF Stations under "live conditions" by competent individuals. He concluded that "a large part of the efficiency of the RDF Chain is lost by poor operators, whose course of training has been curtailed."[38]

All of these problems were unsurprising in view of the way the RDF organization was rushed into service and without the priority for resources it deserved. As Robert Watson-Watt (later Sir Robert Watson-Watt, 1892–1973) remarked in a memorandum to Sinclair on 21 December 1940, "we have not yet proportioned our efforts in the installation of RDF coastal stations to the size and urgency of our programme." He went on to emphasize the "rudimentary state of RDF cover in the West" and "six months' lateness in the East coast programme," in support of his pleas for a larger and more powerful organization. Not surprisingly, in view of Watson-Watt's central role as the government scientist who originally persuaded the government to develop RDF, he made effusive claims for the efficacy of the system. That the "First Battle of Britain [the daylight air battles] was won by RDF and the 8-gun fighter" and that the value of the defense had been multiplied by three to five times were assertions repeated in very similar terms in Montgomery Hyde's influential *British Air Policy between the Wars, 1918–1939*.[39] Using both this and the prevalent assumption that the daytime fighting would resume in the spring, Watson-Watt wanted the War Cabinet to start thinking on a grand scale and with the "highest priority" for resources. What he also required was a single engineering organization dealing with all aspects of RDF installation.[40] The document amounts to an official admission that the system still had many holes and was incomplete. However, exaggeration was necessary if adequate funding was going to be obtained for essential development.

Shortly after this memorandum, yet more training problems were set out by Air Marshal Joubert, who summarized the history of RDF personnel problems and the efforts of the Air Ministry's Signals 4 unit in January 1941. It is unclear who he was writing this for but it was connected with the expansion advocated earlier by Watson-Watt. He described the recruitment of radio officers and radio mechanics/radio operators from January 1940 as "haphazard and mainly on a civilian basis." Consequently, various appeals had been made for recruiting over one thousand technicians that could not be accommodated within the existing training facilities. This resulted in Air Ministry embarrassment and opposition from the Ministry of Labour on the grounds that the recruitment had removed too many men from industry. However, a limited number of radio mechanics was eventually obtained but shortages of key personnel in other signals fields led to some of these being relocated. Adequate numbers of radio operators "up to the capacity of the training facilities" were secured, but by the end of June the sources of recruitment for radio officers and radio mechanics were almost exhausted and an attempt was made to obtain one hundred Canadian signals officers. An unsuccessful attempt was made to set up a Canadian school and investigating the options for placing a school out of enemy bombing range had consumed too much time. This meant that an additional school at Cranwell would not be operational until April 1941. The deficiency in facilities meant that a "serious bottleneck" was expected within the training system if any more personnel were to be recruited. More positively, Signals 4 had been "instrumental in recruiting 200 Signals Officers (Radio) and over 2,000 Radio Mechanics in the past eleven months." Fighter Command's demand for sixty filter officers was only met with difficulty, inferring that quality standards had suffered. If there was going to be continuing expansion, then overseas recruitment would be needed but even "a minor success [in expanding recruitment] would seriously embarrass our training facilities." Canadian radio officers and radio mechanics had rescued the system from "serious difficulties" but Joubert still felt a Canadian school was necessary. Expansion plans could only be met with a relaxation of the criteria and he was forced to recommend a shortening of the radio operators course from four to three weeks. Alternatively, some reorganization might bring about more efficient deployment of existing personnel, but this was doubtful. Plans for expansion also took no account of the requirement—expected to be burdensome—for heavy airborne equipment"[41]

So despite the Stanmore Research Section's complaint from the previous year, the Radio School Course was going to be reduced again. It must be remembered that Williams thought the original length of the course was too short. The general dilution of recruiting standards reluctantly advocated by Joubert should be read in parallel with Williams' earlier comments regarding the unsuitable standard of recruits. But Joubert had to take an overall view of the problem and a degree of panic over the Luftwaffe resuming daylight operations was clearly discernable. This later correspondence written after the major day battles places the recruitment and training problems for RDF personnel up to the end of the Battle of Britain within the context of an essential long-term grand expansion. Because RDF had to compete with other sectors of a rapidly expanding manpower-consuming war economy with a voracious appetite for all types of resources, it seems unlikely the RDF chain was at anything like the state of efficiency usually assumed and was still a long way from achieving this. Like the training of fighter pilots in 1940, much "muddling through" and desperate expedients were being resorted to, because events forced the pace of change faster than planners could provide for a steady and systematic expansion. Most importantly, it was necessary for Watson-Watt to trumpet the alleged achievement of RDF in helping "win" the Battle of Britain if he was going to win the battle for resources with competing organizations such as Bomber Command. No doubt the radar chain was far better than anyone could have imagined in 1934 when research had begun.[42] Yet the "manning" problems in 1940 were significant and the evidence shows it could not have functioned well with the existing low caliber of personnel and training.

To these problems must be added that of calibration, a factor also exacerbated by the poor quality of many operators. RDF stations were particularly inaccurate in their measurement of height and this deficiency tended to complicate the process of filtering. Filterers would often receive wildly conflicting height estimates from two separate RDF stations and, as striking an average between the two readings was clearly useless, they had to work out which station was likely to have given the most accurate report.[43] An operation requirements report in June stated that "interception over the sea usually failed because CH [Chain Home] was not accurate enough, and CHL [Chain Home Low] had no capability to measure height as it had originally been designed as a Coast Defense Set."[44] In June 1940, SRS provided notes indicating that RDF stations needed to calculate the elevation between one and a half and fifteen degrees, but owing to a lack of suitable equipment, most stations could only measure between one and a half and six degrees. RDF could accurately detect aircraft flying between 5,000 and 25,000 feet, but if the elevation was outside the one and a half to six degrees band a wildly inaccurate height reading would be given, especially if the operator was inexperienced.[45]

Another problem regarding the accurate estimation of height related to the proximity of enemy air bases and assembly points within the maximum range of CH. According to Watson-Watts' memoirs, "it was sometimes made more misleading by our very success, because the first height reports might be made on formations which had not yet completed their climb to operational height."

Doubtless, a second inland chain would have helped the defenders keep track of any subsequent changes in altitude.[46] As previously seen, height was an extremely important factor for a fighter pilot and the difficulties of night interceptions increased considerably if the precise height of attackers could not be established. The notes of an Air Ministry meeting chaired by Joubert toward the end of the battle reflected an attempt to address some of the difficulties. He stated that the "requirements of calibration were stated on 3rd April, before the full extent of expansion was under way." These requirements were "ignored or disputed . . . and [are] only now being taken seriously," and he believed that all the calibration problems stemmed from this "underlying cause." Another indication as to how Fighter Command's effectiveness was being handicapped by a lack of cooperation from Bomber Command can be seen in the provision of resources for the radio maintenance units. Joubert stated that crews for radio maintenance units were inexperienced, and that flight crews provided for test aircraft did not have the necessary training in blind flying as a result of recently coming out from training schools. Aircraft were not fully equipped with oxygen or blind flying gear and lacked standard equipment such as parachutes and life-saving jackets. The tasks demanded a very high standard of training for all aircrew, particularly wireless telegraphy (W/T) operators, but it had not been provided. Joubert also raised complaints about the inadequacy of the Blenheim aircraft, as they were difficult to service and insufficient in number. Limited resources and bad weather had made accurate calibration impossible throughout the preceding winter and had led to the majority of stations being only partially calibrated throughout the air battles.[47]

Again, Dowding and his colleagues had not been able to secure adequate resources from the Air Ministry for essential work. Even in 1940, the Blenheim was a poor aircraft but inexperienced crews and cast-off aircraft were all that Bomber Command was prepared to release for testing Fighter Command's systems. The system did not yet work as Dowding "dreamed it would," but it was gradually improving. Vital radar parts including a cavity magnetron were later shipped to the United States as part of Tizard's technical and diplomatic mission intended to help secure the vital continuing cooperation of that country. Although invented in February 1940, the first cavity magnetrons only started production in August 1940 and became the basis of a new radar system entering service in 1942. U.S. scientists were very impressed and the magnetron was a major offering to the United States in 1940.[48] Dowding, Watson-Watt, and Churchill all had their reasons for not fully acknowledging the limitations of the Dowding system, but relying so completely on this brilliant but as yet un-perfected technology was unwise and may have blinded the C-in-C to a number of tactical initiatives.

On his own admission to Liddell Hart in 1943, Dowding played little part in directing the battle once it had begun: "During the Battle of Britain," he wrote, "I was personally more occupied with the development of Night Fighting defence than with the Day Battles." Indicating that he wished to be remembered more for his work in pre-war technical development, he continued, "I had made my contribution to the former in the 4 previous years."[49] Dowding was talking about AI, or night fighters carrying special radar sets to make them less reliant on ground control. Given what the Luftwaffe did to British cities at night, AI was of crucial importance but there was no obvious reason why it could not have been delegated to another officer, and this is indicative of Dowding's tendency toward micromanagement of technical aspects. His isolation from the nitty-gritty of fighting the air battle would have unfortunate consequences. Dowding's system revolved around centralization, yet having set up a heavily centralized system, in true "hobby-manager" style, he relinquished control where he was least comfortable and left it to his group commanders to conduct the actual fighting. This is not to say that a "hands-off" management style is not a perfectly valid way of running an organization. The style worked well for Admiral Nelson but he did not allow differences between key subordinates to escalate beyond control to the extent that the outcome of the battle might become seriously prejudiced. Fortunately, the subordinate officer on whose shoulders lay the burden of fighting the Battle of Britain was a competent man. Sir Keith Park would later establish himself as the victor in the air battles over Malta, and with the freedom to conduct the defense as he saw fit Park proved to be a flexible commander. However, Park's effectiveness during the Battle of Britain would be limited by a damaging squabble over the so-called "big-wing" with his opposite number in 12 Group, the equally strong-minded Trafford Leigh-Mallory. The balance of serious historical writing is that Dowding should have intervened in the dispute before it got out of hand. Historian John Ray believes that the C-in-C was merely being indecisive in choosing between Park—struggling to implement the Dowding system—and Leigh-Mallory, whose tactical ideas were more in tune with the C-in-C's thinking than generally acknowledged.[50] After all, it was Dowding who was responsible for the large formations of fighters sent over Dunkirk to cover the evacuation of the BEF, with mixed results. Whatever the real reason, the affair says little for the C-in-C's ability as a manager of people.

Leigh-Mallory's position on the subject of two or more squadrons operating in the air as a "big wing" appears to have stemmed from Douglas Bader's frustration at being on the periphery of the action, together with Bader's admiration and possible misconception of Manfred von Richthofen's so-called Flying Circus of 1917–18. Bader was a forceful and volatile character probably more temperamentally suited to the individualistic style of the World War I flyers he admired. The role of the Geschwader (air force wings), in the words of the German chief of staff in 1917, was "to attain and maintain air supremacy in Sectors of the Front as required."[51] The reason for the introduction of this concept in 1917 was clearly more strategic than tactical. Back in 1917–18 air fighting rarely involved intercepting large formations of bombers. The role of the German fighter aircraft was mainly to intercept Allied two-seater aircraft engaged in reconnaissance or artillery-spotting over German lines. Bombing and ground attack only gradually emerged as a secondary activity. The Royal Flying Corps engaged in fighter sweeps by flights of five to six single-seat scouts to clear the way for vulnerable two-seaters, and this led to "dogfights." Air supremacy was then more about gaining or denying the freedom to see what was happening on the ground than about bombing, as bombers were severely limited in range and bomb-load. Large-scale fighter-versus-fighter battles were rare in World War II and did not occur in the Battle of Britain because the RAF declined to meet the challenge of the Luftwaffe fighter sweeps.

The essential weakness of the "big-wing" plan was in the time it took to assemble the aircraft in order to meet an incoming raid. Though the significance should not be over-emphasized, an official war game fought after the war attempting to re-create the Battle of Britain using big-wings indicated these tactics did not work.[52] Proponents were relatively unconcerned about the targets being bombed so long as the German bombers were severely mauled going back. When the targets were important sinews of 11 Group's command and control system, this view was intolerable. Unfortunately, the forming up of so many aircraft out at sea also tended to flood the radar screens, blinding RDF to the approach of enemy raids. As will be realized from the earlier discussion on filtering, sudden incursions of fighters into a neighboring group's territory without pre-arranged flight plans was bound to sow confusion. What Park required from 12 Group was for their fighters to guard 11 Group's airfields while his own fighters engaged the Luftwaffe.

As Bader is universally recognized as the instigator of the "big-wing" concept, it is important to assess his defense of these tactics. Through his biographer and brother-in-law, P. B. Lucas, Bader complained that none of the "experts" on this tactical controversy ever discussed it with him before relating their own interpretations. If three squadrons were to be used, he would take them to 20,000 feet, their optimum operating altitude. Meanwhile a squadron of Spitfires would be climbing to 25,000 or 26,000 feet above in order to deal with high-flying German fighters. He claimed that on average it took four to six minutes to assemble the formation at battle height. Bader claimed that 11 Group often failed to call the Duxford wing in good time for interception to be made. Furthermore, having to guard 11 Group's northern airfields "wasn't much of a main dish."[53] Well-known ace "Johnnie" Johnson was reputed to have said that "the Duxford wing had recently taken 17 minutes to leave the ground and a further 20 minutes before it set course from base," with a remark that concentrating so many aircraft in this fashion left the Midland industrial belt vulnerable to air attack.[54] Lucas, speaking for Bader, denied Johnson ever said such a thing, claiming he was a lifelong friend of Bader.[55] Johnson, he said, never served with the Duxford wing in 1940, only moving within the 12 Group perimeters to rest and regroup. Johnson was then praised in the text as one of the great "Allied wing-leaders of the war" before the reader was advised that Johnson and Bader did not fly together until

1941. Naturally, Johnson did not mention these criticisms in his history of air warfare, *Full Circle,* and would hardly have made such a reference in the book he co-wrote with Lucas, *Glorious Summer.*[56] The earliest reference to Johnson's alleged remarks was in 1969, but as neither author referenced their sources in line with current practice, it is now impossible to check. Probably Johnson once made a casual remark he could not repeat because of his friendship with Bader and Lucas. Another author mentioned that the Hurricane took seventeen minutes to reach 20,000 feet. If a Luftwaffe bomber formation only took twenty minutes to reach Croydon after crossing the coast, then it is hard to see how these tactics could have worked in any area south of London, especially when a further period of time on top of the seventeen minutes was clearly necessary to sort the aircraft into a battle formation.[57] This further period of time would inevitably increase in cloudy conditions.

Bader and Lucas went on to deny that assembling the big-wing ever took fifty-five minutes during August or September. Duxford to Tilbury (the border with 11 Group) was forty-seven miles, and the Duxford wing "invariably" got there at 18,000 feet "within 18–19 minutes of setting course."[58] In practice a lot would depend on the wind. When the Duxford wing made their well-known interception over London on 15 September, a 90-mph wind from the northwest had propelled their aircraft down from East Anglia while German bombers slowly struggled against the headwind.[59] If the warning from 11 Group was indeed too slow during the "critical period," it was because the technical and personnel flaws in the RDF chain had not been ironed out yet. Therefore, it was up to Leigh-Mallory to devise alternative strategies taking this limitation into account, particularly when 11 Group had at least the moral right to expect his aircraft to be in the right place at the right time. Unfortunately, with the system set up by Dowding, Park could not *order* Leigh-Mallory to comply with his tactical needs, and this led to conflict.

It is also reasonable to query whether it was desirable for all of the Duxford squadrons to arrive simultaneously, as it has been denied that having so many aircraft airborne would dramatically add to effectiveness. Using his own logbook as evidence, Allen stated that "whenever a squadron of twelve aircraft were ordered into the air, only six fired their guns." In the Duxford wing, which sometimes comprised forty-eight aircraft, this might mean that only fifteen of these would see action, or in other words fire their guns. Because of the "difficulty" in controlling such a large formation, the interception rate was likely to have been even less. Allen also alleged that unlike Bader's fighter sweeps into France during 1941, the basic formations used in 1940 did not allow for as many pairs of eyes to scan the sky for enemy aircraft, thus increasing the chances of being "bounced" by enemy fighters.[60] Johnson seems to confirm this. While relating his personal experience of leading larger formations in sweeps over the Low Countries, he stated his preference for leading two squadrons, rather than three. "I found we got in each other's way in a fight, and only the leaders were able to bring their guns to bear," he wrote. "I also found that a single, common radio frequency made it difficult to control the activities of more than four or five sections."[61]

Park was understandably incensed about what he came to see as Leigh-Mallory's attempts to dictate tactics, while the latter merely saw these objections as indicative of 11 Group's parochial attitude to fighting the campaign. Relations between the two groups became so bad that Park was unable to rely on 12 Group to guard his airfields while his fighters were airborne. Thus North Weald and Hornchurch were badly hit on 24 August and Debden was hit the following day. On 30 August, Bader's Duxford wing was told to cover Biggin Hill but failed to intercept, with the result that the airfield took heavy damage including thirty-nine dead and twenty-six injured.[62] The debate on larger formations did lead to the compromise of having two squadrons fight together in the air. As Dowding noted in his post-battle dispatch, "when time was the essence of the problem, two squadrons were desirable. Otherwise, fighter formations in the greatest strength should be used." In other words, he was claiming that when the Luftwaffe was concentrating its effort in the area of 11 Group, there was value in slightly larger formations, but when London became the principal daylight target, the more extreme methods of Leigh-Mallory and Bader were more effective. Dowding mentioned that 11 Group "have now developed the technique of using wing formations. These enable as many as 20 squadrons to be concentrated rapidly in the air."[63] It must be remembered that he was writing this in 1941 and it is not a reference to the Battle of Britain, but to the policy of his successor, W. Sholto Douglas (and Leigh-Mallory, who replaced Park at 11 Group) in making large-scale fighter sweeps over France. Dowding might also have mentioned the need for squadrons working in pairs to be using compatible equipment. When Allen's squadron attempted this pairing with a faster climbing Spitfire Mk II squadron, they were left standing "in a haze of 100-octane petrol fumes, and we were on our own, which is how we preferred it."[64]

Dowding's dispatch was likely to have been informed by Park, who distributed a note to 11 Group's sector stations in October 1940. Reacting to Leigh-Mallory's criticisms and betraying some fears about morale, the note was defensive in tone and the introduction made it clear he was responding to feelings that using wings of three squadrons "is the only way to defeat the enemy raiders." This was done during the campaign in France but those circumstances were different in that operations were carried out according to pre-arranged plans. Even then, the best results were obtained by fighting in two pairs, two to engage the fighters at higher altitudes and two to engage the bombers. The experience over recent weeks had shown that short warnings, adverse cloud conditions, and lack of time made the use of three-squadron wings generally unsuitable. When there were two or more cloud layers, these squadrons had difficulty making a rendezvous and maintaining contact afterwards. Park's experience was that enemy fighters often attacked RAF fighters as they struggled up below them. Sometimes in clear weather, flanking sectors formed up larger wings to meet a third incoming wave or to cut off the retreat of escaping bombers. Such decisions had to be at the discretion of the group controller, who was the only one with the complete picture. Most commanders believed that until very high frequency (VHF) radio was fitted throughout all units, it was impractical for three squadrons to work together on a common frequency, a comment substantiated by Johnson's remark reproduced above.[65]

Yet even if Leigh-Mallory's methods were at fault, at the heart of 12 Group's dissatisfaction was a justified complaint that the full resources of Fighter Command were not being deployed. Dowding's policy was not to apply his full resources in case the Germans launched an invasion, a policy for which he has received fulsome praise. Yet as has been suggested, he could have used his entire fighter force to strafe the Luftwaffe aircraft on their bases in northern France before the Battle of Britain had begun. Adolf Galland expressed surprise in his memoirs that the RAF did not take advantage of Luftwaffe vulnerability immediately prior to the Battle of Britain as they assembled near the Channel.[66] Since the Germans were without established warning systems and adequate telephone lines, and had only limited AA defenses, the RAF's success was reasonably assured. Even a force of inadequately trained and inexperienced Luftwaffe pilots flying obsolete machines managed to achieve complete surprise against Allied airfields in January 1945, destroying two hundred (Allen claims four hundred) aircraft on the ground by strafing operations. Of course the Luftwaffe in 1945 were operating in far less favorable conditions than the RAF in 1940, and their own losses were catastrophic, but it showed how a heavy blow could be delivered by these means. Such an operation against French airfields in 1940 could well have severely damaged the German effort before it had even started.[67] Unfortunately given the number of aircraft required for such an operation, only Dowding could have authorized it. No doubt sensitive to these criticisms, Dowding's former aide claimed the C-in-C did ask the Air Ministry for attacks to be launched by Bomber Command against various targets during the early (contact) phase of the battle. These were intended to "slow up the impetus of the German air attack" and included airfields, aircraft on the ground, industrial plants, and oil stocks.[68] Only after the air campaign began in earnest did Bomber Command launch some limited raids on French airfields but the opportunity had gone. The most obvious conclusion to be drawn from this is that the Air Ministry could not have seriously believed that the forthcoming German air offensive was capable of knocking Britain out of the war. As previously explained, the Air Staff was predisposed to be overprotective of the bomber force because they still believed this to be the main war-winning asset.[69] That Bomber Command was not prepared to accede to this suggestion did not mean Dowding could not have gone ahead using his fighters in a ground strafing role.

Allen has suggested that another option open to Dowding might have been to send his fighters over to France as soon as German formations were seen assembling over the promontories of the French and Belgian coasts. However, as one writer has pointed out, the bombers would more often assemble at low altitude behind the coast and out of RDF range, only using the promontories as rendezvous points with their fighter escorts. If everything went to plan, then the German aircraft would already be in formation by the time the rendezvous point was reached, suggesting that RDF alone would not have provided many opportunities for this strategy.[70] Nevertheless, 421 Squadron—equipped with faster Spitfire Mk IIs—did undertake effective missions on behalf of the Royal Observer Corps to estimate the size, height, and direction of enemy bombers behind the enemy coast, thus providing even more information about the buildup of raids than radar alone could have given. German escort fighters with notoriously low fuel capacities would conserve fuel by delaying takeoff, thus leaving the bombers in a vulnerable position. Had squadrons been scrambled to intercept at first sighting, Allen—with his flying combat experience—predicted the bombers would have been thrown into chaos, with British fighters back at base before the Me 109s could arrive.[71] Perhaps Dowding was concerned over the German fighters following his aircraft back to base and catching them on the ground without fuel or ammunition, but no consideration seems to have been given to these options. Such tactics were similar to suggestions made by Bader, later successfully adopted by Park during the air defense of Malta. In this situation, fighters were successfully sent out on offensive sweeps well out to sea and over Sicily to intercept massing bombers. Without doubt, Dowding's well-known aversion to sending his fighters over the sea militated against these sorts of schemes.

Dowding's system was not perfected by 1940. At the end of the "critical period," Park found it necessary to supplement the system by using VHF-radio-equipped Spitfires "to shadow enemy raids, and report to Sectors, who report to Group."[72] Commenting on this to the Air Ministry, Dowding supported the need for this supplementary measure. So important did Dowding feel this supplement to be that he requested an additional flight in 66 Squadron to fill this need without delay "as the need is immediate."[73] This, taken with the introduction of standing patrols in the final stage of the battle, represented something of an admission of failure for the RDF system. The defense adopted was not proactive but reactive. In fact, Dowding took an enormous risk in leaning so heavily on a modified command and control system from World War I that now relied heavily on inadequately tested new technology. This system had already been compromised from the outset by the German occupation of northern Europe where maximum warning was unattainable because enemy bases were already within the maximum range of radar. This left the Germans to take the initiative in each phase of the battle. Dowding's actions were not what would normally be expected of a senior executive in virtually any large organization. That Fighter Command survived at all had more to do with the efforts of Keith Park, pilots, and countless support staff, but also because of German decisions relating to the wider campaign that released the pressure just in time. Unfortunately Dowding was not a team player. He was not fired as a result of a dastardly plot by "big-wing" proponents, as claimed by former aide Robert Wright, but because of a stubborn attitude and inability to compromise that manifested itself in a negative attitude to several issues, including the decentralization of the filter room and night air defense.[74] As Churchill had been subjected to many complaints about Dowding's negative attitudes from the Air Council, his chairmanship of the Night Air Defence Committee gave him an opportunity to closely observe Dowding's poor relationship with colleagues.[75] Apart from good relationships with General Alfred Pile, head of AA defenses, the controversial figure of Lord Beaverbrook at the Ministry of Aircraft Production, and Sir Henry Tizard (already eclipsed by Professor Frederick Lindemann), Dowding seems to have irritated almost everyone he had to work with. On 14 November, Coventry was virtually obliterated in exchange for only one German bomber, and immediately afterwards large tracts of London were destroyed for minimal enemy loss. This was the last straw.

Fortunately for the C-in-C's reputation Churchill saw no advantage in denigrating Dowding after the sacking and obtained a Grand Cross in the Order of the Bath (GCB) and a baronetcy for him. He also arranged a further appointment in the United States as head of a technical mission, though it should have been obvious from the start that Dowding lacked the sort of public relations skills required. Sir John Slessor wrote to Newall from Washington on 4 December warning that Dowding should avoid any comment outside of a carefully prepared statement concerning the nature of his immediate duties. The message confirmed the intense interest of the American "man in the street" in the exploits of the RAF, and that Dowding would find the questions of the American press "distasteful to him," but nevertheless answers should "be given with as good grace as possible."[76] However, Dowding's posting to the United States must have seemed a shrewd move given that the Americans had now seen the Luftwaffe abandoning its large-scale daylight bombing campaign, together with a general consensus that the invasion had been thwarted by Fighter Command's continued survival. For all this, Churchill was clearly grateful. When the HMSO booklet *The Battle of Britain* was produced in 1941, Churchill argued (albeit unsuccessfully) against the non-inclusion of Dowding's name in it. A *Daily Herald* article covering the pamphlet's release and making some mild criticism that Dowding's name was not mentioned had clearly stung Churchill. However, this was the only article making the comment, and the Air Ministry files record satisfaction that HMSO was predicting sales exceeding a million, which would be "an all time record for such a pamphlet. A similar response is believed to await it in the United States."[77] The official attitude was that everyone knew who the C-in-C was anyway and that the pamphlet was about how a thousand anonymous young men had "fought one of the decisive battles of the world." This was entirely consistent with a long-standing official policy of not glorifying individuals in case it detracted from the efforts of the many. In 1914–18 there was no official glorification given to successful British airmen such as Mick Mannock and Albert Ball. The press ensured these names were well known but the publicity did not compare with German equivalents such as Manfred von Richthofen, who enjoyed widespread celebrity status. In the Battle of Britain, it was again left to the press to make the names of aces known, and it was common for children to avidly listen for the names of "fighter-pilot heroes" on the BBC and look for their photographs, "especially those being decorated at the Palace."[78] Dowding's concern to protect his reputation did not mean he was a glory-seeker, and the file indicates that Dowding did not wish for any personal publicity.[79]

Following his return to the UK, Dowding won the admiration of Basil Liddell Hart, one of the foremost military historians and theorists of the day. A letter from Liddell Hart to a contemporary admired Dowding's honesty, his empirical approach to scientific problems, and his "eagerness for new ideas." Liddell Hart even went so far as to wish that Dowding had been "in charge of our defence policy as a whole." The letter also revealed an enthusiasm for Dowding's unorthodox spiritual ideas, and his other "hobby horse" of a common world language, indicating they were well attuned to each other's wavelength.[80] The pair subsequently met and became friends, with Dowding being consulted for Liddell Hart's subsequent publications including his *History of the Second World War*. Unfortunately, this distinguished writer may have also blinded himself to Dowding's faults. Subsequent authors such as Robert Wright have done the same. The ability to work in a team with senior civil servants, politicians, and service colleagues was surely fundamental to the type of committee system run by the British for determining policy. Certainly Dowding had no interim solution to night raids and was dismissive of suggestions. Later in the war, the Luftwaffe disproved the impossibility of an interim solution to night raids. When the RAF temporarily blinded the German Himmelbett system, Allied bombers were silhouetted with flak, flares, and searchlights so that high-flying day fighters could attack at night from above with visual sighting. Though unpopular with the Air Ministry, Dowding retained the affection of his pilots. Yet both Allen and Lucas believe this only spread after the campaign and deny he was widely loved during the battle itself, claiming that this was an image promoted by the media in a repeatedly published photograph of Dowding surrounded by his "chicks" at an anniversary celebration.[81]

Dowding was perhaps the best available officer to lead Fighter Command in 1936, and if he had been replaced by Sholto Douglas at an earlier date, then the latter's attempting to fight the air campaigns with big-wings was likely to have damaged the defense. On the other hand, Sholto Douglas may have proved sufficiently flexible to modify the idea before 11 Group was dragged to disaster, but ultimately this is speculation. It is hard to imagine many commanders being as obdurate over centralized filtering and night air defense as Dowding. Those subscribing to the psychological model of convergent/divergent thinkers will not be surprised to see Dowding fitting into Liam Hudson's convergent thinker category typified by engineers, while divergent thinkers were said to make better managing-director material and to be better placed to "think outside the box" and to thrive in a milieu of fast-changing situations demanding flexible responses.[82] Perhaps this is why Dowding excelled in the pre-war period, but seemed too rigid, uncommunicative, and unimaginative to be a great field commander. At fifty-eight, Dowding was perhaps too old for this appointment anyway, and while he deserved high marks for supporting the development of RDF and the eight-gun fighter, there is no real evidence that he deserved the mantle of "tactical genius." While this chapter has suggested that Dowding's reputation is over-exalted, the next will examine his naval equivalent and ask whether the relatively unknown Admiral Forbes deserves greater recognition than Dowding for his contribution toward national defense.

CHAPTER SIX

Wrong–Way Charlie's Navy

He [Forbes] was in my opinion quite one of the soundest and best of our war admirals, and was never given credit for his doings.[1]

Admiral A. B. Cunningham

Compared with that of Lord Dowding, the reputation of Admiral of the Fleet Sir Charles Morton Forbes (1880–1960) is clouded in obscurity. For the reasons detailed in the two previous chapters, Dowding's name is synonymous with the Battle of Britain but it is rare for Forbes to be accorded even a cursory mention. Even publications dealing with the Norway campaign of 1940, an action in which he played a major part, have made surprisingly few direct references to the C-in-C Home Fleet by name.

An article in the *Sunday Post* dated 21 April 1940 observed that prior to the commencement of the Norway campaign "hardly anyone knew his name," despite the fact that the war was now seven months old and Forbes had been in command of the Home Fleet for two years. While the article was naturally positive about Forbes' qualities as a commander, it also contrasted his anonymity with naval predecessors Admirals of the Fleet John Arbuthnot Fisher, John Rushworth Jellicoe, and David Beatty, all of whom were household names in 1914.[2] No attempt was made to analyze the reason for this. Lord Nelson's dramatic victory at Trafalgar in 1805 heralded the so-called Pax Britannica (1815–1914) and was a hard act to follow.[3] The failure to impose the same crushing defeat on the German High Seas Fleet at Jutland in 1916 had proved a great disappointment to the press and public. Though by now out of the Admiralty, Churchill also suffered (and allegedly accepted) some public criticism over Jutland for failing to appreciate the value of aircraft as spotters for the fleet when he was First Lord.[4] This is not to say the British had lost touch with their maritime tradition in 1940, as is said to have happened in the second half of the twentieth century. The Royal Navy was still a source of pride but since Jutland, German Gotha bombers had bombed London and the great technological strides in aviation accompanied by doomsday scenarios of destruction from the air had focused attention away from the sea and toward the sky.[5] The diversion of staggering amounts of public money into the RAF—inevitably at the navy's expense—during the 1930s can therefore be seen as a reflection of the public's unspoken yet diminished regard for the senior service and its leaders. Nothing much happened to change this view during 1940. Churchill proclaimed the RAF's victory in the Battle of Britain and by November 1940 severe parliamentary criticism of the navy's leadership was being reported in the British press.[6] One historian wrote that until "March 1941 the RAF with its triumphant record in the Battle of Britain, the only great pivotal battle to be witnessed by half the nation, had attracted the greatest acclaim among the three services."[7] None of this fully explains Forbes' continued obscurity. His colleague, Admiral A. B. Cunningham, has enjoyed well-deserved fame to the present day. Taranto was a battle that caught the world's imagination, and in gaining a spectacular success with Fleet Air Arm aircraft against Italian capital ships in November 1940, Cunningham could only benefit from the validation this bestowed on British airpower, especially when it was turned against warships. In turn, this can only have reinforced the perception of the Battle of Britain as a decisive victory won by airpower alone.[8] Forbes never had the opportunity of delivering a similar success, and unlike Cunningham and the majority of senior military men he did not bother to write memoirs after the war. In consequence, the historiographies of the "finest hour" and the Royal Navy in World War II do not hold Forbes in any position of prominence.

Belying many of his actions in 1940, Winston Churchill wrote that following his second meeting on board HMS *Nelson*, he "formed a strong feeling of confidence in the Commander-in-Chief."[9] The official historian of the Royal Navy summed up Forbes by noting that "his fifteen months bought no great sea victory . . . as might catch the public's imagination." However, despite many constraints he felt that Forbes' policy and strategy were "generally justified by subsequent events, and that his steady hand on the reins contributed greatly to bringing the country through this anxious period."[10] However, for another writer, Forbes was "guilty of not backing his hunches" in the matter of ship dispositions during the Norway campaign. Along with Admiral William Whitworth and others, he was among the "decent men doing a very competent job" but who were "not going to set naval warfare alight."[11] A more controversial critic considered Forbes shared Cunningham's characteristic "unshakability" but quoted a subordinate's opinion that the C-in-C lacked "panache."[12] A book aimed at the general reader stressed the C-in-C's "ill-luck" to be in charge during "a period of setbacks and uncertainties," but praised his strategic grasp and noted his command "immobilized the bulk of the German surface ships during the Norwegian conflict." Concluding that he was a scapegoat for the navy's ill-preparedness at this time, the author pointed out that Forbes later handed over a stronger fleet than existed at the commencement of hostilities.[13] Some praise was given by Admiral Dudley Pound's biographer, who stated that it was Forbes rather than the Admiralty who read the invasion situation correctly. He also absolved Forbes from blame over the sinking of *Royal Oak* in 1939 by pointing out that he "had moved heaven and earth to get the Scapa Flow defences improved."[14] The only academic to examine Forbes' career in any detail has been the American scholar James Levy, who praised Forbes as "a solid strategist and a fine admiral" but who could not be considered a "great commander" owing "to his inability to see through the intelligence muddle [during the Norway campaign] and guess his enemy's actions and intentions."[15] Levy considered that Forbes would have made a better First Sea Lord than Dudley Pound, except perhaps for an outspokenness that antagonized Churchill and contributed toward his eventual dismissal. As far as most naval historical literature is concerned, Forbes remains a figure with only tangential significance.[16]

Ultimately, the reputation of military commanders should rest more heavily upon how they dealt with the constraints placed upon their operational tenure rather than upon the glamour surrounding their branch of the armed services. Both Forbes and Dowding had served in senior appointments for many years and the efficiency of the RAF and Royal Navy (RN) was partly the result of their pre-war efforts to modernize their organizations. Forbes therefore shared collective responsibility with his colleagues for the state of the Royal Navy during the early phase of the war. In this respect, there has been a tendency among some writers to portray the navy as a backward-looking organization obsessed with the so-called lessons of Jutland during the inter-war period.[17] However, there is an opposing school emphasizing the pragmatic way in which the navy adapted to financial and technological constraints by making radical changes to tactics and gunnery. Whichever of these views one accepts will inevitably influence how Forbes is perceived. Also relevant to his reputation was the propensity of Churchill and the Admiralty to interfere in operations with the justification of "superior" knowledge as it fundamentally related to his ability to contact and destroy enemy ships. As we shall see, it also reflected a clash in temperament that existed between Forbes and his immediate superior at the Admiralty, First Sea Lord Dudley Pound. A detailed blow-by-blow account of the Norway campaign is not covered here, but the operation is discussed in order to highlight the "intelligence muddle" and the problems of excessive interference with Forbes' command. Yet the C-in-C's crippling of the Kriegsmarine around Norway and the giving of sound strategic advice during the invasion crisis did not save him from the sack. Why then was Forbes' contribution to victory so diminished?

Forbes was born into an expatriate Scottish family in Ceylon (now Sri Lanka) in 1880. It was a family with naval traditions—hence his father's intention for his son to join the navy. This was fine by Charles and his early education at Dollar Academy in Scotland proved a happy one.[18] Forbes entered the navy in 1894, and in passing out from his training program with a reported five out of five first-class certificates gained a twelve-month seniority advantage over many of his peers.[19] He was then posted to a series of sea-going appointments but in 1903 served on the staff of the gunnery school *Cambridge* at Devonport. This was undoubtedly a shrewd career move given the primacy of big-gun specialists that would prevail for years to come. A variety of other postings followed and in 1916 he was present at the Dardanelles as commander of the battleship *Queen Elizabeth*. At Jutland he was flag commander to Sir John Jellicoe in the battleship *Iron Duke*, where he won the Distinguished Service Order and a mention in dispatches.[20] His relationship with Jellicoe was clearly a positive one. Now captain of the light cruiser *Galatea*, Forbes commiserated with Jellicoe over his dismissal as First Sea Lord in December 1917 and thanked him "for all that he has done for me."[21] In August 1919 he became a naval member of the Ordnance Committee and was deputy director of the Royal Naval Staff College from August 1921 to May 1923. From 1923 he served in flag captain appointments in the Atlantic and Mediterranean before serving as the director of Naval Ordnance with the rank of rear admiral in 1928.[22] From October 1925 to May 1928, Forbes was considered by Vice Admiral Ernle Chatfield (First Sea Lord, 1933–38, and minister for co-ordination of defence, 1939–40) to be "exceptional." Chatfield wrote that Forbes would probably make a "brilliant Controller" and a "fine Flag Officer" but tempered his praise with the observation that his cautious approach could make him unsuitable for the Naval Staff. In 1930, Forbes became rear admiral (destroyers) in the Mediterranean Fleet and Chatfield considered he fulfilled these duties "admirably" but thought he was "better at consolidating a position than capturing it." However, this was "without intending to detract from the fact that his abilities are of a high order."[23] He next became Third Sea Lord and Controller of the Admiralty, and was promoted to vice admiral on 21 January 1933. This post was considered by Vice Admiral Clifford Caslon to be one "calling for exceptional qualities of technical knowledge and ability in committee."[24] It covered responsibility for materiel including ships and armament, and oversaw the directors of Naval Construction, Dockyards; Naval Ordnance; Torpedoes and Mining, Armament Supply; Compasses; Scientific Research and Experiment; Electrical Engineering; and the Fleet-Engineer-in-Chief.[25] Later second-in-command of the Mediterranean Fleet, he received the Knight Commander of the Order of the Bath (KCB) in 1935, the year prior to being promoted to admiral. His appointment in the Mediterranean Fleet was a key appointment as this was the Royal Navy's most important tactical formation—a place where the naval tactics that would be used in World War II were developed during the interwar period. The appointment as C-in-C Home Fleet was made in April 1938, shortly after the Anschluss crisis drew to a close.

His "Captain's Confidential Reports," taken from his service record, cover the period from 1914–40 and portray an extraordinarily talented officer. While Chatfield's remarks about Forbes' cautious approach cannot be put aside lightly, it may be significant that Chatfield was the only reporting officer to interpret his calm and thorough approach in this manner. Nevertheless, this criticism may have prevented him from gaining the First Sea Lord's chair in 1939. His *Times* obituary article claimed there "was nothing spectacular . . . nor on first acquaintance did he give the impression of possessing outstanding personality." Nevertheless, it acknowledged "no man ever saw him 'rattled . . . he had full confidence in himself, and he inspired it in those under his command.'" It went on to say that those in "closest contact with him knew best the reserves of power . . . the clear vision, sound judgment, and strong sense of proportion," while also likening him to "a tower of strength."[26] Obituaries, by their nature, focus on the positive aspects of the deceased but not without hinting at the subject's perceived shortcomings. By emphasizing that those in "closest contact" knew his virtues the impression was given that many people were unaware of these qualities. Many years after the war, his former flag officer wrote to the official historian about him. Godfrey Style stated that "he [Forbes] dodged the publicity cult like mad." An aversion to publicity was a disadvantage when there were problems with the morale of the fleet at the end of 1939, resulting from the perception that the public was not appreciating the navy's efforts.[27] The same source also remarked upon "his *extreme* loyalty both upwards and downwards. . . . [H]e stood on his own bridge, always calm, always the same and ALWAYS CORRECTLY DRESSED without mufflers or other fancy gear." This behavior contrasted with another admiral against whom it was claimed, if there was a problem on the bridge, "would come in and push one out of the way."[28] The sartorial comment was probably made to support the remark about Forbes' aversion to publicity. Style was doubtless thinking of egocentric self-publicists such as Lord Louis Mountbatten, a controversial but well-connected officer with enough influence to take him from the captaincy of a destroyer to Supreme Allied Commander, South-East Asia, by the end of the war.

Commander J. A. J. Dennis' papers also remarked that "poor Admiral Forbes came in for a lot of criticism—indeed it is said that some called him 'Wrong-Way Charlie.'" While Dennis went on to defend Forbes, stating that the fault lay with the higher command and Churchill himself, these recollections were almost certainly influenced by hindsight and subsequent reading.[29] An interview with Ron Babb, who served as an engine-room artificer on HMS *Rodney* before and during the Norway campaign, suggests that Forbes was not badly thought of by the personnel of the Home Fleet except that it was always considered he wasn't doing enough to push the war effort forward. He did not "come over as a striking force" at the time and people thought he was a little more cautious than he should be. When questioned directly about whether the "lower deck" had confidence in Forbes, he replied that to the best of his knowledge they had. He "never heard anyone knock him on the lower deck." A suggestion (originally made by Admiral John Tovey) was put to Mr. Babb that Forbes failed to visit his ships enough. As far as he could recollect, Forbes did come on board and make regular inspections. Much of the problem appeared to be rooted in the sailors' frustration at the relative inactivity during the opening months of the war, and they took it out on their superiors.[30] The relative inactivity was perhaps inevitable as the Draft Hague Rules of Air Warfare (1923) did not permit the harrying of German coastal traffic, despite the fact that these rules were self-imposed, unratified, and not part of international law.[31] Nevertheless, the Allies decided to adhere to them until the Norway campaign and it is clear this ruling put a severe restraint upon the activities of the Home Fleet at this time.

Forbes' career showed a steady rise through the strata of naval hierarchy and, as the *Times* pointed out shortly after his death, his career shadowed closely that of his predecessor as C-in-C Home Fleet, First Sea Lord Sir Roger Backhouse, a fact suggesting Forbes was being groomed for Backhouse's job. This may well have happened after the death of Admiral Dudley Pound in 1943, had circumstances been a little different.[32] Unlike colleagues such as Pound, Forbes was neither a centralizer nor an advocate of "orthodox" tactics. One Royal Navy officer has stated that it has "become very fashionable" to blame the predominance of gunnery officers in the 1930s for some tactical misdirection, because of assumptions that U-boat attacks would only be made in shallow waters and because anti-submarine (A/S) officers exaggerated the success of their Asdic anti-submarine detecting device. While acknowledging that Asdic failed partly as a result of the navy's failure to audit their systems properly, he believed that it was more a "freak application of a generally satisfactory [administrative] system." Gunnery officers seemed to have not understood the problems because submariners tended to "have minimal interface with other branches" and because of a natural "slight bias" to their own interests. He also indicated that the disappointment with Asdic was more the result of a tactical misconception during the early phase of the war than the failure of pre-war development. It was also acknowledged that other navies including that of Germany made the same mistake of over-emphasizing the importance of big guns, yet there were certainly grounds for asserting the primacy of gunnery in Britain.[33] The kind of battle for which big guns, battleships, and their tactics were developed would later occur at the Battle of Calabria against the Italian fleet in 1940.[34]

Like the majority of great naval battles before it and with the notable exception of Trafalgar, Jutland was characterized by the opposing fleets forming up into parallel lines against each other. As historian J. T. Sumida explained, there were mechanical weaknesses relating to British gunnery, making the Grand Fleet of 1916 relatively ineffective at long range. Despite subsequent improvements to this equipment, financial and treaty constraints resulted in the navy losing some ground in the technological competition with other powers during the interwar period. With the Japanese thought to be achieving proficiency at 30,000 yards, well beyond anything the British could achieve in 1934, experiments were conducted in the use of short-range actions of 10,000 to 15,000 yards.[35] By 1935, not long after Forbes' term as Third Sea Lord and controller in charge of materiel, a memorandum was distributed advocating short-range actions, reflecting the many successes obtained by this method in the past.[36] Other simulations also indicated the possibility of controlling the ranges at which combats would be fought utilizing smoke screens and night-fighting techniques. According to Sumida, night fighting became standard under the Mediterranean Fleet commanders of the 1930s, and this fleet was recognized as the navy's "premier and tactically most influential force."[37] As Forbes commanded the destroyer flotillas of this fleet during 1930–31, and was vice admiral in the Mediterranean commanding the first battle squadron, and second in command, Mediterranean Fleet, 1934–38, his role in developing these tactics must have been significant.

According to Admiral of the Fleet Sir John de Robeck, divisional tactics had been practiced by Forbes as captain of the battleship *Queen Elizabeth* during 1923–24 with "great success."[38] Later, these divisional tactics gradually superseded the single line-ahead or in other words, the division of the line-ahead into components ranging from one to five ships. The Tactical School emphasized the importance of "individual action" by divisional commanders in 1935, recognizing that torpedoes launched from destroyers threatened the battle fleet.[39] It was also recognized that developments in carrier design and torpedo bombers also threatened the line of battle, which was seemingly proved in a 1937 exercise where torpedo bombing attacks on a seven-ship line resulted in heavy damage and disruption, whereas similar attacks against more agile two-ship battle-cruiser formations were ineffective. However, it ought to be stressed it was not being suggested that divisional tactics were a complete antidote to the effects of massed air attack, but in many circumstances they would "greatly reduce the danger."[40] None of this resembles the actions of a moribund and backward-looking organization, though it did represent the pragmatic response of a navy with very limited resources.

Postwar critics of the Royal Navy, focusing on the supposed obsession of the "fleet action," may have taken their cue from Dowding's wartime *Sunday Chronicle* article in which he claimed that it was the Admiralty's fault the navy had been supplied by the Air Ministry with inadequate aircraft. It was the Admiralty that insisted on a "plurality of roles" and on hybrid types "doomed to inefficiency before pencil was laid to drawing board." He claimed "the role of naval aircraft was completely subordinated by this [fleet action] conception." Dowding had been provoked by Admiral Herbert Richmond's earlier newspaper criticism of the Air Ministry, but it was only natural that where the Air Ministry was holding the purse strings, the Admiralty could not have expected (or got) a series of different aircraft each designed for separate purposes.[41] The Fleet Air Arm was only returned to full Admiralty control in May 1939, and the story of how it started the war with inadequate equipment in terms of both numbers and quality is well known. In reality, a multitude of factors was responsible for the limitations of the Fleet Air Arm's aircraft. The most fundamental was the strategic priority for "strategic" bombers and the Admiralty's tendency to stress the naval rather than the aerodynamic design aspects. Both the Air Ministry and the Admiralty shared responsibility for the problems, but fortunately the limitations of the Fleet Air Arm did not fatally weaken the fleet's ability to operate in the teeth of enemy airpower.

In 1942, the retired Admiral R. H. S. Bacon explained the tactics being used by the navy to the general public in surprising detail, in the book *Britain's Glorious Navy*. Principles of division and subdivision were affirmed but placed within the context of divisions operating within the line-ahead for fighting. The advantage was in allowing each heavy gun to fire over an arc of 120 degrees. Other positions were considered less satisfactory because of obstructions from the ship's super-structure. However, Bacon drew a distinction here between fighting and cruis-ing, acknowledging that line-ahead was too vulnerable to torpedo attack. "The best cruising formation in wartime is with one or more divisions abreast of each other." Such a formation represented a far smaller target area on an attack from the beam, and was relatively easy to maneuver into "line-ahead" when enemy surface units were to be engaged.[42] In another section by Admiral Sir Studholme Brown-rigg, the advantages of night fighting were espoused by stating that a "weaker or numerically inferior force well skilled in night fighting may well score a success over a stronger opponent less well skilled in night fighting." The obliteration of two Italian cruisers in the Battle of Matapan in 1941 was cited as an example of the success of these methods.[43] This wartime book written by senior naval officers indicates that much of what was learned in the interwar exercises was actually put into practice.

After the war, Forbes told the official historian: "I think the Navy's ideas on the whole were fairly, in fact very sound." He conceded that some tactical mis-takes were made, for example, anticipating wrongly the Germans would employ torpedo-bombing attacks against warships. This meant that in the initial contact phases, destroyer screens protecting capital ships spread too far outward, weaken-ing the barrage of protective fire. It also meant outlying ships were vulnerable to conventional bombing, but this was soon remedied by bringing the destroyers close in to the big ships.[44] The legacy of Forbes' Mediterranean experience and pragmatic approach was also apparent in his chairmanship of pre-war naval dis-cussions on the relative merits of speed, armor, and firepower, sensibly observing that warship design could only ever be a compromise between the three.[45] Levy has remarked that in true Nelsonian tradition, Forbes' management style was to let his captains know what he wanted to achieve and let them work out the precise details of how it was to be done.[46]

It is also easy to see the parallels in attitude with Nelson's actions at Trafal-gar. Nelson was willing to go against conventions by delegating authority to his captains and abandoning the traditional line of battle in favor of two columns of ships aimed at breaking the enemy line in order to place their ships in cross fire. Forbes, who also believed in delegation, opposed the traditional line-of-battle tactics laid down in the *Fighting Instructions* in favor of the more recently developed divisional tactics. Ironically, the *Fighting Instructions* of 1939 had been co-written by Forbes and Pound before the war, representing guidance rather than "orders."[47] That Forbes was co-author might be seen as a reflection of his tactical expertise built up between the wars or, more simply, that the co-authors happened to possess recent experience of senior command in the tactically important Mediterranean Fleet. However, these instructions cannot be represented as an important contribution to naval warfare. According to historian A. J. Marder, the feeling in the navy was that they were "all rubbish."[48] There were perhaps two reasons for this. First, the history of the *Fighting Instructions*—or *Articles of War*—was embarrassing for the Royal Navy as Admiral John Byng's zealous adherence to them was blamed for the British defeat at Minorca in 1756 and led to his execution for failing to do his utmost against the enemy.[49] Second, the co-authors seem to have had fundamental disagreements. For example, Pound was said to have written them with a view to a fleet action against the Japanese and thus envisaged two parallel lines of capital ships slugging it out with heavy guns. As already stated, a pitched battle similar to that envisaged by Pound did take place in the Mediterranean at the Battle of Calabria, indicating that the line of battle was not completely redundant. However, this concept was inappropriate to the circumstances of 1939 as they pertained to home waters. The Kriegsmarine was too small for a large fleet action and saw no advantage in fighting one. Even in the Pacific, it was unlikely that the Royal Navy could ever have amassed enough ships to deal with the Japanese in this sort of fleet action while Germany and Italy represented major threats much closer to home. Marder has noted that Forbes opposed large fleet actions strongly.[50] With the blessings of hindsight, it may have been more useful to have written two sets of instructions for the radically different conditions in each theater, but in the event, even the Pacific war did not run to the sort of fleet action envisaged by Pound.[51] As one historian has remarked, the problem of dealing with a triple threat from Germany, Italy, and Japan with a single power fleet was one that "defied solution."[52]

With Forbes' experience of command in the influential Mediterranean Fleet, it would have been easy to put his differences with Pound down to contrasting experiences, but Pound had been C-in-C there between 1935 and 1938 and must have drawn other conclusions from his tenure of command. Ironically, Pound's entry in the *Dictionary of National Biography* made a point of emphasizing that in this post he had trained "officers to use their initiative and not to wait for orders."[53] This stands in stark contrast to the reality of Pound's micromanaging personality, a factor that would complicate the relationship of these men in the early stages of World War II. In the circumstances, it would be surprising if the *Fighting Instructions* of 1939 seemed at all coherent. Nevertheless, they did allow for discretion on the part of commanders. When Pound wrote to him in August 1939, reserving the right to intervene in operations, Forbes responded "that it must be left to my discretion at the time whether or not I carry out these [Admiralty] orders, in the same way that Captains are given this discretion in Clauses 2 and 6 of the *Fighting Instructions*."[54] These instructions confirm that captains "without 'specific directions'" or "faced with unforeseen circumstances . . . must act as their judgment dictates." Clause 6 stated that if orders from a senior officer would result in losing touch with the enemy, consideration must be given to the senior officer "not being in full possession of the facts."[55] Accurately predicting what would later happen around Norway, Forbes argued that if he were maintaining radio silence at sea, then too much radio traffic (including inappropriately detailed orders) would give away his position to the enemy. His view was that the Admiralty should advise a course of action, leaving the decision to him as to whether the suggested action should be complied with. Forbes would later write "never answered" on the file copy of his letter to Pound.[56]

Perhaps the most serious obstacle to Forbes' reputation is the unfortunate "Wrong-Way Charlie" tag applied by some personnel. This was because of his inability to intercept German surface raiders at the beginning of hostilities and later, for failing to immediately grasp that an invasion of Norway was under way. Forbes was initially distracted by the need to stop German naval surface raiders from breaking out of the Baltic into the Atlantic, and indeed the pre-war naval plans of both countries had been based on the assumption that this would be attempted by Germany at the first available opportunity. Yet the poor information received by him did not mean the navy was backward in appreciating the value of good-quality intelligence. According to a former producer of a signals intelligence system known as Ultra, "the war at sea presents the sharpest possible contrast to the war in the air from the intelligence point of view," and the navy was ahead of the other services in this respect. During 1914–18, signals intelligence had developed to a high standard but atrophied between the wars, a problem illustrating the wider problem of insufficient long-term service funding. However, complex organizations cannot be quickly resurrected at full efficiency simply by sudden injections of large cash amounts. The problems manifested themselves in an inability to understand the significance of the decrypts. Bomber Command showed little interest in signals intelligence throughout the war because it did nothing to confirm the validity of Air Chief Marshal Arthur "Bomber" Harris' strategic bombing theories.[57] Ultra played little part in Fighter Command's campaign and there is still doubt over whether Dowding was on the list of persons approved to see the decrypts. Consequently signals intelligence, including Ultra, was of little help to the Allies at this stage of the war, but there is no real evidence that this was simply down to "Admiralty complacency."[58] In the event, Kriegsmarine signals could not be read by the British until 1941.[59]

Undoubtedly needled by the situation and probably aware that the lower decks were frustrated at his inability to find the German ships, Forbes complained to the Admiralty in January 1940 about the contradictions in Operational Intelligence Centre (OIC) intelligence and demanded an improvement. He complained that the reports of 4 January 1940 confirming the *Deutschland* was under repair at Kiel on 20–21 December had not been received by him until his return from sea on 10 January. His message also claimed that reports could be anything up to fourteen days old when posted to the base. Furthermore, if the reports were correct, then which pocket battleship was it that came through the Great Belt early on 21 December, bearing in mind one report said that *Gneisenau* and *Scharnhorst* were at Wilhelmshaven on 18 and 21 December? From these contradictory reports he concluded wrongly that the *Deutschland* and a cruiser must have been responsible for the much-publicized sinking of the *Rawalpindi* and second, "the *Admiral Scheer* and a cruiser are not abroad." In conclusion he urged that signals should be sent to him on a daily basis giving the last known location of enemy battle cruisers, pocket battleships, and cruisers, with copies to other commanders.[60] It is hard to say whether he was fully justified in drawing the wrong conclusion about which ship had sunk the *Rawalpindi,* but the complaint about delays resulting from having the reports posted to his base is a reasonable one. Unfortunately, as will be seen, increases in signals traffic would further assist the Germans in their own intelligence gathering. It was, in fact, the *Scharnhorst* that sank the *Rawalpindi* on 23 November between the Faeroe Islands and Iceland. Forbes' report does not make clear that he had also received a report direct from the *Rawalpindi* correctly identifying the battle cruiser *Scharnhorst*. Within minutes of receiving this, a contradictory report from the *Rawalpindi* claimed it was the *Deutschland*. It must be noted here that Stephen Roskill, the official historian of the Royal Navy from 1949 to 1960, has remarked on the difficulties of distinguishing pocket battleships and battle cruisers because of similarities in construction and the poor visibility in northern waters. Forbes accepted the second report because it was already known the *Deutschland* was abroad, and while she was back at Kiel on 15 December the Admiralty did not discover this until later. Forbes confessed to being "a bit muddled" about the *Deutschland*'s whereabouts by 27 December, but an OIC report dated 29 December told him that a neutral ship had seen her badly damaged and approaching Kiel on 21 December. Even this contains an anomaly with the date recorded by the official historian. As Roskill has concluded, the mistake in identifying the *Rawalpindi*'s assailant confused Admiralty intelligence on enemy dispositions for a significant time.[61] In the circumstances, it is hard to blame anyone for the confusion. Interception problems were compounded by the speed advantage of most German heavy ships and by the temporary loss of Scapa Flow as a base while its anti-submarine and anti-aircraft defenses were being overhauled. Forbes' heavy ships were now positioned on the Clyde, farther south and on the wrong side for operations in the North Sea. During March, however, the Home Fleet returned to Scapa Flow.

There can be no doubt that Forbes and the navy were let down by poor intelligence at this early stage of the war, as there were a number of indications that a full-scale invasion of Norway was under way in April. A signal intercepted in early April 1940 revealed that all ships heading for Bergen were told to regularly report to OKH in Berlin. The cryptographer, Christopher Morris, was told that the signal must have been incorrectly decrypted because ships would not report to the army. Morris later wrote, "The ships were of course troopships, and the signals would have given advance warning of the invasion of Norway." Other indications supporting the signal included Coastal Command sightings and a report on unusual German naval wireless activity during 6–7 April within the Baltic. As these reports went to different departments in Whitehall, they were not appropriately collated.[62] There was no such thing as a German naval Ultra in home waters until August 1941, although a certain amount could be learned of enemy shipping movements in the Channel and the Atlantic using RDF and the decryption of low-grade keys. This meant that German troops were able to land in mainly undefended Norwegian ports and gain a significant foothold before Allied naval and land units arrived on the scene. It was an extremely bold and daring plan. Using the Luftwaffe to offset their naval inferiority, the Germans would eventually take the country by force. Not only could they secure the supply of essential iron ore from Sweden but also the opening of several hundred miles of coastline to German shipping undermined the Allied blockade and allowed more bases from which German warships and aircraft could operate. However, once he had figured out the German intentions, Forbes ordered his destroyers to attack the German disembarkation at the port of Narvik and prepared to bombard troop landings at Bergen. Sadly, Churchill and Pound cancelled the Bergen plan at the last moment though this may have been the last realistic chance to check the German advance in central Norway.[63] Although the land fighting resulted in a humiliating debacle for the Allies, it must be remembered that the naval balance sheet at the end of the fighting favored the British, who had sustained heavy but manageable losses. German losses were three cruisers, one gunnery training ship, eight U-boats, one torpedo boat, and ten destroyers, representing around 50 percent unit losses. British losses were two cruisers, nine destroyers, six submarines, and an aircraft carrier. Bombing was the main single cause of the British losses, although these amounted to less than one-third of the total.[64] Admiral Raeder would later write in his memoirs, "The losses it [the Kriegsmarine] suffered in doing its part weighed heavily upon us for the rest of the war."[65]

In the circumstances a heavy dependence needed to be placed on air reconnaissance provided by the RAF. Sadly, the Norway campaign tended to show up the RAF's shortcomings. A frustrated Forbes signaled the Admiralty on 15 June 1940: "The quite unexpected appearance of enemy forces . . . in the far north on 8th June which led to the sinking of the *Glorious*, two destroyers, and a liner . . . shows that our scheme of air reconnaissance should be overhauled." Peevishly, he added, "The enemy reconnoitre Scapa daily if they consider it necessary. Our reconnaissance of the enemy's bases are few and far between."[66] This begs the question as to whether

Forbes was trying to scapegoat the RAF for these disasters. Roskill believed there was an atmosphere of obsessive secrecy covering the final phase of the campaign responsible for the failure to make Coastal Command sweeps for enemy ships, and criticism of the Admiralty reported in the *Times* on this very point in November 1940 tends to confirm the woeful state of internal communications within the Admiralty at this time.[67] Roskill, who then worked in the Admiralty, maintained the Air Officer C-in-C had been told unofficially about the evacuation from Norway, but the information did not filter down to a lower level.[68]

Unfortunately, with only some 170 largely obsolete operational aircraft in home waters on its strength, Coastal Command may well have failed to locate the *Scharnhorst* anyway. Why the *Glorious* (an aircraft carrier) did not carry out its own reconnaissance missions is unknown but may have had something to do with a lack of operating deck space for its own aircraft after receiving several RAF fighters withdrawn from the fighting the previous day.[69] The real reason may never be known, but the fact that RAF reconnaissance was inadequate at these longer ranges can hardly be doubted. Even in 1941, Admiralty papers revealed little confidence in Air Ministry intelligence.[70] While the sinking of the *Glorious* had something to do with a lucky break on the part of the Germans, Forbes was unfortunate in having to operate in a milieu where German naval intelligence was having remarkable success at this stage of the war. Writing to Captain Roskill after the war, Forbes wrote: "One of the most dreadful things that has come to light since we captured all the German documents is the way they had 'broken the ciphers' so early in the war, whereas we were still a long way from that goal, and when one comes to think of the mass of stuff that went out over the air from our War lords at the Admiralty, just giving away our dispositions at the slightest provocation."[71]

The irony of this complaint is in Forbes' earlier demands that signals regarding the location of enemy ships be widely disseminated among commands. Another irony was contained within Foreign Office advice to war correspondents that a warship has "to keep its radio silent, unless it wants to reveal its whereabouts to the enemy."[72] It was not until August 1940 that the Admiralty suspected the Germans were reading the naval codes and changed them, thus depriving the enemy of an important intelligence advantage during the period a cross-Channel invasion was most likely to have been made. Unfortunately, German expertise at reading the strength and direction of British naval traffic meant the problem was not entirely removed. By contrast with its British counterpart, during the period 1940–41, the reputation of B-Dienst (German naval intelligence) was high.

Given the Admiralty's relative enthusiasm for intelligence activity and the postwar publicity regarding Ultra, it seems hard to comprehend that B-Dienst was so successful. Captain Heinz Bonatz, former head of B-Dienst, attributed the German success to "long years of effort" rather than any technological breakthrough. Peacetime Royal Navy codes gave them few difficulties, as they were not re-ciphered on a regular basis. Familiarity developed with British routines and the phrases used within wireless transmissions. The adoption of secret cipher and secret code increased the complexity. However, Bonatz also claimed that German expertise in analyzing the broad range of wireless traffic soon re-established the initiative. Traffic analysis in this sense includes all of the material that can be gathered through a W/T receiver and that is susceptible to analysis, including changes of frequency band, monitoring the appearance of ships maintaining W/T watch, "corrections, calling-up procedure, acknowledgments, the interpretation of numerous call-up signs and delivery groups." This sort of analysis did not require cryptanalysis but Bonatz claimed it later enabled a cryptanalysis breakthrough based largely on the experience gained regarding the character and vocabulary employed in British signals along with accurate assumptions regarding message contents taking into account whether or not the message was routine.[73] In this situation, any unnecessary W/T traffic was likely to have deleterious consequences. Forbes undoubtedly considered that too much information was being sent over the air because the Admiralty was trying to micromanage the campaign from London.

Unfortunately, Churchill had undermined Forbes in the Norwegian campaign by dividing his ships between the C-in-C and another officer. This was the elderly Admiral of the Fleet William "Ginger" Boyle, Lord Cork and Orrery, appointed as flag officer, Narvik, and finally supreme commander of the operations around Narvik. Thus, for reasons that are not completely clear, but probably connected with the First Lord's desire to "divide and rule," Narvik was treated as a separate operational area from the rest of Norway. Yet it was not completely unrealistic to have one commander to focus on attempting to cut the enemy supply lines at sea, while another commander concentrated on amphibious landings around the crucial Narvik area. Forbes may have felt resentment about this treatment but he did not let this interfere with the job in hand. The official historian suggested there were difficulties arising from Lord Cork's dependence on Forbes for support, as each commander could not properly appreciate what the other was doing in their respective spheres. However, a letter to Forbes from Rear Admiral L. H. "Turtle" Hamilton conveys Lord Cork's wish for Hamilton to emphasize "how grateful he was to you for the AA cruisers and escort vessels, which have undoubtedly saved the situation." Not too much can be read into this but it is at least an indication that the naval commanders ended the campaign on cordial terms.[74]

The allegation that Churchill had interfered in the Norway operation probably originated in Roskill's official history drafts, in which he suggested the First Lord's tendency at certain times "to spend long hours in the Operational Intelligence Centre" encouraged "him to assume direct control therefrom" and "sometimes confused the conduct of operations."[75] This comment clearly needled Churchill as he had already written about the operations around Bergen: "Looking back . . . I consider that the Admiralty kept too close a control upon the Commander-in-Chief."[76] So sensitive did the matter become that Roskill's accusations spawned an internal government investigation, which concluded that the Admiralty had tended to interfere "too freely" but not as a result of Churchill's interference.[77] His exoneration was perhaps unsurprising in view of the reverence in which Churchill's name was then held. Temperamentally, Churchill could not help himself but his insistence on pressing dubious strategies on the military professionals drove even loyal colleagues to distraction.[78] Roosevelt's envoy Harry Hopkins held the impression that Churchill ran the British war effort from strategy down to the details. A man of considerable paradox, Churchill found the whole business of war exciting, envied the younger men their direct involvement, and yet still found room to empathize with the human suffering that war entailed.

Yet if Churchill had a tendency to meddle in the conduct of operations, then his First Sea Lord was no less guilty. There is abundant evidence to show that Dudley Pound's instincts and actions were to centralize and control to an extreme degree. At an academic level, Pound was sometimes prepared to acknowledge the right of a C-in-C to run his own show, but in practice he found it difficult to "let go." The culture of excessive secrecy within the Admiralty over which he presided is a further indication of a micromanaging personality. As the Admiralty was an operational center as well as a department of state, Pound had a technical right to intervene. General Hastings Ismay, in charge of the military wing of the War Cabinet secretariat during 1940, has commented on how this function differentiated between the chief of naval staff on one hand and, on the other, the chiefs of the Imperial General Staff and the Air Staff, who did not issue executive orders to their organizations. But it was obviously a matter of degree.[79] According to a former director of Operations Division (Home)—DOD (H)—Captain (later Admiral) Ralph Edwards, Pound was the "arch-meddler." Edwards expressed amazement to Roskill at the degree to which Pound intervened in operations at sea, and claimed he (Edwards) was repeatedly ordered to signal detailed instructions to fleets and ships regarding where their destroyer screens were to be placed. Edwards, who was involved in the investigation exonerating Churchill from interfering, claimed "his interference was negligible compared with Dudley Pound."[80] Admiral John Tovey, Forbes' successor as C-in-C Home Fleet, complained that Pound fancied himself as a great tactician and strategist who was in turn adversely affected by Vice Chief of Naval Staff (VCNS) Tom Phillips, a man who was inexperienced, "narrow-minded, very self-opinionated, and even more obstinate and pig-headed than you [Roskill] accuse me of being."[81] Pound was also a worrier. At the conclusion of the *Altmark* affair, Pound wrote a lengthy letter to Captain Philip Vian, commander of the *Cossack*, who boarded the German supply ship in Norwegian waters to successfully rescue prisoners taken by the *Graf Spee*. After a brief sentence offering Vian "hearty congratulations," Pound scolded him at length for not updating him with situation reports and complaining how he and Churchill spent "many anxious hours" at the OIC, waiting for news. Forbes, who had reason to feel aggrieved about the way the Admiralty had given orders to Vian directly over his own head, also received a letter from Pound stating that "no doubt you also spent a good many unnecessarily anxious hours." In the margin Forbes scribbled, "No, I went to bed. I know Vian."[82]

The clash of opinions between Forbes and his "warlords" was clearly shown during the invasion crisis. His views on invasion were clearly laid out for them on 4 June 1940. He complained of the difficulty in making an appreciation, having been "kept in ignorance of the size and disposition of the Royal Air Force and Army," asserting "the repelling of invasion is a matter for all three forces working in the closest co-operation. . . . [H]istory," he argued, "has proved beyond all shadow of doubt that invasion is to all intents impossible without local control of the sea." In this he emphasized the importance of airpower and how local control of the sea during the Norwegian campaign and minimal Norwegian resistance still cost the Germans ten thousand men. He also went on to stress the irrelevance of German naval power in influencing the Polish campaign and in the Dunkirk operation; also how the air situation had greatly influenced the recent fighting in Europe. If an invasion was launched, he argued "it would be a great opportunity." He did not see why the army could not fulfill its traditional function of holding up the enemy until the navy could cut their supply lines. It was not worth diverting too many naval resources for this purpose and since the Norwegian campaign he had increasingly thought that Germany would go all out to sever British communications by air and submarine, as there was no way of achieving this with "surface forces." Consequently, "no first line troops should be kept in England if required elsewhere," he continued. Forbes was also concerned that British ports might be prematurely sabotaged to prevent their use by German forces. The immediate problem, as far as he could see, was to protect the "sea communications of London (including its docks) against mines, both magnetic and contact . . . and against air attack." He suggested increasing the strength of defensive mine barriers and dared to propose that "all small craft now allocated to inshore squadrons for invasion be diverted to sweeping."[83]

The opinions expressed were sensible and vindicated by events. That the Germans now had even easier access to the Atlantic since the fall of France and were in control of the "gate" between Denmark and Norway could only increase the potential for imposing economic blockade upon Britain. He also knew that if destroyers, cruisers, and submarines attached to the bases at the Nore (Sheerness and Harwich), Portsmouth, and Plymouth failed to prevent a landing, then he could be in the Channel from Scapa Flow within thirty hours with the heavy ships of the Home Fleet. It must also be said that having been on board HMS *Rodney* while under air attack at Norway and having his operations constrained by the German air superiority there, he was irritated by ill-informed criticisms about lack of naval aggression. He was also annoyed that his destroyers and most of his light cruisers had been taken away and placed under the control of base commanders responsible for flotilla defense. Scattering ships around the Channel bases would only bring them within Luftwaffe bombing range, and while these were not sitting ducks, there was no point in exposing them to the risk of air bombardment without strategic gain.

Forbes' memorandum dismayed the Admiralty. The DOD (H) described the arguments as "unconvincing" and quoted a Joint Intelligence Committee conclusion that the enemy had enough resources for an invasion despite his "other commitment."[84] While it was generally acknowledged that Forbes may only have been thinking in terms of a mass invasion, it was also felt the possibility of a raid was being ignored despite the fact that successes in France, Belgium, and Holland allowed the enemy greater scope for amphibious operations. Raids held the potential to disrupt internal communications and make life unbearable for the civil population.[85] No doubt recalling the naval theories of Sir Julian Corbett, these officers were worried the launching of small raids at different points would cause British defenders to exhaust themselves attempting to defend the whole coastline. After all, this was part of Liddell Hart's "British way in warfare" that had been used successfully in Britain's eighteenth-century wars. However, these officers apparently overlooked the fact that for such a method to succeed, naval superiority was required for the attacker in order to utilize the mobility that such a condition might confer.[86] The German conquests did of course open up the possibility of raids over short distances from a greater number of foreign harbors than had ever hitherto been the case. But even a raid in the circumstances of 1940 would have been a hazardous undertaking with ambiguous results. A raid, however successful in military terms, ultimately involves the withdrawal of troops and equipment plus the abandonment of fallen comrades, and this would have been represented as the foiling of a mass invasion. After the war, Churchill admitted that no steps were taken to contradict the persistent rumors that arose in 1940 concerning an invasion attempt that had been foiled as a result of forty German bodies being washed up along the south coast. In the event, no German amphibious landings, other than the unopposed Channel Island occupations, were ever attempted on British territory.[87]

Forbes' arguments were not entirely disregarded as a meeting called in Pound's office on 7 June resulted in the battle cruisers *Hood* and *Renown*, plus one destroyer flotilla, being based at Scapa rather than Rosyth in order to deter a German northward breakout.[88] The argument between the C-in-C and the Admiralty raged over the next few weeks, with the latter trying to convince Forbes that an east coast raid was likely, despite his arguments to the contrary. The Norwegian port of Trondheim had now become the main Kriegsmarine base for heavy ships, meaning that the main surface threat now came to the Northern Patrol or even to Ireland. By the end of June Forbes was being told with increasing force to consider an invasion likely.[89] A desire to bring home to Churchill the potential effects of attacks from the air upon warships may well account for a curious episode related by General Ismay. An early invasion conference attended by Forbes and Churchill discussed the part to be played by the Home Fleet. The C-in-C shocked the conference by immediately making it clear that his heavy ships would not operate south of the Wash "under any circumstances." Instead of erupting into rage, the prime minister merely remarked mildly that "he never took much notice of what the Royal Navy said they would or would not do in advance of an event." Smiling indulgently, he said "since they invariably undertook the apparently impossible whenever the situation so demanded . . . he had not a shadow of doubt . . . we should see every available battleship storming through the Straits of Dover."[90]

Why did Churchill react in this uncharacteristic manner? Forbes had already shown he was quite capable of resisting the prime minister's bullying and knew well enough that if matters came to the crunch, then he had to run the gauntlet in the Channel. There is also reason to think that Churchill secretly agreed with at least some of Forbes' strategic ideas. Churchill must have realized he had underestimated the potential of air attack upon shipping during the Norway campaign, and knew that taking away Forbes' destroyers to serve in the Channel meant the heavy ships lacked adequate protective destroyer screens. The prime minister had never been entirely consistent on the ability of Germany to launch an invasion anyway. Erskine Childers' *Riddle of the Sands*, a novel in which Germany planned a surprise invasion using boats hidden in the Frisian Islands, caught Churchill's imagination in 1903.[91] So seriously did he take this idea that when First Lord, he was said to have made it required reading for naval officers prior to 1914. Later, Churchill's speeches of 4 and 17 June 1940 were widely reported and raised invasion fears.[92] However, on 18 June he was saying that the Royal Navy makes a mass invasion impossible, but they "have never pretended to prevent raids by 5,000 to 10,000 men . . . thrown ashore . . . some dark night."[93]

The somewhat alarmist Pound told Churchill on 12 July: "It appears probable that a total of some hundred thousand men might reach these shores without being intercepted by naval forces." Yet, if Churchill was to be believed, the prime minister remained confident that such a force was "well within the capacity of our rapidly-improving Army." It is easy to criticize Pound for being unduly pessimistic, though he later revised this figure to 200,000.[94] According to John Colville, Churchill's private secretary, the prime minister said he did not believe the Germans could bring troops over from Norway in fishing boats, and that he doubted if an invasion was a "serious menace" but thought it useful in terms of keeping everyone "tuned to a high pitch of readiness." He did not want the invasion scare to abate yet and was going to continue giving the impression of imminent danger by talking about "long and dangerous vigils" in his forthcoming broadcast.[95]

Pound's biographer has suggested that the First Sea Lord and VCNS Tom Phillips were persuaded by an idea emanating from military intelligence in the War Office (who had obviously read Erskine Childers) suggesting the Germans might commandeer a flotilla of fast motorboats each carrying a tank. Admiral Godfrey, the director of Naval Intelligence, was one who did not accept this scenario and it must have been galling for his opinion to have been rejected in preference to that of other service colleagues.[96] Nevertheless, Pound had the support of base commanders such as Admiral Drax at the Nore who naturally wanted maximum resources under their control, bearing in mind the responsibility for preventing an enemy landing impinged more immediately upon them than on Forbes and the Home Fleet. Furthermore as a member of the Chiefs of Staff, Pound must also have been adversely affected by the attitudes of the army, who did not relish the prospect of getting to grips with the potentially immense power of German land forces.[97] A considerable amount of equipment was lost at Dunkirk and a humiliating defeat inflicted on the BEF. In his relations with the other services, Pound has been described as having a philosophy of "compromises must be found," an attitude that even the sometimes critical official historian found himself in broad agreement with.[98]

Two days earlier Churchill had written to General William Edmund Ironside, C-in-C Home Forces, along the lines that Germany would face great difficulties launching an invasion, and arguing for more troops to be moved from a defensive role in the UK to offensive operations abroad, thus suggesting he had taken Forbes' comments on board about not keeping "first line troops in England if required elsewhere."[99] He also quoted Forbes' reply to a War Cabinet question concerning the possibility of German heavy ships covering an invasion. This was that only heavy ships not under repair are based at Trondheim and superior British naval forces guarded this base. It is not too much to say that Forbes had indirectly made possible Generals Archibald Wavell and Richard O'Connor's spectacular offensive in Egypt and Libya against the Italians later in the year. It is also hard to imagine that Churchill's aggressive temperament would have left him sympathetic to the passive defense policy advocated by the Admiralty. Neither was he oblivious to what was happening in the Atlantic while so many potential escort vessels were tied up in the Channel. As early as November 1939 he wrote to Pound expressing serious concern over the "immense slowing down of trade . . . during the first ten weeks of the war."[100] By 7 July 1940, his concern over "rifle convoys" from the United States was being strongly expressed in a minute to the secretary of state for war.[101] On 4 August 1940, the prime minister sent Pound a haranguing minute about "repeated severe losses in the North-western Approaches," and speculating that "this is largely due to the shortage of destroyers through invasion precautions." He then went on to demand information on the numbers of "destroyers, corvettes, and Asdic trawlers, together with aircraft" tied down in these duties. "Anyhow, we cannot go on like this," he continued.[102] Churchill's own tables show that total British, Allied, and Neutral shipping losses surged from 273,219 gross tons in May 1940 to 571,496 gross tons in June and would not fall back to the May figure during 1940.[103] Had the Kriegsmarine not been plagued with unreliable torpedoes, these figures would have been much worse.

Nevertheless, there were limits to Churchill's power and the country did "go on like this" for several weeks. When his military commanders occasionally united against blustering attempts to press ill-conceived strategies upon them, the prime minister invariably backed down. This had been demonstrated during the Norway campaign when he urged the attack upon Trondheim. Concerned about being hemmed into a narrow thirty-mile-long fjord by mines dropped in his rear, Forbes forcefully argued against the order to attack. Churchill was furious but after a long and heated argument he eventually retreated when the advisors surrounding him backed Forbes' judgment.[104] The Chiefs of Staff would become more adept at this as the war progressed. As none of the services was prepared to accept the burden of risk-taking it probably suited all of the senior figures involved to use the navy as a visible deterrent to German amphibious landings by encouraging the spread of destroyers and light cruisers around the east and south coasts. The general lack of faith in the ability of the RAF to provide early warning also contributed to this over-cautious attitude, although it was far easier to watch the Channel coast from the air than it had been to patrol Norwegian waters at extreme ranges. There was no German naval Enigma yet and as most of the Luftwaffe's communications were being made via landlines not enough information could be divined from intelligence sources to ascertain precise German intentions. Consequently, a large flotilla of small craft mainly commandeered from the fishing fleet was being misemployed on sentry duty outside foreign ports instead of being utilized for anti-submarine work. As Forbes could see no reason why the other services should not be engaged in the initial stages of the invasion it is unsurprising that colleagues treated his views with alarm. Churchill probably saw advantages in these dispositions in terms of maintaining a state of visible readiness that would impress U.S. journalists and exaggerate the danger of invasion to manipulate American insecurities.

By September, when the likelihood of invasion was at its height, Forbes' views had not fundamentally changed and he was still arguing the navy "should not be tied down to provide passive defence to our country, which has now become a fortress."[105] However, on 4 September, the chief of Naval Staff scared his service colleagues by warning that if the Germans captured the coastal batteries at Dover, they could control both sides of the Straits and deny it to British naval forces. During a meeting of the War Cabinet Defence Committee on 31 October, when autumn should have virtually ruled out the threat of invasion for 1940 anyway, Churchill asked for Forbes' opinion. "While we are predominant at sea and until Germany has defeated our fighter forces, invasion by sea is not a practical operation of war," he replied.[106] Only at this point and with overwhelming evidence from other sources did the Defence Committee agree that Forbes could have his ships back. Churchill had been present when Group Captain Winterbotham of the Secret Intelligence Service had passed on a decrypt during September to the effect that air-loading equipment at Luftwaffe airfields in Holland was being dismantled. The chief of Air Staff then announced it marked the end of the invasion threat for 1940.[107] In the circumstances, the prime minister could not have been in any doubt about the issue and must have been using Forbes purely for the benefit of convincing the War Cabinet.

Sadly, the reward for his record of sound advice was the sack. Replaced by Sir

John Tovey in December 1940, Forbes later served as commander of the naval base at Plymouth between May 1941 and August 1943. As this establishment had already declined in importance with the transfer of the headquarters of Western Approaches Command to Liverpool in February 1941, it was hardly an expression of continuing confidence. No official reason for his dismissal remains. However, Pound wrote to Admiral Cunningham on 20 September suggesting there "seems some chance C. M. F. will be relieved in the near future, not because he has not done well but because there is a growing demand for younger people."[108] It was undeniably true that the press was constantly demanding the promotion of younger officers at this time and at sixty, Forbes was one of the older field commanders. Yet he was younger than Pound and outlived him by a further seventeen years. The real reasons, according to Levy, were "his independent outlook, unsolicited opinions, and fearless critiques of the Pound/Churchill regime."[109] This analysis is broadly correct but Levy's thesis also surmised that Churchill wished to pursue an "aggressive policy in the Mediterranean, while hedging his bets with a more defensive posture at home," and this was why Forbes was continually ignored.[110] While Cunningham later told Roskill that Churchill and Minister of Information Brendan Bracken both disliked Forbes, his advice was useful to the prime minister in helping him pursue initiatives in the Mediterranean even if he may sometimes have resented the outspoken way in which it was being given.

Long-standing tensions between Forbes and destroyer Captain Lord Louis Mountbatten centering on the latter's reckless handling of HMS *Kelly* cannot have helped. Having only been "mentioned in dispatches" instead of winning a Distinguished Service Order (DSO) for bringing his shattered ship back from an engagement in the North Sea, Mountbatten was convinced that Forbes was plotting against him. *Kelly* had suffered terrific damage as a result of Mountbatten's decision to ignore instructions and embark upon a fruitless U-boat pursuit. Mountbatten was the king's cousin and a bad potential enemy to make. He was also a friend of Churchill's, and according to the mischief-making Lord Beaverbrook was sent this message: "Tell Dickie [Mountbatten] that Winston warned me that Forbes means to break him." Forbes probably disapproved of Mountbatten's ostentatious lifestyle, but Forbes was "much too big a man" to let that interfere with his professional judgment.[111] The poison Mountbatten dripped into the ears of Bracken, Beaverbrook, and Churchill may never be known, and whether the latter could separate personal feelings from professional judgment is perhaps another matter.

Despite this it was perhaps Pound who represented the main driving force for replacing the C-in-C. Undoubtedly aware that pressure was growing for even the apparently heroic figure of Dowding to be dismissed, he must have calculated that the time had come to replace his own "difficult" subordinate with an ostensibly more suitable—but in reality a more pliable and easier to control—C-in-C. Having picked up on some of the frustration within the fleet, including perhaps Mountbatten's sense of injury, he must have represented these feelings to Churchill as lack of confidence in the C-in-C. It also needs to be stated that Churchill did not criticize Forbes in his memoirs and even made a point of expressing confidence in him.[112] Forbes later wrote to Godfrey Style that he met a slightly inebriated Churchill at a Navy Club function and was assured privately that he never thought the Germans would invade in 1940. They had now "made it up."[113] There were no witnesses to this conversation but much of what Churchill said and wrote from 1940 is consistent with this. Forbes' successor as C-in-C Home Fleet later responded to Roskill's comment that in 1939 there was no suitable alternative to Pound for the post of First Sea Lord, stating that: "Charles Forbes was . . . in every way better equipped." Tovey said that Pound's report that "Forbes lacked the confidence of the fleet was, I consider, most unfair," except Tovey had an "idea" that he did not inspect his ships enough but "confidence in his ability and courage was unquestioned."[114]

First Lord A. V. Alexander found himself defending Forbes at an English-Speaking Union luncheon in October 1940, where he "deprecated . . . the general assumption that whenever there was a new appointment . . . reflection was thereby implied on the officer who was relieved." Forbes was then allowed some positive praise but it was also stated that the navy's leadership needed to be in the hands of those who were "equipped technically and scientifically to meet and defeat new threats." The statement belied Forbes' considerable technical expertise but it was probably meant to reinforce the idea he was "too old," and the fact Alexander was mentioning this at a public function suggests some morale-damaging gossip was going around.[115] A later report in the *Times* concerning parliamentary attacks on the Admiralty also indicated that Forbes had gone as a result of criticism.[116] No doubt Alexander also felt the need to impress the Americans present that the navy would be more effective in the future.

Despite their obvious clash of temperaments, Churchill might have defended Forbes had the latter been in a position to secure a tangible victory for American opinion. While the Norway campaign can now be seen as a naval victory, that country still fell to the Wehrmacht. The whole affair had only provoked embarrassing questions in the American press about Britain's ability to wage war.[117] While it was true that Forbes had failed to divine German intentions in time to avert the invasion there, he was severely handicapped with the intelligence initiative in enemy hands. His later conduct of the campaign was also prejudiced by the undue interference of Churchill and Pound. The abject failure of the navy to intercept German surface raiders further embellished the picture of British incompetence, yet Admiral Tovey proved no more successful at this until the quality of British naval intelligence improved.[118] Forbes had also been wrong about the whereabouts of German surface units in the *Rawalpindi* affair but there is no reason to think anyone else would have achieved more in the circumstances.

On the credit side, he helped build a navy that was much more forward-looking and resourceful than some writers have allowed. Insufficiently emphasized in most accounts is the crippling damage to the Kriegsmarine's surface fleet by units under his overall command that would soon have prejudicial consequences to Operation Sea Lion.

His strategic advice was sound and might well have reduced the impact of the U-boat's "happy time." Forbes was also unfortunate in having to command the Home Fleet at an initial stage of the war when there was no recent experience of commanding the fleet in wartime conditions. Circumstances had changed radically since 1918 and misjudgments were inevitable until the necessary practical experience had been acquired. Yet it could only have been succeeding generations of wartime officers able to benefit from this. While he may have needlessly antagonized Churchill and Pound by his outspoken tendencies, and some naval officers disagreed with his views, Admirals Whitworth, Tovey, and Cunningham acknowledged his wisdom and held him in high regard. This contrasts with Dowding, who antagonized most of his colleagues and with less justification. Neither officer sought publicity but Dowding gained sympathy from the public, politicians, and press because he had ostensibly delivered a decisive victory that was being sold to American opinion. Forbes was indeed a fine admiral and the more deserving of the two figures. But with no tangible victories to point toward and lacking the flair for flamboyant publicity that might have engaged the journalistic instincts of Churchill, Beaverbrook, and Bracken, there was little incentive to protect him. Sadly, he had nothing to offer the crucial campaign for winning over the United States.

CHAPTER SEVEN

Why We Fight? The Battle of Britain

> The story is told in vivid scenes, but facts and figures are carefully and accurately recorded, and it will surprise many people who have lived through these tremendous years to see, for the first time, laid out in order, what happened and why. . . . Things have been said about what we have done and how we behaved, which we could never have said about ourselves.[1]
>
> *W. S. Churchill*

There can be no doubt that the positive contributions of the Merchant Navy and the Royal Navy toward preventing an invasion did not achieve full recognition because of their relatively passive and unpublicized roles in the summer of 1940. Their activities could not compete with newspaper headlines showing the enormous (and inflated) tally of downed German aircraft, and it is now time to assess the relative propaganda values of the maritime and air dimensions. The Battle of Britain became an Anglo-American media construct but the determining factors shaping this and the role of politicians, media figures, and others still require closer examination.

From the moment he became prime minister, Winston Churchill's actions were geared toward bringing to bear the enormous industrial potential of the United States of America in the cause of the Allies.[2] When France sought an armistice a few weeks later, the only realistic prospect of Britain continuing the struggle lay with the willingness of the United States to increase the flow of essential war supplies. In the longer term, the only chances of winning were either with the Soviet Union joining the fight (a seemingly remote prospect given the Ribbentrop-Molotov Pact of 1939) or an American decision to send their army to Europe as in 1917–18. But with American opinion set firmly against direct involvement this could not be anticipated within the foreseeable future and might never happen. Churchill's considerable oratory powers using highly charged emotional appeals would not persuade the cabinet to carry on the struggle unless he could hold out the prospect of continuing and increased tangible material assistance from this quarter. Government members such as Lord Halifax were initially in favor of negotiating with Germany but not without Halifax insisting "he would fight to the end if Britain's integrity and independence were endangered, for instance if Hitler demanded the fleet or the RAF."[3]

Unfortunately, Churchill had been given little or no encouragement from the United States since he had taken over as prime minister, and even the re-election of Roosevelt in November held out no prospect of significantly greater participation in the near future. At the end of 1940, Sir Walter Layton of the Ministry of Supply warned his superiors that U.S. industry had still not fully mobilized because they lacked full appreciation of the effort required. Consequently, American aid would not peak until 1942, hardly an edifying prospect for Churchill, who needed to hold out the prospect of imminent heavy assistance.[4] Unfortunately, Churchill's temperament and history were not ideal for the task of persuading the United States. Most Americans preferred Britain to Nazi Germany but the British Empire roused ambivalent feelings in those molded by the tumultuous events of 1776 and Churchill was the arch imperialist. Churchill and Roosevelt had met once during World War I but his rude manner had upset the U.S. naval secretary.[5] As First Lord of the Admiralty at the time of the sinking of the *Lusitania*, Churchill was held by conspiracy theorists to have engineered the incident to inveigle the United States into World War I.[6] Unfair as this was, it could only mean that Americans could only view his words and actions with varying degrees of suspicion. It probably did not help that Great Britain had long stopped repaying the 1914–18 war debt to the United States. Along with other debtor nations, Great Britain had ceased repayments to the United States in 1934 because of Germany's repudiation of the Versailles Treaty and the need to re-arm. This still left an outstanding balance of $4.368 billion from Britain but as Churchill was out of office in 1934 he could not be held personally responsible for this.[7]

However, President Roosevelt had offered to correspond on matters of mutual concern when Churchill was at the Admiralty, giving the First Lord an opportunity of manipulating American fears of German expansion into U.S. spheres of control. As an enthusiast of all things maritime and dedicated disciple of A. T. Mahan, the president had earlier suggested sending Captain Royal E. Ingersoll of the U.S. Navy to London to set up contingency plans for staff talks in 1937.[8] These spluttered out in an atmosphere of mutual distrust before hostilities commenced, but the signing of the Anglo-American Trade Agreement of 1938 following the Munich Agreement also demonstrated that both countries recognized the need for some broad display of Anglo-American solidarity.[9] Roosevelt was broadly sympathetic to the British cause and may have been even more concerned than British politicians about Nazi intentions during the late 1930s. But he was by no means uncritical of British motives where the empire was concerned and was also looking to the "main chance."[10]

In an American presidential election year, public opinion counted for a great deal. A vast number of American newspapers might be studied for insights into "public opinion," including several written for ethnic communities in languages other than English. However, the question as to whether newspapers reflect or create "opinion" in liberal democracies is probably irresolvable. When most British newspapers were family-run concerns, the Fleet Street of Beaverbrook and Alfred Harmsworth, 1st Viscount Northcliffe, was dedicated to propaganda rather than financial gain.[11] Deference to the upper classes was another problem tending to undermine confidence in the British press. The British social survey organization known as Mass Observation revealed little confidence by the British in their newspapers in early 1940, and it was also suggested in a *Time* article that current problems—including competition from informal newsletters—might make the temporary loss of confidence engendered by the British reluctance to report on the abdication crisis of 1936 more "long lasting."[12]

Unlike Britain, the United States has never had a "national press," and even if it could be accepted without reservation that newspapers reflect rather than shape opinions, no single newspaper could encapsulate the full diversity of American opinion. With a long and poorly protected western seaboard containing sizeable Asian minorities, Californians shared similar concerns over German intentions with the residents of Washington, D.C., but balanced these with equally substantial worries about Japanese expansion.[13] However, some reasonable idea of the relevant American concerns of 1940 can be gleaned from the pages of the *Washington Post*. It was (and continues to be) regarded as an influential newspaper with a national readership, and includes syndicated columns to be found in other American newspapers. Rescued from bankruptcy in 1933 by financier Eugene Meyer, the *Washington Post* espoused high-minded principles including objectivity, independence, and being "fair and free and wholesome in its outlook on public affairs and public men." Such worthy sentiments do not necessarily guarantee sales, which explains the modest circulation figures—54,000 in 1933 to 162,000 in 1943—and the fact it was continuing to lose money.[14] Fortunately for the British, Meyer was friendly with British ambassador Lord Lothian (Philip Kerr, 1882–1940), who is generally credited with giving Meyer the scoop on the Mrs. Simpson–Edward VIII affair heralding the British abdication crisis. For all the *Washington Post*'s sentiments of independence and non-alignment, the tone of writing was pro-Roosevelt, and it is probably no coincidence that President Truman appointed Meyer the first president of the International Bank for Reconstruction and Development in 1946. This newspaper usefully recorded Gallup polls relating to U.S. feeling throughout the country regarding aid to Britain, and its articles gave opinions about the international situation and how it was being influenced by factors such as the Battle of Britain.

The actions and attitudes of media figures including American war correspondents covering the Battle of Britain are very significant. These range from Eric Sevareid, an American journalist from the isolationist Midwest, to international media magnate—and British cabinet minister in 1940—Max Aitken (Lord Beaverbrook). As a controversial World War I minister of information and a press baron with interests in British and North American publishing concerns, it is unsurprising that Lord Beaverbrook became minister of aircraft supply during 1940. Churchill's private secretary claimed "many people thought he was evil."[15] But this petulant Canadian entrepreneur with a reputation for dubious dealing was a successful propagandist. Beaverbrook confessed to preferring power to profit and ran his newspapers to that end. "What I want is power," he said. In 1948, he told the British Press Commission, "I run the paper for the purpose of making propaganda and with no other purpose."[16] For these reasons alone his value to Churchill transcended his ministerial duties and his propagandist activities are examined here rather than his better-known role in aircraft production.

Brendan Bracken (1901–58) was Churchill's former private secretary from the Admiralty before he became minister of information in 1940. Bracken had also been Beaverbrook's protégé, giving the prime minister a wealth of journalistic expertise within his inner circle.[17] Beaverbrook's personal papers have been scrutinized for insights into the campaign to secure American aid and these reveal an interest in filmmaking as a method of putting the British case to the American public. Later on, it may have been Beaverbrook and Bracken who helped persuade Churchill to allow American film director Frank Capra to film him introducing the propaganda series *Why We Fight*. Churchill's short introduction urged British cinema audiences to accept the series as a factual interpretation of the events up to the current stage of the war. Film number four in this series entitled *The Battle of Britain* was shown to U.S. servicemen and distributed in British cinemas in late 1942 after the U.S. had entered the conflict. As one revisionist writer has claimed, "no film about the events of 1940–41 in Britain reached such a vast audience."[18]

There is no doubt that U.S. sympathy was on the side of the British. A letter to the editor of the *Washington Post* in July 1940 described a newsreel shown in a Washington, D.C., cinema portraying a German aircraft being shot down in flames by the guns of an aircraft carrier. To the embarrassment of the correspondent, the incident was "occasion for loud applause from almost the entire theater."[19] However, turning sympathy into positive action was another matter entirely. Although a significant amount of space in the *Washington Post* was devoted to stories of the air war and concern was expressed that the British might not hold out, there is little indication the air war was considered fundamental to this during July. An end-of-year summary article charting the rise of aid-to-Britain sentiment, written by Dr. George Gallup, director of the American Institute of Public Opinion, and based on polling data, does not use the term "Battle of Britain" as such, but he did indicate a 2 percent rise in sentiment—from 15 percent favoring the United States entering the war on 19 July "following re-organization of British strength in England" to 17 percent in October, following the "aerial blitzkrieg on Britain." The high point of intervention sentiment was shown as being 19 percent on 14

June "following Italy's entrance," which was greater than the 14 percent recorded on 6 July "following collapse of France" and much more than the measly 5 percent polled in October 1939. The greatest fall in sentiment occurred in December 1940, apparently as a result of the successful British offensive in North Africa and despite the continuing virtually unopposed night bombing of London and other cities.

The only tentative conclusions to draw from these figures is that only a small minority of those polled favored entering the war and British "successes" did not necessarily encourage U.S. war entry. In fact, as Gallup stated, "because of recent British successes, and because many think that our increased material assistance will turn the tide," those favoring entry are now less than at the "height of the blitzkrieg last fall [the night blitz]." The interpretation of Dr. Gallup in terms of relating the question of immediate war to the 50 million Americans who voted in the November presidential elections meant that if a war vote were taken in December 1940, only 6 million would be in favor.[20] Even after a further year of Axis triumph, a Gallup poll of 22 November 1941 revealed that only 26 percent surveyed were in favor of immediately declaring war.[21] This suggests that even Pearl Harbor would not have been enough to prod Americans into the fight without Hitler's declaration of war on the United States in December 1941.

Possibly, victory in a North African campaign resembling a "colonial war" was not something high-minded Americans could wholeheartedly approve, and while success in standing up to bombing evoked considerable sympathy and admiration; it was still something of a negative achievement. The "Britain-Can-Take-It" line employed by propagandists had limitations, and American correspondent Larry LeSueur has been quoted that it could not be used forever and he had never seen a boxer win a match simply because he could "take it."[22] Some shift in American opinion can be noted but it is clear that direct American intervention could never have been in the cards during 1940. Realistically, the British could only hope that an increasing number of Americans would favor more aid to Britain. In fact, the overwhelming numbers of Americans—approximately 88 percent—in July 1940 were in favor, and by November this had slightly increased to 90 percent.[23]

A trickier question was whether "it was more important to keep out of war ourselves, or to help England win even at the risk of war?" Undoubtedly, the British were heartened to see this steep climb in favor of helping Britain and risking war, from a modest 35 percent in May 1940 to a comforting 60 percent in November 1940. Support on this question had briefly stalled in the period immediately before the American presidential campaign when both candidates had tended to emphasize peace for the United States.[24] This support had risen significantly through the period of the air campaigns but it seems likely the respondents were also weighing the risks to U.S. shipping and recalling the role that U-boat campaigns had allegedly played in U.S. entry to World War I. This does not imply a general acceptance that naval matters had played the dominant role in bringing America into this war. The causes of U.S. entry had been hotly debated in the 1930s, with the Senate's investigation of the munitions industries (1934–36) blaming industrialists and munitions makers for dragging America into war.[25]

It was also asserted in the *Washington Post* that U.S. rearmament was failing to meet requirements, meaning that Americans always had to bear in mind British prospects of survival in deciding whether it was better to help Britain or keep the fruits of existing war production for the use of U.S. forces.[26] A letter from fellow press baron Harold Harmsworth, 1st Viscount Rothermere, in North America to Beaverbrook in July 1940 stated the "pressure to rearm is terrific" and stressed the anxiety of people in government. Rothermere then accurately predicted the difficulty in getting "really big assistance from them." Only when the Americans "have appreciated what this war means for them and when they fully understand this I think you will *get a move for* closer co-operation."[27]

Another article gave useful information on the geographical diversity of attitudes relating to the United States entering the war. "Southern States" were most in favor of going in at 17 percent with the "West Central States," perhaps because of their German communities and traditional conservatism, less enthusiastic at 9 percent. On the question of helping England, but at risk of war, it was again the southern states most in favor at 75 percent and again the Midwest states less favorable at 54 percent.[28] Nevertheless, it was significant that even in the cautious Midwest there was still a majority in favor. It was certainly the feelings of the Midwest giving the most concern to the British-organized Inter-Allied Information Committee (New York) in June 1940. Their representatives, Mr. Hall and Mr. Powell, had toured this area and found "sympathy with the Allied cause is extremely unsatisfactory." The people had been influenced by pro-German sources that were "extremely successful in promoting a feeling which is anything but favourable to the Allied cause."[29] The extent to which these figures reflected a "black vote" is unknown. It would be wrong to assume that black Americans automatically wished to support a fight against a radical racist state such as Nazi Germany. One newspaper focusing on "black interests" tended to view the conflict as "just another clash among rival groups of white exploiters" but how typical this attitude was among black people is impossible to say. The racial problems of the South were severe and it cannot be assumed that black people were permitted to participate in polling while "Jim Crow" was still in the driving seat. Black people would have been underrepresented anyway because of their low education opportunities. Critics have also claimed that "pollsters did not ask the 'right' questions, specify the characteristics of the respondents as precisely as one might wish, or repeat questions over time at suitable intervals."[30] None of this completely invalidates the results, but scientific polling was still in its infancy and whatever the limitations, Roosevelt needed to take these into account with an upcoming election.

Another Gallup article published as the air battle neared a climax suggested that an intensification of the crisis in Europe would aid Roosevelt's election campaign. "If England is defeated between now and election time and it looks as though the United States might have to fight Germany, which candidate would you prefer for President—Wilkie or Roosevelt?" went Gallup's ponderous question. If the election had been held then, while Britain was still undefeated, 51 percent would have voted for Roosevelt, but otherwise the result was 58 percent, a contrast showing a "substantial increase in Roosevelt's popular strength in case war seems imminent."[31]

An edition of the *Washington Post* on 20 December raised a concern that recent British successes, far from keeping Britain in the war, may ultimately have the reverse effect. It noted that some Englishmen in favor of a negotiated peace remained within the British government and these were the "propertied and hitherto privileged classes who fear social revolution in England that war threatens to cause, even if Great Britain wins decisively." Arguing that Britain had stood up to air attacks, frustrated invasion, and beaten the Italians in the Mediterranean, it claimed British prestige had risen. As Hitler had put out peace feelers thus revealing his own lack of confidence in ultimate victory, then a favorable peace to Britain was obviously attainable. The alternatives would be more destruction, living like "wild animals," loss of financial empire to the United States, and the possibility of social revolution at home. The source of this information was claimed to be diplomatic reports indicating "certain groups" were increasingly expressing such sentiments, and the columnist suggested these sorts of views might have influenced Ambassador Joe Kennedy's pessimistic reports about Britain continuing the war.[32]

This represented a convincing scenario, and the "diplomatic reports" might provide some explanation for Roosevelt's favorable response to the British government's cash crisis at the end of 1940. It also provides considerable justification for the speculation surrounding the later flight of Rudolf Hess to Great Britain where it has often been asserted that Hitler was trying to contact the "Peace Party" within the British establishment.[33] None of this appears in Churchill's lengthy review of Britain's position and appeal for financial aid to Roosevelt dated 8 December 1940, as he had learned the importance of not stepping too hard on American sensibilities.[34] His earlier attempts in May 1940 to "blackmail" the United States for aid by using the possible fate of the British fleet in the hands of "appeasers, bargaining amid the ruins" had not been successful, and had led to serious U.S. discussion of seizing British and other European possessions in the Western hemisphere.[35]

Enough of this debate had seeped into the public domain by July 1940 for Gallup to poll the U.S. public on the question of seizing European possessions near the Panama Canal. This was conducted against the background of a U.S.-sponsored conference at Havana with the twenty-one American republics debating the fate of these territories. The poll showed a heavy majority—87 percent—in favor of the United States taking over these areas in the event of a German victory over England. A similar number—84 percent—were prepared to fight to keep the Germans out of these areas. Again a large majority, 81 percent, were prepared for the United States and the American republics to buy these possessions should Britain require more money for the war.[36] These figures represented a mandate for action on the flimsiest of pretexts and it is not difficult to see how these results might have encouraged the significant Destroyers-for-Bases deal agreed in September. On the day the poll results were published the text of the Act of Havana was also announced. This revealed an agreement whereby, in any emergency, any country "shall have the right to act in a manner required for its defense or the defense of the continent."[37]

In the circumstances of this forthcoming conference, Lord Lothian had already determined that offering these Caribbean bases to Washington "spontaneously" and generously might counter uncompromising American demands for rights in British possessions and gain something in return.[38] Lothian was right about the Americans being prepared to demand these bases but important British figures including Lord Lloyd, the colonial secretary, were heavily opposed to making a deal as they saw the only way to involve America in the war was to maintain fears about security.[39]

Another article linked the Battle of Britain with Havana. Columnist Walter Lippmann (1889–1974) was an influential political columnist with his Today and Tomorrow column, syndicated nationally. Lippmann was also a friend of the British ambassador to the United States, Lord Lothian. As assistant to Woodrow Wilson's secretary of war in 1917, Lippmann helped draft the Fourteen Points Peace Program. It is indicative of his standing that Lippmann was a delegate to the Paris Peace conference of 1919 and helped draft the Covenant of the League of Nations.[40] His German-Jewish ancestry and the socialism of his youth obviously pre-disposed him against the Nazi regime.

Lippmann saw the measures agreed at Havana as deriving "their whole significance from the struggle between Great Britain and the Nazi domination of continental Europe." If it were not for the possibility of breaking the blockade, and the Axis achieving "something like naval supremacy in the Atlantic Ocean" and adding the British assets of "industry, shipbuilding, foreign investments, and finance into the totalitarian system, the problems discussed at Havana would not exist." The rest of the article dealt at length with how British naval power was protecting the United States from the problems of competing on equal terms with a "totalitarian monopoly." The fall of Britain would mean the disappearance of "the last free market outside the Americas." Axis naval supremacy, including control of the massive British merchant fleet, would mean the South American states "especially of the temperate zone" would then have to carry on three-quarters of their trade with the European monopoly. The crucial importance of sea power was asserted in the "battles around Great Britain and Gibraltar." These were stressed heavily as they would "decide whether the independence of the nations of this hemisphere can be defended in the future as it has been in the past." There were also references to the west coast of Africa, the Cape Verde Islands, the Azores, and Greenland all being used as "stepping stones to domination of any part of this hemisphere." Economic dependence would also mean "fifth column" uprisings in South America, all of which would be further prejudicial to American security. Lippmann went on to claim that "the Battle of Britain will therefore decide whether the United States must maintain permanently a very large army and whether American industry must be regimented permanently on military lines." In the circumstances of a British defeat, very little prospect was seen of the United States achieving "even parity, much less mastery in the Atlantic Ocean." Consequently, the United States would be driven to maintaining a large army, introducing conscription, and changing its way of doing business.[41]

The precise impact of this article cannot be gauged and it may not have resonated with high-minded Americans preferring moral arguments to those centering on economic self-interest. However, it did home in on traditional American insecurities. It also showed signs of being influenced by Lord Lothian's speech to Yale University alumni (which included Lippmann) on 19 June 1940, where very great play was made of the historical importance of the Royal Navy to the United States.[42] Lippmann's emphasis was very much on how a British defeat would impact on U.S. economic interests and the American way of life. As the worst deprivations of the Depression were only a recent memory, sensitivity to threats to American recovery was particularly high. In any case, the shibboleth of "free trade" has always been central to any discussion of American foreign policy, and concepts of regimenting economic life are even more alien to the "American way" than to the British.[43] Conscription is controversial in most liberal democracies but the prospect of maintaining a large standing army in "peacetime" was as awkward for 1940s Americans as it had been for earlier generations of Britons. As many Americans were descendants of British colonists, they retained some shared cultural memories with the British in that, unlike navies, large standing armies were potential instruments for powerful minorities to inflict their tyrannical will upon the majority. Furthermore, compulsory military service concepts inevitably impinge on individual freedoms, raising tricky constitutional issues. Roosevelt had undermined this during the 1930s by forcing a quarter of a million young males into the Civilian Conservation Corps under semi-military conditions, and his alleged dictatorial tendencies had already been spotlighted in his infamous clash with the U.S. Supreme Court over abuses of presidential power.[44] The power of these fears of fifth-column activity in South America helps to explain their successful manipulation by British intelligence in order to gain an easing of the Neutrality Act later in the war. One intelligence specialist believed Roosevelt was happy for this disinformation to be circulated in 1940–41 and turned a "blind eye."[45]

Also reacting to Havana and American press attitudes toward these U.S. fears, Reichsmarschall Hermann Goering gave an interview to one of the few pro-German American journalists, Karl von Wiegand. Goering stressed that although

"German air power is supreme in Europe" the United States is isolated by "ponds" more than "3,000 miles wide and another 5,000 miles on the other, [the United States] cannot possibly be invaded either from the sea or air." Scorning the idea that Greenland could be used as an air base, he pointed out that it was so unsuitable it was given up as a base by commercial firms running the transatlantic air route. Showing his awareness of U.S. industrial potential he stated that America "will be a match for any Power or combination of Powers." Characteristically, Goering also boasted about German airpower dominating the Atlantic but conceded that airpower was very young and "has certain limits."[46] The article made valid points, and even though Greenland was not the only potential "stepping stone" it was still a fairly accurate assessment of the situation. However, it seems to have made little impact on American thinking.

These articles were written when the air campaign was in an early phase, but this initial American view of the Battle of Britain was far more wide-ranging and naval determinist in nature. Airpower was not prominent in any context whatsoever. For Americans, this naval dimension was at the very core of their concerns. For all the encouragement given by Churchill to Roosevelt regarding British determination to win, even the Battle of Mers-el-Kébir near Oran on 3 July 1940 did not seem to have completely calmed American fears. Here the Royal Navy had ruthlessly removed any possibility of the French fleet joining an Axis combination by bombarding and sinking their former ally's warships at anchorage. In retrospect, some of the fears articulated by Lippmann and others seem vastly exaggerated and underrated the nation's vast industrial potential to out-build any enemy fleet combination. Numbers alone could not properly evaluate the potential superiority of a combined European fleet, and the difficulties of welding together a massive fleet of disparate nationalities and equipment and with questionable loyalty to Germany would have been significant factors.

American fears about the future use of the British fleet were finally laid to rest with the announcement of the Destroyers-for-Bases deal reported in the *Washington Post* on 4 September 1940. The British were reported as "rejoicing" over the deal and American congressional opinion was cautiously quoted as "evoking commendation," though isolationist leaders expressed anger. According to Sen. David Worth Clark, Democrat from Idaho, "[t]ransfer of the destroyers amounts substantially to an act of war." The only adverse aspect of the deal that Roosevelt's presidential opponent, Wendell L. Wilkie, seized upon was the secrecy surrounding it. Given that his policy was also for "helping the British," it was perhaps his only opening for exploiting Roosevelt's weakness of perceived dictatorial tendencies. Secrecy was inevitable given the fact that negotiations had been protracted and marked by mutual distrust. The British Foreign Office, clearly worried about the effect in Britain of being seen to conclude a poor deal, described the pledge never to sink or surrender the fleet if UK waters became "untenable" as a "parallel development," but it seems doubtful if anyone was fooled. Roosevelt had already prepared for internal criticism by submitting the report of Attorney General Robert Jackson supporting the deal. Apart from allowing some temporary encouragement to the British public in terms of allowing a sense of transatlantic solidarity, it is hard to divine very much tangible long-term political or practical advantage to Britain from this deal, given the appalling state of the American destroyers and Jackson's opinion that "the acquisition from Britain implies no future promise from the United States. It is not necessary for the Senate to *ratify* an opportunity that entails no obligation."[47] Roosevelt was emboldened by the deal's "success" to propose subsequent aid packages such as Lend-Lease while continuing to press for the liquidation of British overseas assets, but the extent to which this agreement paved the way for such initiatives is impossible to ascertain.

Without doubt, "the fleet guarantee was exceedingly important to Americans" and Churchill was thinking "in terms that allowed him to consider the exchange as a down payment on further aid."[48] Nevertheless, the "intangible factors" argument is not an entirely convincing one even if staff talks between the nations intensified from then on. The deal did not mean that Americans were necessarily confident that the worst was over and Britain would win, but might easily be viewed as encouraging the British to divulge as much useful military information as possible before British capitulation. An end-of-year article focusing on Churchill's revival of British spirit remarked that "Britain has just about weathered 1940, but 1941 promised to bring an even greater ordeal" and mentioned that most military writers expected an invasion attempt the following year. Much of the article praised German military achievements and noted that Hitler's detractors were still waiting for him to make a mistake.[49]

While the above articles viewed the Battle of Britain in naval terms, the *Washington Post* was not always consistent about this, especially as fears of Axis naval power began to decline. Reviewing the conflict on 1 September 1940, another article asserted that the "great air battle is not a prelude, a preliminary round in the Battle of Britain. It is the main bout." It was claimed that if the "British can take it" and the "Royal Air Force can continue to dispute the skies with them until the bad weather sets in, Adolf Hitler may rue the day that he drew his sword and marched into Poland." It was further suggested that time was on Britain's side as warplanes and aircrew were now increasingly being provided in the United States and countries of the British Empire. This was only partly true as very few aircraft came to the RAF from America in 1940.[50] September was certainly the month most likely to see an invasion and the air conflict was now moving toward its climax. But on 1 September, Hitler was still holding back the Luftwaffe from all-out terror bombing on London and other cities. However, as the RAF was already attempting this over Germany, retaliation must have been expected soon.

As shown in previous chapters, the air campaign was going badly for the RAF at this time, but censorship in Britain and the American desire to provide upbeat pro-British coverage were clearly having a subtle and cumulative effect on writing. This was understandable as it was much easier for reporters to cover the air war. Typical of the coverage derived from American war correspondents was an article dated 3 September by "an International News Correspondent," its front-page headlines stating, "Pilots Have What It Takes: RAF Oblivious to Odds, Small Force Takes on 200 Nazis." Here the correspondent described his witnessing of a fearless attack by a "small force of Spitfires and Hurricanes" against "200 roaring German bombers and fighters and beat them." A captured German fighter pilot was dubiously quoted: "These Spitfires are really terrible. They're much too good for us."[51]

The previous day, the *Washington Post* had given front-page coverage to Churchill's message to Bomber Command that "the command of the air is being gradually and painfully, but nonetheless remorselessly wrested from the Nazi criminals." This was ostensibly meant to express cabinet satisfaction "that so many important military objectives in Germany and Italy have been so sharply smitten." The article also claimed that Messerschmitt "was once a word to conjure with" in England however, it "has lost much of its luster today." On the other hand, this piece did allow a sharp decrease in the ratio of German to British losses—now less than 2 to 1 as opposed to earlier battles of "3, 4 or even 5 to 1," and noted an improvement in the German technique of increased fighter protection.[52]

An article reinforcing American perceptions of heroic (if eccentric) British stereotypes told of a Hurricane pilot who left his cockpit to accept the commanding officer's offer of a cup of tea. Within a few minutes German bombs had destroyed his plane on the tarmac, implying the quaint British tea-drinking habit had saved his life. This pilot later told the war correspondent he had just scored his twenty-second victory. Commenting further, the pilot mentioned that a captured German airman recently told him that his bombing missions were personally motivated by a desire for revenge over the British bombing of Cologne, his home city.[53] This piece could only promote the idea that German participants were acting out of base revenge motives and, despite the irony, highlight evidence that RAF bombers were striking back.

With grossly exaggerated scores reported in British and foreign papers climaxing to between 175 and 185 German aircraft destroyed on 15 September, when the actual figure was closer to sixty, "the few" must have seemed like superheroes to the newspaper readers of Britain and America.[54] Indeed, an end-of-year article reviewing the conflict stated "England could not be defeated until Germany could control the air over the islands, and the 'tough guys' in the air force went aloft daily and drove the invader away." It continued: "Some observers felt the British fighting planes were superior to the German. Others did not. But all agreed the English airmen were superior to the Nazis."[55] No wonder that Sir John Slessor had written from Washington about the "intense interest" of the American press in the exploits of the RAF in December 1940.[56]

While these stories put British pilots in a very positive light, it would not have been obvious to more reflective readers that the RAF was going to survive—indeed the reality of the situation in early September was that Fighter Command was losing the battle over Kent and Sussex. An Air Ministry claim that the Luftwaffe had lost nearly two thousand warplanes over Britain in the first year of war was recorded on page five of the 3 September edition of the *Washington Post*. Most of these were claimed within the previous two and a half months. No direct mention was made of the pilot crisis, but British losses were acknowledged as "considerable" even if the "ratio was in Britain's favor" and "many British pilots are saved even when their machines are lost." However, the newspaper balanced the British claim with German counter-claims that nearly 1,200 British planes had been destroyed in August alone. Success was claimed in the "steady night bombing of Germany" and it was here that the American public was probably most misled.[57]

Notwithstanding the role that raids on Berlin allegedly played in changing the focus of Luftwaffe attacks to London, it is now generally accepted that these early British efforts to bomb Germany were ineffectual. This was because of problems relating to lack of fighter escort, small bomb loads, poor defensive gunnery, navigation, and bomb aiming. Air Chief Marshal Sir Richard Pierce concluded in late 1940 that "on the longer-range targets only one out of every five aircraft which [he] despatched actually found the target."[58] A *Washington Post* report on 31 August claimed that "Berlin shook this morning and late last night under the most intensive Royal Air Force bombing raids since the war began." The raids were described as "one phase of a tireless mass offensive." Numerous military targets were claimed as hit.[59] A report on later raids, stating that hidden armaments factories and munitions stores were hit in dense woodlands on the outskirts of Berlin, suggests a positive spin was being put on RAF bombs exploding harmlessly into rural areas outside of Berlin.[60] It was naturally very important that the British were not seen merely as passive victims of German attacks. Being seen to simply soak up punishment could not maintain a favorable impression indefinitely. Yet the bombing offensives of the two combatant nations were not yet remotely comparable in terms of actual efficiency, and coverage of the RAF bombing offensive did not reflect the limited damage caused.

Another story on page one of the same edition mentioned a British claim that the Germans were using "four-motored flying barns" in the assault on London.[61] In fact, there were no Luftwaffe aircraft in 1940 that could be described as such. In all probability, this was a British attempt to scare the more "jittery" members of East Coast communities into thinking the Luftwaffe had large long-range aircraft capable of raining bombs on cities such as New York and Boston. The prospect of new Luftwaffe bases in Britain and Ireland could only increase this possibility. A letter in July from Beaverbrook's fellow press baron and former wartime cabinet colleague Lord Rothermere suggests this rumor may have been in circulation for some time. "I have spoken to Americans who talk about moving 100 and 200 miles away from the coast. To me these fears are whimsical."[62]

Despite the above, Americans would surely have been reassured by Secretary of the Navy (and publisher of the *Chicago Daily News*) Frank Knox's statement in Honolulu dated 7 September that "Britain has a better than even chance now of withstanding the blitzkrieg." He reportedly stated "he would not have said this 30 days ago." Significantly, he attributed his confidence to "Britain's superior navy." He also said that Germany would not "gain complete mastery of the air to launch an invasion," a remark failing to convey the damage already done to Fighter Command's infrastructure mentioned in the previous chapter.[63] While he was at Honolulu, Knox told Admiral J. O. Richardson, C-in-C, U.S. Pacific Fleet, that he thought the United States would be at war by the following spring, which suggests he was genuinely upbeat about British survival prospects and was assuming Roosevelt's re-election would soon lead to direct U.S. participation.[64]

As the year drew to a close, the more optimistic predictions of British survival seemed to have been vindicated not so much by events but by non-events. The Germans had not invaded and the British did not seem about to drop out of the war as a result of the bombing. Further reassurance was given by Major General James E. Chaney (1884–1967) of the U.S. Army Air Corps on his return from England in December. By now, Chaney was the latest of a long list of U.S. civilian and military advisors sent to assess British prospects of survival and to obtain technical information useful to the American rearmament program. It was essential for Roosevelt to show the public tangible benefits for the support he was giving the Churchill regime, and Chaney would not have disappointed him. Great play was made of the "information that will aid us in our own rearmament efforts . . . things that might be worth hundreds and millions of dollars to us." Speaking in some detail of the "aerial blitzkrieg," he said that the early phases were decisively won by the "speedy fighters of the RAF" but "a large measure of the success . . . was attributed to the plane detecting system employed." Without mentioning any of the RDF/command and control shortcomings detailed in an earlier chapter, Chaney described a "thorough and able" system for aircraft detection that allowed fighters to remain in position until they knew details of the enemy height, speed, and direction. The current phase of night bombing and daylight fighter-bombing attack was described as causing "much material damage but could never win a war." He also believed the current loss ratio was "1.9 German craft for 1 British plane." This would only have been a small exaggeration had he meant the whole period but Chaney was wide of the mark for the current fighter-bomber/night-bomber phase, in which German losses were much reduced. A valuable lesson drawn from the conflict was that American fighters and bombers all needed more guns.[65]

Mostly this statement was accurate but the claim that any phase was "decisively won" was dubious. Much valuable information was being given away for very little tangible benefit. He was right about the current German bombing tactics not winning the war on their own, although it was rather early for Chaney to draw this authoritative conclusion. British RDF research was ahead of the Americans at this time but the claims for the efficiency of the command and control system originating from Watson-Watt and Dowding were clearly being taken at the same face value as the inflated scores of downed aircraft. The extent to which British expertise and more tangible assets were being surrendered was the subject of a letter from Beaverbrook to Churchill a few weeks after Chaney's departure. Beaverbrook's immediate concern was articulated over an American demand for "our South African gold" and the proposal "to collect and carry it away." In no uncertain terms he stated, "That is a decision which I would resist very strongly and seek to destroy by every means in my power." The Americans "have conceded nothing . . . they have extracted payment to the uttermost," and Beaverbrook further complained "they have taken our bases without valuable compensation." He also fulminated over the delays in the American armament programs resulting in "negligible" deliveries, but at the same time "we find ourselves, having provided the necessary money for munitions and aircraft, with deliveries delayed but no suggestion of any return of moneys advanced on the basis of performance of contract." A series of examples were then provided, including the surrender of machine tools for the manufacture of 700 Hispano Suiza 20-mm guns a month. Some 650 were to be manufactured for Britain but the administration later refused to supply these on the grounds they were needed for U.S. forces. "So we lost our machine tools and we lost our guns too." Reference was also made to the Tizard mission "and all the secrets transferred to the Americans." Beaverbrook was also scathing about the supposed "benefits" of the Purvis Mission, the British purchasing mission in Washington led by Arthur Purvis, who "has nothing to his credit except a kindly position on the part of Mr. [Henry] Morgenthau [U.S. secretary of the treasury] and that is easily bought at such a price." His suggested solution was typical of the entrepreneur's distrust in the ability of bureaucratic agencies to handle crucial matters. His proposed independent mission dealing directly with the American public would advocate a fairer deal for Britain and put pressure on the Roosevelt administration "to carry out some of the pledges and promises so freely given."[66]

Beaverbrook's files also include a document apparently prepared by Churchill's secretary back in June. This asked for advice on the question of a "policy of full and frank exchange with the U.S.A." It indicates that the prime influences on Churchill to agree to this came from the political heads of the navy and RAF, Mr. A. V. Alexander and Sir Archibald Sinclair. Their argument was summed up as a need to overcome an American feeling about "our stickiness" about British secrets and the fact that the enemy now knew many of these anyway. The benefits of cooperation would be having essential RDF parts made in the United States as "insurance" (presumably against bombing), and the British would get information on ultra-shortwave technology should the Americans know more about this. Finally, as the Americans wanted to know about British gun-turret technology, "If we could tell them, they could fit [the technology] into machines to be delivered to us."[67]

This correspondence reflects Beaverbrook's discontent with—as he saw it—the one-sided treatment that Britain was receiving from the Roosevelt administration. Beaverbrook's own advice to Churchill back in June is unclear but his continued possession of the "Précis for Prime Minister" suggests he was holding it as ammunition against Sinclair and Alexander in case—as seemed likely—their policy backfired at a later date. The arguments articulated by this Précis are vague and not altogether convincing, but only Alexander and Sinclair could have said whether they had been accurately quoted. Of course, the ultimate responsibility belonged to Churchill, who tried to hold a quid pro quo bargaining position that could not be sustained.[68] It meant the "kindly position on the part of Mr. Morgenthau" was essential even if he was probably already scheming to replace the pound with the dollar as the prime international currency for trade. The *Washington Post* reported that Morgenthau had testified to the House Appropriations Subcommittee in Washington on 17 December 1940 that Great Britain would be unable to place further orders for war materials without financial assistance.[69] Despite the alleviation of U.S. naval fears in the summer, a London *Times* report inferred there was still enough mileage in these insecurities to ease the passage of Lend-Lease through the American government machine. In January 1941, and probably at Morgenthau's instigation, Knox was supporting this in front of the Foreign Affairs Committee by stating that the United States "would be heavily outnumbered by the fleets of the Axis, if British sea-power should be destroyed."[70] Whatever his true motivation, Morgenthau needed to make efforts to convince his skeptical countrymen, as an earlier message from the British ambassador in Washington confirmed. In defending himself against criticism for revealing the British cash crisis to American reporters, Lord Lothian claimed that American public opinion "is saturated with illusions to the effect we have vast resources available which we have not yet disclosed." He also recounted a third-party conversation with Roosevelt whereby the president "believed we could go on paying to July 1943."[71]

The same edition of the *Washington Post* contained Roosevelt's announcement on his proposed scheme to lease the British war equipment using the parable of the fire-hose, but it would be March 1941 before the Lend-Lease bill gained Senate approval.[72] In the circumstances of late 1940, Churchill was in no position to resist U.S. demands for anything. The emphasis on personal testimony from American military and political leaders such as Knox, Chaney, and Morgenthau about British prospects (and value) was likely to have had more impact upon the American public than official "propaganda" press releases from Britain's Ministry of Information. Yet it was the work of the neutral war correspondent most likely to sway opinions among the public. After the air campaigns had subsided, the Council of the Newspaper Proprietors' Association entertained many of these correspondents at the Savoy Hotel, with Quentin Reynolds and Harry Hopkins on the guest list. Esmond Harmsworth, 2nd Viscount Rothermere, then chairman of the council, expressed his admiration for the way American correspondents had worked through the dangers of the blitz "to see things for themselves." They had been "the best propagandists of Britain in America." Mr. John Gilbert Winant, the American ambassador to the UK, concurred, pointing out that the London correspondents "more than any other group . . . taught America to be forewarned and forearmed." Alluding to the problems of official censorship, another American speaker demanded "news when it was news and not some time after the Germans had had a chance to put their coloured interpretations before the public."[73]

Despite British attempts to flatter the correspondents it was clear that representatives of the British and American press were using the occasion to take a public swipe at the Ministry of Information and the official procedures for controlling the flow of news. Substance was given to some of these complaints by correspondence with the chairman of the BBC. Back in April 1940, Mr. W. Will, chairman of the Newspaper and Periodical Emergency Council, had complained to Sir John Reith criticizing the chaotic censorship system, the preference given by the Air Ministry to the BBC over newspapers, and unnecessary delays with Admiralty censorship. Some censorship reorganization subsequently took place but it was still not enough for American correspondents.[74]

Mr. W. G. V. Vaughan of the MoI General Productions Division had forwarded this criticism in July to the MoI Policy Committee. He stated there was a "considerable demand, particularly from the USA, for stories from RAF pilots or the Navy of exploits." Unfortunately, the RAF was said to have delayed these for up to a month and even then sometimes produced unsuitable material. The Admiralty was slightly better but could still take a fortnight.[75] In November, Drew Middleton of the Associated Press of America had published a long list of complaints in American newspapers, citing rigorous censorship and "British capacity for understatement working overtime." The London-based *Times*, however, did not think the censorship was as severe as the Americans described; journalists were allowed to be direct in military matters and American correspondents often failed to balance bad news with British successes abroad.[76] British successes in the Mediterranean did not seem to be as newsworthy to American correspondents as a "review of the dark days at home." Despite these peevish British claims there was some justification for American complaints. It was the job of the MoI to "present the national case to the public at home and abroad," and it was also responsible for "the preparation and issue of National Propaganda" together with the issue of "news" and to control information in accordance with the requirements of security.[77] One problem for the MoI appeared to be the initial lack of interest in propaganda shown by Churchill, from whom one minister of information claimed,

"No interest was ever shown in the subject."[78] The role of the MoI in managing news was inevitably going to be seen as an impediment to correspondents, and as Churchill, Bracken, and Beaverbrook had all worked within the British media, it was unsurprising there was skepticism over the ability of bureaucracy to handle the task of persuading the United States.

The Royal Navy did not allow war correspondents on board their ships and "throughout the war naval censorship remained the toughest."[79] At first, the RAF did not allow them at their airfields but in any case the fighting was clearly visible from most parts of southeast England. In general, soldiers and politicians have been wary about allowing civilian reporters close to the fighting because of the potential security threat they represent, and the possibility of unwelcome criticism from these quarters. On the other hand, civilian reporters had become a "necessary evil," as a well-founded public cynicism over the accuracy of official pronouncements required some third-party validation.[80] A great deal of pressure has often been placed upon correspondents to "toe the official line" and the pressure is often effective. Unsurprisingly, correspondents from neutral countries proved more difficult to handle, and those from the United States were much less willing to accept censorship than their British counterparts because of their aggressive reporting culture. Minutes of the MoI Policy Committee show that U.S. correspondents wanted "as many facilities as they could get" and they wanted to be able to broadcast their own personal verification of people's suffering. However, disquiet was raised about a possible public "revolt against making an exhibition of our sufferings from air raids." It was finally agreed that more facilities be granted to the Americans but not without expressions of concern over the potential loosening of control over the British press.[81]

Fortunately, since the Anschluss crisis, the Foreign Office recognized that "a large part of the [American] press is very sensible and there is widespread genuine friendliness toward us, and genuine dislike of the totalitarian systems."[82] It has been pointed out that "by far the biggest volume of reporting came from American war correspondents" and they were pro-British "to a man." This sentiment "naturally coloured American reporting and it prevented most correspondents from giving their readers a balanced view."[83] From what has already been said together with a perusal of the memoirs of a correspondent from the "isolationist heart of the United States," this seems largely correct. Eric Sevareid clearly disapproved of many aspects of 1930s British life, writing at length about the iniquities of the "English class system," but none of that stopped him from describing approvingly the "hysterical adulation" showered on the "average Londoner" from the United States. Neither did it prevent him from describing the pilots as "a small group of the semi-professional, the elite who seemed to us like shining knights, the airmen who could come to grips with the enemy," The others, he said "could only take it and resist with their hearts and minds, not their hands."[84] Edward R. Murrow had originally hired Sevareid to make radio broadcasts from London to

New York in 1939, and it is Murrow that Sevareid credits with best representing the British cause to America, claiming he was not only more influential than the American ambassador in London, but he *was* the ambassador. For Sevareid, it was the Columbia Radio Network (for which Murrow was the London chief) that first recognized that the "rigid traditional formulae of news writing" had to be discarded and replaced with "a new kind of pertinent contemporary essay [that] became the standard form."[85]

Sevareid comes over as a hopeless romantic for his view of a vicious air war that had little in common with notions of chivalry. But the slightly effusive claims made on behalf of Murrow had some basis. Apart from his innovative skill in the presentation of news reports to the American public, Murrow was influential not only as an associate of the president's envoys to Churchill, Harry Hopkins and "Wild Bill" Donovan, but also of Roosevelt himself.[86] In fact, it was probably one of Murrow's broadcasts in October 1940 that made it easier for Americans to sympathize with the British cause. Here he suggested the old Britain, for which Americans still had ambivalent feelings, was now dying as a result of the social pressures brought on by the blitz. Ordinary people were now questioning authority and demanding answers to questions like: "Why must there be 800,000 unemployed when we need shelters?" Broadcasts like this seemed to prove that American correspondents had more freedom than their British equivalents in getting information past the censor.[87]

A further contender to Sevareid's nomination of Murrow for the title of unofficial ambassador to the UK would have been Quentin "Quent" Reynolds (1902–65), associate editor and war correspondent to *Collier's Weekly*. Reynolds was sufficiently important to merit a London *Times* obituary on the occasion of his death in 1965. Reynolds became popular with the British public through the BBC's *Postscript Schicklgruber* broadcast. The obituary claimed he "identified himself wholeheartedly with the British war effort" but noted that "not all American journalists were seen to be sympathetic to the British cause."[88] Strangely missing from the obituary is Reynolds' narration of the eight-minute film documentary *Britain Can Take It!* (1940). This graphic depiction of London during the blitz was widely credited with helping Roosevelt gain public support for helping the British, and according to Beaverbrook was "the finest piece of propaganda that I have ever looked upon so here are my congratulations."[89] Reynolds later used his fame to make an introductory tribute to the feature film *Eagle Squadron* (1942) about American flyers in the Battle of Britain and with a theme of Anglo-American cooperation. Although some Americans fought in the RAF during 1940, the Eagle Squadron was not operational until 1941 and attempts to use the real pilots as actors were frustrated by the deaths in combat of all those selected to play the leads. Though viewed as a propaganda success, historian Nicholas J. Cull noted the Hollywood treatment offended the real members of the Eagle Squadron.[90]

Reynolds' personal involvement in *Eagle Squadron* suggests the theme may have developed from the circumstances surrounding a telegram to Walter Winchell, a well-known columnist of the *New York Daily Mirror* during August 1940. It conveys Reynolds' enthusiastic nature and indicates that there was a "certain number of American newspaper men here who as individuals are extremely well aware that Britain is fighting our battle." The document also reveals Reynolds and Lord Beaverbrook's collusion in an illegal fund-raising scheme for newsmen to buy a Spitfire out of their own pockets. Eight hundred dollars had been raised from them so far and a Spitfire was thought to cost $20,000. Reynolds credits Beaverbrook, who had only joined the War Cabinet on 2 August, with the idea for it to be flown by one of the twenty-six Americans in the RAF and have it "christened" by the king. In a typical Beaverbrook flourish, he suggested naming it after the "great newspaper man Heywood Broun" (1888–1939). It was also emphasized that the fundraising had nothing to do with the Association of American Correspondents, London. The telegram acknowledged it was "contrary to outdated neutrality laws but this [is] not [the] time [to] split hairs."[91]

What became of this scheme is unknown and it seems likely either the legal problems mentioned by Reynolds may have proved insurmountable or the monetary sum proved too great a strain on the pockets of a few individuals, but it illustrates his commitment to the British cause. Winchell was influential in media circles and corresponded regularly with the director of the FBI. More significantly Winchell has been linked to William Stephenson, who led British secret intelligence service operations in the Western hemisphere, and also to the White House.[92] For all the potential snags, including the blow to morale if (or more likely, when) the "Heywood Broun" aircraft was shot down, it was still a clever idea with the potential for strengthening Anglo-American ties bearing in mind Heywood Broun's father was an English immigrant to the United States.[93]

Official agencies were working in the same direction at this time. As Cull notes, RAF heroism seemed Britain's "greatest propaganda asset" by late August. The Foreign Office wrote to Sir Maurice Peterson of the MoI on 17 August mentioning a BBC broadcast by an American pilot. The memo stated "publicity of exploits of individual American pilots in our service, even if exaggerated, would have an excellent effect, and would give the hero-worshipping public of the United States a feeling of identity with the conflict."[94] The plan was to build up the image of Pilot Officer William Fiske III of New York. Unfortunately, the death of Fiske the very day of this memo as a consequence of an earlier encounter with supposedly vulnerable Ju 87 Stukas restricted the propaganda opportunities considerably.[95] Perhaps wisely, with the heavy attrition rate for airmen, the British made no attempt to find a propaganda substitute for Fiske. Given the "hero-worship" paid to the American aviator Charles A. Lindbergh by the American press and public, the idea for promoting an American air ace in the British cause was understandable, given that the pro-Nazi Lindbergh was using his fame to speak against American aid to Britain in 1940.[96]

The advantage of the air battle was the ability to clarify the "British predicament in the United States" and express British prospects "in a simple statistic: the ratio of the losses of the Luftwaffe to the losses of the RAF." Lord Halifax at the Foreign Office wrote to the Air Ministry: "Whatever you can do to give the American correspondents an inside view of your organisation and personnel, may, I firmly believe, have the most important influence on the help we get from the United States in the near future."[97] Some of the pro-British correspondents were still skeptical of Air Ministry claims. Gottfried Keller, president of the Foreign Press Association in London, once demanded to check the British score of twenty-six by seeing and counting the German wrecks. Having been told to cooperate fully with neutral correspondents, Barry Cornwell, south-eastern regional press and liaison officer of the MoI, drove Keller around the countryside. After fourteen wrecks, Keller was exhausted by scrambling around fields and fences and conceded defeat.[98] There was simply no viable way to validate either Luftwaffe or RAF claims and most correspondents seemed content to swallow reservations and publish British figures without qualification. No wonder that following the "urging" of the Foreign Office, Churchill made his now famous tribute to "the few" in his House of Commons speech on 20 August 1940.

It was probably the medium of film that proved the most useful tool for communicating with ordinary people, and the popularity of the cowboy film helped identify American cultural preferences for British propagandists. Bill Boyd (who played Hopalong Cassidy) and Roy Rogers were among the best known actors of the period and it is a testament to the popularity of the cowboy genre that Boyd and Rogers appeared in twelve films during 1940 alone. Nevertheless it was a genre in need of modernization and it seems likely that Americans mentally projected their cultural values onto "the few" by putting the cowboy into an aircraft cockpit. The references by more than one senior British figure to the "hero-worshipping" tendencies of the Americans and the American press indicates a sharp culture clash between upper-class Britons and ordinary Americans during the 1940s. But these cultural preferences had to be accommodated and manipulating the image of the RAF pilot provided a golden opportunity. Back in 1916, the French had astutely exploited the old American revolutionary alliance by forming a squadron of American volunteers and naming them the Escadrille Lafayette after the Revolutionary-era French military advisor to the United States, the Marquis de Lafayette (1757–1834). Painted on the aircraft fuselages and resplendent in war paint and feathers was a whooping Native American symbolizing not just the links between France and the United States but also between the aviator and the Wild West. In 1918, "balloon-busting" American ace Lieutenant Frank Luke Jr. from Arizona would die heroically clutching his smoking revolver in the classic manner of the Wild West hero after refusing to surrender to surrounding German troops.[99] It was surely these virtues of self-reliance, fearlessness, and rugged individualism inherent in the American pioneers and cowboys that helped modern Americans readily identify with "the few" in 1940. Americans were not alone in this. Aviation appeared so modern and exciting between the wars that Germany, Italy, and Great Britain also seemed to be projecting their cultural ideals upon the aviator.[100]

Much of the support given to Britain from the United States in 1940 came from individuals acting either on their own initiative or willingly complying with the activities of British agencies. Reynolds' role in *Britain Can Take It!* was partly to conceal the Ministry of Information's Crown Film Unit authorship. He was originally recruited by the film entrepreneur Sidney Bernstein through the latter's contacts with the American press corps in London, and this was said to mark the climax of MoI efforts to secure cooperation with the Americans.[101]

It must not be supposed that films covering aspects of the "aerial blitzkrieg" made up the entire cinematic propaganda output. Lord Louis Mountbatten had a lifelong interest in film and founded the Royal Naval Film Corporation. It was his adventures portrayed by Noël Coward in the feature film *In Which We Serve* (1941) that went some way to restoring the navy's reputation with the British public after the "failures" of 1940.[102] *The Sea Hawk* was premiered in London on 1 August 1940, shortly before the Luftwaffe intensified its campaign over England. This adventure starring Errol Flynn showed how Elizabethan England had raised its fleet specifically to counter Imperial Spain's ambitions for world domination. The parallels were obvious as the *New York Times* noted: "Count on Warners to inject a note of contemporary significance."[103] Warner Brothers was an American company and Beaverbrook's letter of invitation to the premiere asserted the company was "whole-heartedly devoted to the British cause." *The Sea Hawk* was recognition that "more than 350 years ago, England faced conditions similar to today's: King Phillip of Spain set out to conquer the world, and only England stood in his way." England then created "the foundation of today's navy." The film was made in the United States but it was stressed that "its setting, its spirit, and most of the principal players are British."[104] The text of Queen Elizabeth's climactic final speech was an example of "classic propaganda" designed to resonate with "high-minded" Americans and talked of one man's ruthless ambition engulfing the world.[105] The motivations for making *The Sea Hawk* were clearly altruistic in part. Harry M. Warner's anti-Nazi feelings undoubtedly stemmed from his Jewish background, though Jewish producers were initially cautious because of fears of an anti-Semitic backlash.[106] The theme of Jewish film producers turning America against Germany was one frequently asserted by isolationists such as Lindbergh.[107] *The Sea Hawk* was in a similar genre to the later *The Young Mr. Pitt* (1942), made in Britain, where comparisons between Pitt (an eighteenth-century prime minister) and the Napoleonic Wars and Churchill and the Battle of Britain were made very plain. The British connections were obviously stressed in the hope that Beaverbrook, as a well-known figure on both sides of the Atlantic, might give the takings a boost by publicly endorsing it. The slightly desperate tone of the letter also reflects the resistance put up by the MoI against Warner's overtures owing to the fear of alienating his competitors.[108] Attempting to "arouse the world to the active and ever-expanding menace of Nazism in every country from within," *Confessions of a Nazi Spy* presented a semi-documentary account of "actual facts of German operations in America" even before the war had started. It was emphasized that Warner Bros. did not make it for financial rewards, and where German coercion had caused some countries to ban the film, Harry M. Warner had tried to undermine the pressure by offering to give the box-office takings to the Red Cross. These films effectively put out ideas to Americans with reflective temperaments and an interest in historical precedent but may not have connected with the rest of the population.

One novel feature of the *Why We Fight* series was Churchill's personal filmed appearance commending the films as an authoritative version of events. A clear break with precedent was now being seen. Unlike the media-conscious public figures of the late twentieth century, newsreel appearances by British politicians were something most of them wanted to avoid partly because the British media had never demanded this of them. A letter to Beaverbrook in June 1941 from Commander A. W. Jarratt, deputy chairman of the Royal Naval Film Corporation, complained bitterly of the "lukewarm support given by the Ministers of His Majesty's Government to the efforts of the British Film Industry for propaganda films to be sent to the United States." Jarratt claimed the MoI had been told that Americans needed to see the ministers speak in newsreels occasionally but also, "not only did the Ministers refuse to be photographed but the Prime Minister was not favourable to the idea." Harry Warner was quoted as being particularly concerned that Foreign Secretary Anthony Eden had refused to appear. Fortunately, Jarratt managed to see Brendan Bracken who persuaded the prime minister to speak from the screens of America. He warned that unless politicians changed their attitude "Americans will lose all their enthusiasm with [British films on] the screens of America and we shall find ourselves shortly in the position of making films and not having them shown." A further grumble lay in the lack of coordination in distributing film propaganda, with all departments having their own film propaganda.[109] All this confirms an Anglo-American culture clash in terms of a British failure to project personality and emotion on film together with the existence of a celebrity culture more strongly established in the United States than the UK. Deference was still a defining characteristic of British society, and public-school-educated politicians, more inclined to make a virtue of hiding their feelings, found the American media culture intrusive.

Perhaps more than any other individual, the American film director Frank Capra was most responsible for cementing the concept of the Battle of Britain as an exclusive air campaign to prevent invasion. The reasons why Capra had made the *Why We Fight* series are clear and some appear within his autobiography *The Name Above the Title*. A well-known director of feature films during the 1930s, Capra had been charged by General George S. Marshall, the U.S. chief of staff, with making documentary films for the purpose of showing *why* we are fighting and to explain the principles.[110] Without prior experience of documentary film-making, Capra viewed Leni Riefenstahl's Nazi propaganda classic *Triumph of the Will*, together with other enemy newsreels, and borrowed from them the exciting techniques of German filmmaking in war. The *Why We Fight* series was aimed at recruits to the U.S. Army but was also used by the other armed services in America, Britain, and the British Empire, and Churchill was credited with the order for it to be shown in British cinemas.

Capra claimed the series became the definitive answer to: "What was government policy during the dire decade 1931–41?" Marshall's advice had been that if Capra was unable to get a clear official answer to what policy was on any aspect during this time—"and this was often"—he was to "make [his] own best estimate, and see if they don't agree with [him] later," inferring considerable latitude in film content. Capra later remarked, "By extrapolation the film series was also accepted as the official policy of our allies."[111] Capra also suggested it was Churchill, whom he had met through Sidney Bernstein, then head of the MoI Crown Film Unit, who put forward the idea to personally present a foreword "to introduce your great films to a grateful British public."[112]

The *Battle of Britain* opened to a "Disney-style" animated map followed by newsreels showing the inexorable march of German troops progressing to Paris, Dunkirk, and Calais. Over this came an American voice stating the British nation was "the one obstacle that stood between him [Hitler] and world conquest." In case the point had not been made sufficiently it was reiterated that Hitler had to "crush the island" as this would be "the way open for world conquest." Yet Hitler had to be careful as "a slip now might ruin the timetable for world conquest." Once Britain was defeated, the combined fleets of Germany, Britain, Italy, and Japan would "hem us in." As the film progressed the narrator described an invasion fleet of "high-speed barges" and spoke over a "Disney" map of the Channel showing animated warships. "The British knew it would be suicide to use the fleet in the English Channel without control of the air." The climax of the day fighting over London on 15 September 1940 was shown with images of swooping fighters accompanied by a statement that 185 enemy aircraft had been shot down, forcing the Germans to adopt night attacks from 6 October. The contribution of RDF was ignored, with the early-warning system represented solely by ground observers using visual and audio detection equipment. While bombs fell at night, "the RAF wasn't much help—just German bombs against British guts." Bombs were said to "fall alike on the East End and Mayfair rich." The Luftwaffe leveling of Coventry was portrayed as vindictive revenge for a successful RAF raid on the legitimate military target of Bremen's submarine yards. Toward the end of the film statements were made to clarify the idea that it was a clash of democracy versus totalitarianism. "In a democracy it is not the government that makes war, it is the people." Also, "they knew it was the People's War . . . a regimented people met a free people in a new kind of war . . . they won for the people of the world."[113] The use of Walt Disney's animation techniques and real action shots of air combat from newsreels made thrilling and compulsive viewing that is just as dramatic today as it was in 1942.

There was enough truth in this account to be convincing, though whether American audiences preferred to believe it was the Battle of Britain that saved the world rather than U.S. entry in the wake of Pearl Harbor may be doubted. Churchill had consistently refused to state specific war aims except for a terse "victory," but the film, indeed the whole series, obviously helped fill a vacuum he was unable to cover as leader of a political coalition.[114] A fight for "freedom" was suitably vague and could mean whatever one wanted it to mean. With its heavy focus on the air campaigns and an unintended diminution of the navy, the "aerial blitzkrieg" was no longer simply part of the Battle of Britain. Now merged with the daylight battles it *was* the Battle of Britain. Although Capra did not mention it, the MoI would have given him the best-selling official HMSO pamphlet *Battle of Britain*, which was officially described as how "a thousand anonymous young men had fought one of the decisive battles of the world."[115] The conspicuous absence of RDF from the film, also missing from the HMSO pamphlet, suggests that Capra may have been heavily reliant on this publication.[116] He would also have been influenced by accounts read in the American press.

The idea that Hitler had a "timetable for world conquest" has already been challenged in an earlier chapter, as has the idea that the British fleet could not survive in the Channel. Far from being made up of high-speed barges, the invasion fleet was an improvised armada of unseaworthy towed river barges. Furthermore, the exaggerated scores of 15 September 1940 and hence the importance of Fighter Command were flawed ideas again rammed home in this film. The undeniable failure of Fighter Command in the blitz was given a positive spin by creating an opportunity for the British to show their admirable stoic heroism in the face of adversity.

Naturally, a propaganda film such as this was hardly going to point out that it was the RAF that had begun the indiscriminate war on a civilian population and that the German decision to do the same only came later. Neither was it mentioned that London's East End working class had suffered disproportionately in the blitz. However, a strict adherence to the actual facts is not part of the propagandist's job. That the British believed these to be the actual facts was because the prime minister had personally assured them that facts had been accurately recorded and the American narration had paid them generous compliments. From this point onward

Capra's view of the conflict set the legend into stone and for this reason the film was undoubtedly far more important to the British public than to the American servicemen for whom it was originally made.

That the Battle of Britain became an Anglo-American media construct is clear but it was less Anglo than American. An aggressive American press culture ensured U.S. correspondents hunted for a wider variety of news angles than the lines fed to them by official sources, and the dearth of quality news forced them to be more innovative in their methods. This culture was characterized by loud and assertive complaints when demands went unmet, something alien to British correspondents in the 1940s.[117] Neither the British nor the American press held implicit faith in the veracity of the controlled information doled out by a necessarily cautious bureaucracy, but desperate political needs ensured that American newsmen received more active cooperation and less official obstructionism when out and about pursuing stories. "Hero-worship" was the perceived American susceptibility that all wished to exploit and the British were dragged along in the wake of the American press' inspired efforts to meet it. This imbalance was less noticeable in the area of film but it was an American film based on an HMSO publication—publicly commended by the prime minister—that was to have the greatest impact on the legend's formulation. With former journalists at the center of British political power there were no precise divisions within the construction. Ultimately it was a fusion of effort by artists, politicians, press figures, academics, and civil servants of both nations all acting within hazy parameters and without a coherent overarching plan for maximizing U.S. involvement.

Analysis of the newspaper articles suggests that for the American press the term "Battle of Britain" was a flexible one. It was largely a generic term but for several weeks simply meant the battle for the British fleet to remain "in being" as an obstacle for Axis expansion into American spheres of interest. Initially it had no air dimension whatsoever and as air activity increased during August the common American press term for the air campaigns was "aerial blitzkrieg." Fears subsided following the mandate for seizing British, French, and Dutch possessions in the Caribbean and Central America, agreed at Havana in late July. These fears fell further with the fleet guarantees given in early September, and Americans could now concentrate on the aerial blitzkrieg that only entered intensive phases during August. Along with the defensive war waged by Fighter Command and covered by sympathetic American correspondents, there was substantial coverage of Bomber Command's parallel efforts to destroy targets in Europe—suggesting that in 1940 at least this was also perceived as part of the Battle of Britain.

With summer passing and the likelihood for invasion receding until 1941, attention naturally focused on whether the British would give way under unprecedented air bombardment and negotiate peace with Germany. Some writers were therefore beginning to see the "aerial blitzkrieg" of London as the real Battle of

Britain. Cinemagoers were also subjected to a series of historical feature films drawing parallels between the naval battles of previous centuries with the Battle of Britain in 1940. For most Americans, including those who did not closely follow current affairs in their newspapers, Frank Capra and Winston Churchill clarified everything in 1942. With America now in the war, everyone needed to fight in order to ensure the success of the "free" over the "regimented." That the struggle had continued was only because the RAF and the British people prevailed in the air campaigns known as the Battle of Britain, allowing the United States time to rearm. This version has proved so attractive to the British public it seems unlikely to be relinquished whatever holes academics might shoot through it.

For all the various stratagems adopted, the propaganda failed to bring the United States into the war in 1940. On the contrary, the opinion poll evidence suggests considerable U.S. public complacency in view of British "success" at the close of 1940. British naval power was the main bargaining chip Churchill had to play with in the first weeks of his premiership but he did not play it with conspicuous skill. As the Americans gradually curbed their naval fears through British concessions, "technical expertise" and "sympathy" became the only political cards left to play. The Foreign Office and the MoI, aided by friendly correspondents, fought for U.S. sympathy by manipulating American hero-worshipping tendencies. In the event, most Americans managed to place their sympathy and their interventionist inclinations into separate watertight compartments. At least helping Britain with aid meant jobs and profits accruing to American industry, together with the "free" research and development information essential for speedy rearmament. It may also have eased any pangs of guilt. For Roosevelt, it was also an opportunity to strengthen U.S. power and weaken imperialism abroad at British expense in line with his navalist beliefs, and his cards were played with more skill. The British experiences of having to fight the "aerial blitzkrieg" assisted the American rearmament program but in the short-term British gains were ephemeral and mainly limited to the boosting of their self-esteem.[118] Immediately prior to 7 December 1941, Roosevelt seemed no nearer to direct intervention—only Hitler's declaration of war following Pearl Harbor achieved this. Where the propaganda had succeeded was in allowing Roosevelt to propose a series of initiatives to circumvent neutrality laws preventing credit for purchasing war supplies. Not that this resulted in much material help yet, but the drive for Lend-Lease had begun, enabling the fight to continue during 1941.

Chapter Eight

Conclusion

Give me the facts, and I will twist them the way I want to suit my argument.[1]

W. S. Churchill

B y the end of World War II, Churchill, Dowding, and the Royal Air Force
had become firmly established in the minds of the British public with preventing German invasion and saving the world from tyranny. The legend
of 1940 has also allowed well-deserved praise to the public for their fortitude
in enduring bombing and privation, all of which was reinforced by a powerful
Anglo-American media construction. However, there was no place for the Royal
Navy or the Merchant Navy within the traditional legend.

As with most legends, there is a basis of fact and it is not my intention to deni-
grate the heroic sacrifices of "the few" or the civilian suffering in the blitz. Western
Europe was finally liberated from Nazi control and this happy event was clearly
rooted in the decision to fight on in 1940. However, the campaigns to make the
public understand the "true significance" of the Battle of Britain often miss an
important point. Sacrifices were also expected from other service organizations and
the Merchant Navy incurred some 25,864 deaths while keeping the all-important
logistical supply lines open in 1939–45. For each month in 1940, some 463 seamen
serving in British registered ships were lost. This meant a loss of approximately
1,730 merchant seamen for the period of the Battle of Britain.[2] Outrageously, these
men were classified as non-combatants despite operating anti-aircraft guns and
sustaining very heavy losses for limited public recognition. By contrast, Dowding
lost approximately 537 men between 10 July and 31 October, showing a wide differential in casualties. Only by including the total for all RAF commands (1,494)
can equilibrium be even approached, but the legend does not usually allow for the
participation of other aircrew. This represents a strong argument for a Battle *for*
Britain memorial encompassing a wider range of participants.

Irrespective of the role that Fighter Command is said to have played in cancel-
ling the invasion plan and despite the advantages of RDF and fighting over home

territory, the RAF could not have defeated a German landing in September 1940 without the other services. The RAF lacked enough competent fighter pilots for the task of defeating the Luftwaffe, though in overall numbers Britain had more single-seat fighter pilots than Germany.[3] Given the circumstances, Fighter Command tried to deploy its limited resources to the best of its ability but it was still no great exemplar of efficiency. Naturally, any organization can be found wanting when measured against some mythical ideal but Fighter Command and indeed the RAF as a whole could never have measured up to the model of efficiency promoted by propaganda agencies and romanticized over the years. In reality, the RAF shared similar problems with other services in that the rapid expansion of the 1930s did not allow enough time for the systematic and orderly implementation of policies essential to organizational efficiency—especially in armament and training. This was rarely the fault of individuals but arguments over distributing limited resources inevitably led to compromise and inefficiencies. Arguably, the only methods that might have engendered an efficient military expansion during the years immediately preceding 1940 were those of totalitarian governments and these would not have reflected Britain's democratic tradition. The British committee system was the time-honored method of managing operational development and while this was reasonably effective in the long term there were short-term disadvantages. Well-run committees comprised of strong "team-players" represent thorough mechanisms for formulating policies but can also be frustratingly slow and indecisive. Consequently they proved poor agents for making the rapid changes required in 1940. This hampered Dowding, who possessed great technical vision but lacked the communication skills essential for this sort of teamwork. Neither did he demonstrate the aggressive characteristics that mark out a great commander. Though deserving considerable credit for introducing technical changes including RDF, Dowding clung doggedly to a reactive defense relying heavily on untried, unreliable new technology—a sort of "air fleet-in-being" strategy—without attempting more proactive options. Dismissed for reasons that owed much to his own shortcomings, Dowding won the subsequent battle for public sympathy by exaggerating the virtues of the RDF chain and befriending a prominent historian. His biographer's portrayal of Dowding as "victim" also aroused traditional British sympathies for the underdog.

If it was not the Battle of Britain air campaign alone that prevented invasion, what then was the Battle *for* Britain? German wartime "opinion," expressed in postwar accounts by former Kriegsmarine admirals, related to a "failure to invade" as opposed to the failure to win control of the air. As Hitler made the crucial decision to invade contingent upon a nebulous concept of control of the air, the traditional argument has been that the invasion fleet could not sail because Germany did not gain air superiority over English skies. Ostensibly this represented a direct causal link between the continued survival of Fighter Command and the cancellation of Operation Sea Lion. But Hitler and an apprehensive German Naval Staff were never disposed to accept they would achieve the degree of superiority required for a landing, despite optimistic Luftwaffe intelligence reports and the reality of heavy damage inflicted upon 11 Group's infrastructure. Hitler appreciated the exceptional risks inherent in launching Operation Sea Lion but his "brittle" hold on the German military could not allow him to back away from military confrontation without a good excuse, and the Naval Staff's negative appreciation of the air situation provided it. Hitler also lacked the necessary ideological motivation to fortify himself for such a task. German witnesses have indicated his admiration for Britain and the empire together with a genuine desire to reach an understanding that long predated Operation Sea Lion. Strong evidence shows that German planners did not wish for a confrontation with the Royal Navy as they never believed the Luftwaffe could adequately compensate for the immense numerical superiority of the Royal Navy over the Kriegsmarine. Despite some Luftwaffe success around Norway, German warplanes had not proved they were capable of offsetting British naval superiority to the necessary degree. The evidence indicates that the Luftwaffe lacked equipment, training, and "spirit" for this particular task. By contrast, the morale of the Royal Navy was high, and despite the limitations of the AA defense, naval warships had substantial passive defense characteristics allowing the Channel flotillas and the Home Fleet to exist as an effective "fleet-in-being." All of this points to a stronger British defensive position than was generally recognized at the time.

Ultimately, the Battle *for* Britain was the struggle to keep Britain in the war as an obstacle to Axis expansion and the outcome depended on the determination of politicians, the British public, the British army, the Merchant Navy, and the RAF—but in my opinion the principal shield was the Royal Navy. Although Admiral Forbes was not called upon to fight his way through the Dover Straits, the Royal Navy maintained pressure upon the Germans by bombarding invasion harbors while struggling to maintain some protection for the hard-pressed merchant fleet. Forbes had worked his way up during the "Locust Years"—a period when the Royal Navy had to make pragmatic and successful tactical revisions to offset the perceived technical advances of foreign navies. Though his ships had badly mauled the Kriegsmarine during the Norway campaign, he also failed to read German intentions in time to avert the invasion of that country and failed to correctly identify the assailant of the *Rawalpindi*. While these errors make it impossible for him to receive the mantle of tactical genius, it must be remembered that even Nelson did not always divine enemy intentions accurately and Forbes was badly let down by the failures of the British intelligence system. Even the Admiralty was not exempt from organizational failures and evidence has been examined that indicates their internal failures of communication led to unnecessary losses. However, the Royal Navy was not a backward or reactionary organization and knew the value of good intelligence.

While both Forbes and Dowding endured interference from superiors during their tenures of command, my sympathy has been reserved for Forbes. With a prime minister who virtually "hobby-managed" the war effort aided by a "meddler" of questionable competence as First Sea Lord, Forbes had much more to endure. Furthermore, the naval structures ensured that a C-in-C's freedom of action would be curtailed whenever Admiralty superiors thought this desirable. By contrast, Dowding had the advantage of having built a complex system with innovative features that few really understood and his special expertise enabled him to resist "interference" until the air situation became intolerable. Dowding's narrow outlook limited his strategic vision but the same could not be said for Forbes, who was perhaps the only senior military figure to accurately read German intentions from June to October 1940. Unfortunately, he failed to impress his superiors but there is some evidence that Churchill was more convinced than he was prepared to publicly admit.

Forbes fell victim to a purge of senior officers in late 1940 and did not receive the recognition he deserved. Arguments with the Admiralty over ship dispositions, a tendency to be outspoken, his criticisms of Lord Mountbatten, and a failure to attend to his own public relations all ensured his downfall. However, the military figures that mattered to Churchill and the clique of journalists at the center of power were those who could project heroic images, essential for maintaining the support of the United States. Dowding was also incapable of this but as the acclaimed victor of the daylight air battles, Churchill gave him the chance to shine as part of a technical mission to the United States. Unfortunately, he was not a success.

The problem for many British figures was their uneasiness with the demands of an American media-friendly culture and a fear that focusing on individuals might detract from the efforts of the many. Strong stoics of yesteryear such as Admirals Horatio Nelson, George Anson, and Edward Hawke had been excellent role models for generations of Britons, but for Americans association with the British Empire tainted these figures. More attractive to American war correspondents were the young men of Fighter Command, not least because some were American volunteers. In the final analysis it was far easier to project American cultural ideals upon modern young aviators than "old" upper-class sailors. While the British were astute in recognizing the "weakness" of the American press for aviation "heroes," U.S. columnists initially saw the Battle of Britain as a naval conflict. The primary American concern was for their national security, and the importance of the Royal Navy as America's traditional shield against foreign interference was recognized and strongly asserted. Only as the threat of the British surrendering naval assets to the Axis diminished did some begin to see the "aerial blitzkrieg" as the "real" Battle of Britain. While Americans (with British help) tended to overestimate the Axis threat to their existence, their initial perspective of the Battle of Britain as a naval affair was the most accurate assessment of the situation to have emerged in 1940. This did not necessarily help the British make their case to America because Churchill raised the prospect of a "Vichy style" British government handing over the fleet to Germany. His overly optimistic hopes of early American intervention were dashed by Roosevelt's iron determination (aided by published opinion polls) to avoid direct involvement in the fighting. But the press evidence also indicates that an exaggerated fear of German naval supremacy could still be deployed in U.S. government circles into 1941 as a means of securing Lend-Lease for Britain. This meant that the trickle of essential war materials to Britain would be maintained and massively increased in subsequent years.

Flattering wartime media portrayals—especially those of American origin—simplified the narrative and with Churchill's direct assistance skewed British perceptions, giving undue emphasis to the air dimensions of 1940. So powerful were these perceptions that in 1945 the British government felt that in recognition of British wartime achievements, Americans would be prepared to make them a staggering $5 billion gift to finance their new socialist welfare state. To their surprise—and to the anger of the British press—Americans did not see the situation in the same light; protracted negotiations merely resulted in a $3.75 billion loan with controversial strings—the so-called "mortgage-from-hell."[4] Despite this, the British continued to cling to the legend. Churchill reinforced these ideas by utilizing his postwar sojourn out of office to write his own "case" with the assistance of an academic team who were left in no doubt that matters of historical interpretation were to be left solely to him. Significantly, his team included Albert Goodwin, the original researcher for the Air Ministry pamphlet *The Battle of Britain*.[5] At least Churchill's memoirs acknowledged that he had been more concerned over the "Battle of the Atlantic" than he ever had been about the air campaigns of the Battle of Britain. As Dowding correctly recognized in a 1942 newspaper article, events had shown that airpower had become an essential adjunct of sea power.[6] But it would have been closer to the truth to have stated that sea power had prevented invasion and was keeping open the possibility of liberating Europe at a future date.

Appendix I

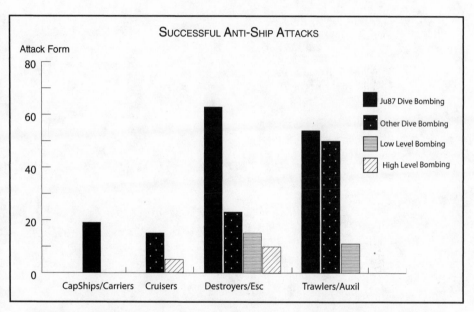

Data in "Tactical Summary of Bombing Attacks by German Aircraft on HM Ships & Shipping, September 1939 to February 1941." TNA ADM 199/1189 /A/NAD326/41

Appendix II

AIRCRAFT DESTROYED

Author	Luftwaffe	Fighter Command	Bomber & Coastal Commands
Richards and Saunders	1,733	915	N/A
Wood and Dempster	1,679	938	N/A
Ramsey	1,882	1,017	N/A
Terraine	N/A	N/A	248 (approx)
Average Loss	1,765	957	248 (approx)

AIR FORCE PERSONNEL LOSSES

Author	Luftwaffe	Fighter Command	Bomber & Coastal Commands
Ramsey	2,662 (approx)	537	N/A
Terraine	N/A	N/A	957/998 (approx)*

RATIO OF LOSS FAVORING RAF

Losses	Luftwaffe to Fighter Command	Luftwaffe to all RAF
Aircraft	1.84:1	1.46:1
Personnel	4.96:1	1.78:1*

*Terraine does not specify a precise number of Bomber and Coastal Command personnel losses. The band of 957/998 losses has been calculated by A. J. Cumming from Terraine's limited data derived from the Roll of Honour in the Battle of Britain Memorial Chapel. The ratio given in the above table uses the lower figure of 957.

Data from sources quoted by J. Terraine, *The Right of the Line* (Wordsworth, 1997), pp. 219–20, and amalgamated in these tables by A. J. Cumming. These sources include D. Richards and H. Saunders, *The Royal Air Force 1939–1945*, vol. 1 (HMSO, 1974); D. Wood and D. Dempster, *The Narrow Margin* (Arrow, 1969); and W. G. Ramsay, ed., "The Battle of Britain Then and Now," *After the Battle Magazine*, 1980.

Notes

Chapter 1: Introduction

1. Winston S. Churchill, Speech in House of Commons, 4 June 1940, as quoted in R. Jenkins, Churchill (Pan Books, 2002), p. 611.
2. TNA CAB 120/438, REF: 95419, Memo from Winston S. Churchill to C-in-C Home Forces, 10 July 1940.
3. ROSK 4/49, Letter from Admiral Charles Forbes to Godfrey Style, 6 February 1947. Forbes is relating a meeting with Churchill at a recent Navy Club dinner.
4. TNA: PREM 4/3/19 and AIR 20/5202, Dowding's "Despatch on the Battle of Britain," par. 106.
5. H. Montgomery Hyde, British Air Policy between the Wars, 1918–1939 (Heinemann Ltd., 1976), pp. 503–4.

Chapter 2: We Can't Simply Swim Over!

1. Vice Admiral K. Assman, "Operation Sea Lion," United States Naval Institute Proceedings 76, no. 1 (1950): 1–13.
2. L. Mosley, Battle of Britain (Pan Books, 1969), p. 35. Galland did not make this allegation in his memoirs. However, when he was asked to be a consultant for the film Battle of Britain, he told one of the producers, Ben Fisz, that "he didn't believe there was any such thing from which it followed that Germany certainly hadn't lost it."
3. A. MacDonald, Winston Churchill and his Great Wars (Scholastic Children's Books, 2004), p. 135.
4. Laurence Rees, series editor, Timewatch: Hitler and the Invasion of Britain (television documentary; Boston: WGBH, 1998). According to the narrator, it was Field Marshal Albert Kesselring who made the remark.
5. K. Macksey, Invasion: The German Invasion of England, July 1940 (Greenhill Books,1980).
6. N. Ferguson, "The Unthinkable," Daily Mail, 26 August 2000, pp. 12–13.
7. G. H. Bennett and R. Bennett, Hitler's Admirals (Naval Institute Press, 2004), p. 14.
8. MoD NID 24.GHS/1, February1947, "German Plans for the Invasion of England in 1940: Operation 'Sea Lion,'" p. 51.
9. "Report of the C-in-C Navy to the Fuehrer on May 21, 1940 at 12:00," signed Raeder, as quoted in J. P. Mallman Showell, Fuehrer Conferences on Naval Affairs, 1940 (Greenhill Books, 1990), p. 5.

10. E. Raeder, *My Life* (United States Naval Institute, 1960), pp. 319–23.

11. From Schniewind to Supreme Command (Air), Fuehrer Headquarters, 26 May 1940; entries of the German Naval High Command War Diary, 30 and 31 May 1940, as quoted in Showell, *Fuehrer Conferences*, pp. 106–7.

12. Raeder, *My Life*, p. 332.

13. "Directive from Fuehrer Headquarters, 7 July 1940," signed Keitel, as quoted in Showell, *Fuehrer Conferences*, pp. 112–13.

14. "Report of the C-in-C Navy to the Fuehrer" on 11 July 1940, signed Raeder, as quoted in Showell, *Fuehrer Conferences*, pp. 113–14.

15. "Directive No.16 Preparations for the Invasion of England," 16 July 1940, signed Hitler and initialed by Keitel and Jodl, in ibid., pp. 116–17.

16. H. A. Jacobsen, ed., *The Halder Diary*, as quoted in E. Kieser, *Hitler on the Door step* (Arms and Armour Press, 1997), p. 95.

17. From the Naval Staff to Hitler, 19 July 1940, as quoted in Showell, *Fuehrer Conferences*, pp. 117–18; Raeder, *My Life*, pp. 324–25.

18. Lord H. Ismay, *The Memoirs of Lord Ismay* (Heinemann, 1960), pp. 188–89. These relationship problems are dealt with in a subsequent chapter.

19. Minsterialdirektor Eckhardt, "Construction of Naval Ports in War," *Nauticus*,1944, and other sources in P. Schenk, *Invasion of England 1940* (Conway Maritime Press, 1990), p. 112.

20. ROSK 5/124, Extract from "An Cosantóir," *The Irish Defence Journal* 1, no.1 (1949), by G. Blumentritt, translated by T. B. Dunne, British Intelligence Section.

21. Vice Admiral F. Ruge, *Sea Warfare, 1939–1945* (Cassell & Co., 1957), p. 85. Ruge's reputation was strong enough for him to participate with General Adolf Galland in a war game simulation of Operation Sea Lion at the Royal Military Academy in the 1970s. Ruge claimed that if Royal Navy units had penetrated the mine barriers, the Luftwaffe would have had serious problems identifying friend from foe within the crossing zone.

22. LH 15/15/149/3, "Notes for History: Talk with Field Marshal von Rundstedt, 26 October 1945."

23. Ruge, *Sea Warfare*, pp. 84–85. Ruge mentions thirty-three tugs each towing two barges. However it is generally accepted that some barge lines would have been much longer and very hard to maneuver.

24. Ibid., p. 85; Schenk, *Invasion of England 1940*, pp. 327–28. These coastal batteries only sank the auxiliary minesweeper *Brighton Queen* in June 1940, although they certainly deterred merchant ships from entering this area. Schenk believed the guns would have taken a heavy toll of larger warships but not the smaller ones.

25. "Conference on 21 July 1940," in Showell, *Fuehrer Conferences*, pp. 119–20.

26. "Conference on 25 July 1940," in Showell, *Fuehrer Conferences*, pp. 120–21. Also see Raeder, *My Life*, p. 327.

27. Raeder, *My Life*, p. 327.

28. J. Adams, *The Doomed Expedition* (Leo Cooper, 1987), p. 176. Adams points out that an unexpected compensatory bonus from the Norwegian expedition was control

of the large Norwegian merchant fleet of 1.5 million tons passing to the British via the Norwegian Trade Mission in London.

29. "Conference on 31 July 1940," in Showell, *Fuehrer Conferences*, pp. 123–24.

30. Showell, *Fuehrer Conferences*, p. 125. Showell's commentary refers to a meeting between Admiral Schniewind of the Naval Staff and Colonel General Halder on 7 August 1940.

31. "Report of the C-in-C Navy to the Fuehrer on 13 August 1940," signed Raeder, in Showell, *Fuehrer Conferences*, p. 126. See Raeder, *My Life*, pp. 328–29, for details of the torpedo problems. See Churchill, *The Second World War*, vol. 2, *Their Finest Hour* (Cassell, 1949), app. 4, p. 639, for details of shipping losses. British losses alone were 82,429 gross tons in May rising to 278,323 gross tons in August 1940.

32. "Directive from the Fuehrer's Headquarters," 16 August 1940, in Showell, *Fuehrer Conferences*, p. 128.

33. Showell, *Fuehrer Conferences*, p. 128.

34. Kieser, *Hitler on the Doorstep*, p. 132.

35. IWM EDS docs, AL1492, Aktennotiz, OKW, 20 August 1940, translation by Dr. I. Roberts, Dartmouth Naval College, May 2004. Dr. Roberts' translation notes advise it is unclear whether the brief is to or from the head of *Wi Rü Amt* (Department for Economy and Armament).

36. Doering personally related this account in *Timewatch: Hitler and the Invasion of Britain*.

37. A. B. Liddell Hart, *The Other Side of the Hill* (Papermac, 1993), p. 220.

38. MoD Naval Historical Branch, NID 24/GHS/1, "German Plans for the Invasion of England in 1940–Operation Sea Lion," February 1947, pp. 77–78.

39. Ibid., p. 56.

40. Report of General Paul Deichmann to Air Fleet II, as quoted by K. Klee, "The Battle of Britain," in H. A. Jacobsen and J. Rohwer, *Decisive Battles of World War II: The German View* (André Deutsch, 1965), p. 83.

41. N. von Below, *At Hitler's Side: The Memoirs of Hitler's Luftwaffe Adjutant, 1937–1945* (Greenhill Books, 2001), p. 73.

42. P. B. Lucas, *Flying Colours* (Hutchinson & Co., 1981), p. 125; J. Terraine, *The Right of the Line* (Wordsworth, 1997), pp. 207–9; H. R. Allen, *Who Won the Battle of Britain?* (Panther, 1976), pp. 124 and 178.

43. MoD, "German Plans for the Invasion," p. 56.

44. H. Macmillan, *Winds of Change* (London, 1966), p. 522, as quoted in E. Ranson, *British Defence Policy and Appeasement between the Wars, 1919–1939* (The Historical Association, 1993), p. 27. According to former British prime minister Harold Macmillan: "[W]e thought of air warfare in 1938 rather as people think of nuclear warfare today."

45. MoD, "German Plans for the Invasion," p. 59.

46. Allen, *Who Won the Battle of Britain?*, p. 204.

47. This opinion of Kesselring's is mentioned in *Timewatch: Hitler and the Invasion of Britain*.

48. Raeder, *My Life*, p. 330. Also "Report of the C-in-C Navy to the Fuehrer in the After noon of 6 September 1940," as quoted in Showell, *Fuehrer Conferences*, pp. 132–36.

49. War Diary entry for 10 September 1940, as quoted in Showell, *Fuehrer Conferences*, p. 136.

50. ROSK 4/86, From M. Saunders, Cabinet office, to S. Roskill, 20 March 1952, alleges mistranslation of p. 98 of the 1940 edition of *Fuehrer Conferences*.

51. MoD, "German Plans for the Invasion," pp. 67–68. A. Martienssen, *Hitler and his Admirals* (Secker & Warburg Ltd., 1948), p. 87, indicated eighty barges sunk at Ostend on 13 September 1940. Schenk sums up losses from all locations as "twelve transports, four tugs, and fifty-one barges, putting them out of action permanently or temporarily." He also mentioned that "nine transports, one tug, and 163 barges were damaged, though they could be replaced from reserves."

52. "Channel Bases Shelled," *Daily Express*, 12 September 1940, p. 1.

53. Ibid.

54. D. Robinson, *Invasion 1940: The Truth about the Battle of Britain and What Stopped Hitler* (Constable, 2005), pp. 262–63. The Air Ministry claimed the credit for destroying these barges in their wartime publication, *The Air Ministry Account of Bomber Command's Offensive against the Axis, September 1939–July 1941* (HMSO,1941), p. 67. Churchill was skeptical about the photographic evidence supporting the Air Ministry case. See "Prime Minister to Secretary of State for Air, 23 September 1940," in W. S. Churchill, *The Second World War*, vol. 2, *Their Finest Hour*, p. 405.

55. "Report of the Naval Staff, 10 September 1940," in Showell, *Fuehrer Conferences*, p. 136.

56. "Conference between the C-in-C Navy and the Fuehrer in the Afternoon of 14 September 1940," signed Raeder, and directives of 14 and 19 September 1940, in Showell, *Fuehrer Conferences*, pp. 137–39.

57. K. Macksey, *Invasion: The German Invasion of England, July 1940* (Greenhill Books, 1980), p. 209.

58. Ferguson, "The Unthinkable."

59. Assman, "Operation Sea Lion." Presumably Assman's questioners had in mind the Hossbach Conference of November 1937, when Hitler vented his frustration with British foreign policy and defined the principles upon which his own policy rested. Assman was head of the Historical Section of the German Naval High Command in 1933 and the official German naval historian for World War I, lecturing on naval strategy at the German Naval Academy.

60. TNA ADM 223/696, Essay by General Admiral O. Schniewind and Admiral K. Schuster, 26 November 1945.

61. Memorandum from Raeder to Hitler, 19 July 1940, as quoted in Showell, *Fuehrer Conferences*, pp. 117–18.

62. Schniewind and Schuster, 26 November 1945; Assman, "Operation Sea Lion."

63. Schniewind and Schuster, 26 November 1945.

64. TNA ADM 1/11397, "Operations XD and XDA: Recognition of Officers and Men." Also Appendix III: "Demolitions Carried Out."

65. A. Calder, *The Myth of the Blitz* (Pimlico, 1997), p. 94.

66. Liddell Hart, *The Other Side of the Hill*, p. 94.

67. LH 15/15/149/3, "Notes for History: Talk with Field Marshal von Rundstedt, 26 October 1945," p. 2.

68. Ibid., p. 3.

69. Schenk, *Invasion of England*, pp. 197–98; LH15/15/149/3, "Notes for History: Talk with Field Marshal von Rundstedt," p. 3.

70. TNA AIR 20/226, Appendix A: "Invasion by Glider-Borne Troops," 24 July 1940.

71. Cato, *Guilty Men* (Penguin Books, 1940), p. vi.

72. I. S. Wood, *Churchill* (Macmillan Press Ltd., 2000), p. 81; W. S. Churchill, *The Second World War*, vol. 1, *The Gathering Storm* (Penguin, 2005), pp. 108–11.

73. Bennett and Bennett, *Hitler's Admirals*, pp. 13, 21. Boehm was a favorite of Admiral Raeder and assisted with the latter's defense at Nuremberg after the war.

74. TNA ADM 223/692, Essay by General Admiral Boehm, 26 October 1945. According to D. Miller, *The Illustrated Directory of Warships* (Greenwich Editions, 2004), pp. 186–87, the *Scharnhorst* class were under-armed and vulnerable even to older British battleships. Displacement was 31,850 tons standard. Details of the Z-Plan are contained in Bennett and Bennett, *Hitler's Admirals*, pp. 23–24. The finalized plan was for "6 battleships of 56,000 tons; 2 battleships (*Bismarck* and *Tirpitz*) of 42,000 tons; 2 battleships (*Scharnhorst* and *Gneisenau*) of 31,000 tons; 3 battle cruisers of 31,000 tons; 3 pocket battleships; and two aircraft carriers." Implementation of the plan was severely handicapped by the lack of an adequate naval infrastructure, hence the long period over which the program was envisaged.

75. TNA ADM 223/690, Essay by Vice Admiral H. Heye, 15 October 1945.

76. TNA FO 371/47018, Essay by Admiral O. Schultze, 1 November 1945.

77. TNA ADM 223/797, Vice Admiral E. Weichold, 26 November 1945.

78. TNA ADM 223/688, Essay by Grand Admiral K. Doenitz, 24 September 1945.

79. TNA ADM 223/689, Essay by Admiral T. Kranke, 2 October 1945.

80. TNA ADM 223/691, Essay by Rear Admiral H. Meyer, 16 October 1945.

81. TNA ADM 223/691, Preface to Meyer's essay by R. G. Rushbrooke.

82. TNA ADM 1/9956, Translation of Vice Admiral W. Wegener, *Seestrategie des Weltkrieges* (The Naval Strategy of the World War), p. 1, submitted by Naval Attaché, Berlin, 1939.

83. A. Herman, *To Rule the Waves: How the British Navy Shaped the Modern World* (Hodder and Stoughton, 2005), p. 220. The phrase "fleet-in-being" was probably first coined by Lord Torrington, who used it to defend himself at his 1690 court martial following the Battle of Beachy Head. Torrington was accused of abandoning his Dutch allies but he was able to argue that by keeping his fleet more or less intact he helped to prevent the French from invading England. Herman argued that the concept became a "hallmark of British naval policy for 200 years" and justified maintaining a large fleet in peacetime.

Reference to the "Belts" seems to mean the channels between Norway and Denmark labeled Lilla Baelt and Store Baelt through which shipping from the Baltic must pass into the Kattegat, Skatterak, and North Sea. The German coastline directly open to the North Sea, including Wilhelmshaven around the Heligoland Bight, is short and susceptible to blockade.

CHAPTER 3: BOMBERS VERSUS BATTLESHIPS

1. Viscount A. B. Cunningham, *A Sailor's Odyssey* (Hutchinson &Co.,1951), p391.
2. F. W. Winterbotham, *The Ultra Secret* (Weidenfeld & Nicolson, 1999), p. 68.
3. For example, Dr. C. Bellamy, "The Battle of Britain," http://www.bbc.co.uk/history/war/wwtwo/battle_of_britain_print.html, BBC (accessed 3 May 2004), and M. Middlebrook and P. Mahoney, *Battleship: The Loss of the Prince of Wales and the Repulse* (Penguin Books, 1979), pp. 17–20, testify to the power of Royal Navy warships in 1940.
4. *Timewatch: Hitler and the Invasion of Britain.*
5. Middlebrook and Mahoney, *Battleship*, pp. 17–20.
6. A. Hezlet, *Aircraft and Sea Power* (Peter Davies, 1970), pp. 155–56.
7. IWM 95/5/1, Papers of Lieutenant Commander J. A. J. Dennis, RN, p. 14.
8. C. Barnett, *Engage the Enemy More Closely: The Royal Navy in the SecondWorld War* (Hodder & Stoughton, 1991), p. 47.
9. Admiral Sir Studholm Brownrigg, "Gunnery in the Royal Navy," in Admiral Sir Reginald Bacon, ed., *Britain's Glorious Navy* (Odhams Press Ltd., 1942), p. 213. Brownrigg was C-in-C of the Nore at the outbreak of war before replacement by Admiral Drax at the end of 1939.
10. J. Campbell, *Naval Weapons of World War II* (Conway Maritime Press, 1985), p. 8.
11. D. Hamer, *Bombers versus Battleships* (Conway Maritime Press, 1998), pp. 41–45; J. Campbell, *Naval Weapons of World War II* (Conway Maritime Press, 1985), pp. 8–18. Quotation from Hamer, p. 45.
12. R. Hough, *Bless Our Ship: Mountbatten and the Kelly* (Coronet Books, 1991), p. 51.
13. TNA ADM 186/338, *C.B 3001/36—Progress in Naval Gunnery—Part VII: Gunnery in Foreign Navies*, 1936, p. 96. This mentions the Japanese practicing at very long range. This included 28,000 meters.
14. TNA CAB 16/137, "Proposed Purchase of Anti Aircraft Guns from Messrs. Bofors (Paper No. D. P. R. 187)," 29 April 1937.
15. Hough, *Bless Our Ship*, p. 48.
16. Lambert, *Sir John Fisher's Naval Revolution* (University of South Carolina Press, 1999), pp. 145, 147–51.
17. Hough, *Bless Our Ship*, p. 49.
18. TNA ADM 199/1189 A/NAD326/41, "Tactical Summary of Bombing Attacks by German Aircraft on HM Ships and Shipping from September 1939 to February 1941."
19. E. Angelucci and P. Matricardi, *World Aircraft: World War II, Part 1* (Sampson Low, 1978), p. 106. Stuka is an abbreviation for Sturzkampfflugzeug, meaning dive bomber.

Strictly speaking this term applied to all aircraft that employed dive-bombing techniques but is popularly applied exclusively to the Ju 87.

20. G. Paust and M. Lancelot, *Fighting Wings* (Essential Books, 1944), pp. 136, 145.

21. TNA ADM 199/66, "Page 2 of Enclosure No. II to Commanding Officer, HMS *Curacoa's* letter No. 0307/19 of 5 May 1940," par. 13.

22. TNA ADM 199/1189 A/NAD326/41, "Tactical Summary of Bombing Attacks by German Aircraft on HM Ships and Shipping from September 1939 to February 1941," Tables I & II.

23. MoD NID 24/GHS/1, February 1947, "German Plans for the Invasion of England in 1940—Operation Sea Lion," Statistics, p. 53.

24. Schenk, *Invasion of England*, p. 246.

25. TNA 95419 CAB 120/438, L. G. Hollis to Prime Minister, 19 October 1946, enclosing "German Preparations for Invasion in 1940," p. 2.

26. TNA ADM 199/1189 A/NAD326/41, "Tactical Summary of Bombing Attacks by German Aircraft on HM Ships and Shipping from September 1939 to February 1941," Table I.

27. IWM HTT 226, Tizard Papers FC/S.18093, Letter from Dowding to Wing Commander J. Whitworth Jones, Air Ministry, 25 November 1939.

28. Paust and Lancelot, *Fighting Wings*, p. 65.

29. J. Terraine, *The Right of the Line*, p. 674. Terraine mentions that on 15 September 1944, *Tirpitz* was attacked and damaged by twenty-seven Lancasters using "Tallboy" (12,000–14,000-pound) and "Johnny Walker" anti-shipping bombs. Only on 12 November 1944 did bombers carrying "Tallboys" finish her off.

30. A Serving Officer in the Naval Air Arm, "The Naval Air Arm—Yesterday and Today," in Bacon, *Britain's Glorious Navy*, p. 127.

31. TNA ADM 199/1189 A/NAD326/41, "Tactical Summary of Bombing by German Aircraft on HM Ships and Shipping from September 1939 to February 1941," pp. 4–5.

32. Ibid., p. 10.

33. M. Griehl, *Junkers Ju 87 Stuka* (Airlife Publishing Ltd., 2001), p. 201.

34. J. Campbell, *Naval Weapons of World War II* (Conway Maritime Press, 1985), p. 276. Precise labeling of bomb types taken from The Royal Engineers Bomb Disposal Officers Club, "A Short History of Royal Engineer Bomb Disposal," http://www.bomb disposalclub.org.uk/BD_history.htm (accessed 27 June 2004). Details of PC bomb from "The Luftwaffe over the Bristol Area—Luftwaffe Weapons," http://www.fish ponds.freeuk.com/nluftbri5.htm (accessed 27 June 2004).

35. Telephone interview with Lieutenant Colonel E. Wakeling on 2 July 2004.

36. A. Galland, *The First and the Last* (Cerberus Publishing Co., 2001), p. 61.

37. Griehl, *Junkers Ju 87 Stuka*, pp.71–72.

38. Ibid., pp. 69,137. Griehl mentions an unspecified number of Italian Ju 87 B-2s bombing on and around Malta around the end of August to early September 1940.

39. J. H. Narbeth and R. H. S. Bacon, "Battleship Construction," in Bacon, Britain's *Glorious Navy*, pp. 110–11.

40. IWM 95/5/1, Papers of Commander J. A. J. Dennis, RN, p. 68.

41. Ron Babb, interview by A. J. Cumming, Bishopsteignton, Devon on 7 April 2004.

42. ROSK 4/49, Letter from "Turtle" Hamilton to Forbes from HMS Aurora, dated 27 May 1940.

43. TNA ADM 1/9920 1536368, Register No. TSD 295/39/G, "Air Attacks on Home Fleet, 26 September 1939," par. 9.

44. Ibid., Minute from G. M. B. Langley for Director of Naval Air Division, 18 October 1939.

45. Ibid., Minute from Director of Naval Ordnance, 11 December 1939.

46. Interview by A. J. Cumming with Sidney Tyas, 25 October 2005.

47. E-mail from J. A. J. Dennis to A. J. Cumming, 27 January 2007.

48. G. B. Mason, "HMS *Gurkha*—Tribal Class Destroyer," in *Service Histories of Royal Navy Warships in World War 2*, http://www.naval-history.net/xGM-Chrono-10DD-34Tribal-Gurkha1.htm (accessed 10 May 2009).

49. G. Sheffield, "Morale," in R. Holmes, ed., *The Oxford Companion to Military History* (Oxford University Press, 2001), pp. 599–600.

50. TNA ADM 1/9920, Minute from G. N. Oliver, Director of Training & Staff Duties, 13 October 1939.

51. Ibid., Minute from Director of Naval Intelligence, 9 November 1939.

52. TNA ADM 1/10225, "Morale in the Home Fleet," Minute from Director of Personnel Services, 13 December 1939.

53. Ibid., Minute dated 20 December 1939 from Admiral Godfrey, Director of Naval Intelligence.

54. TNA ADM 199/66, "Page 2 of Enclosure No. II to Commanding officer, HMS *Curacoa's* letter No. 0307/191 of 5th May 1940," par. 12.

55. Ron Babb, interview by author, 7 April 2004.

56. TNA ADM 199/66, Page 2 of Enclosure No. II to Commanding Officer, HMS *Curacoa's* letter No. 0307/19, 5 May 1940, par. 13.

57. R. Spector, *At War at Sea* (Allen Lane, 2001), p. 169.

58. Cunningham, *A Sailor's Odyssey*, p. 358.

59. Ibid., p. 363.

60. IWM, Papers of J. A. J. Dennis, p. 121.

61. A. B. Cunningham, "Report on the Battle of Crete," reproduced in M. Simpson, ed., *The Cunningham Papers* (The Navy Records Society, 1999), p. 422.

62. ROSK 4/50, Letter from Godfrey Style to Captain S. Roskill, 10 March 1979.

63. Hough, *Bless Our Ship*, p. 159.

64. IWM, Papers of Commander J. A. J. Dennis, p. 56.

65. Cunningham, "Report on the Battle of Crete," in Simpson, *Cunningham Papers*, p. 422.

66. Ibid., p. 423.

67. IWM, Papers of J. A. J. Dennis, pp. 123–24.

68. J. Johnston, *The Complete Idiot's Guide to Psychology* (Alpha Books, 2000), pp. 192–93.

69. Cunningham, "Report on the Battle of Crete," in Simpson, *Cunningham Papers*, p. 181.

70. IWM, Dept. of Sound Recordings, Interview with G. W. Deacon 9316/4/4, as quoted in Spector, *At War at Sea*, p. 183.

71. Signal from Cunningham to First Sea Lord, dated 30 May 1941 as quoted in Simpson, *Cunningham Papers*, p. 417.

72. Cunningham, *A Sailor's Odyssey*, p. 378; Spector, *At War at Sea*, p. 183.

73. Cunningham, "Report on the Battle of Crete," in Simpson, *Cunningham Papers*, p. 423.

74. S. David, *Military Blunders* (Constable and Robinson Ltd., 1997), p. 347. David's estimate of naval losses confirmed in W. S. Churchill, *Second World War*, vol. 3, *The Grand Alliance* (Penguin, 2005), p. 269. Luftwaffe losses from Hezlet, *Aircraft and Sea Power*, p. 172.

75. L. Deighton, *Fighter: The True Story of the Battle of Britain* (Jonathan Cape, 1977), p. 138. Range for the Ju 87 B-1 from Angelucci and Matricardi, *World Aircraft: World War II, Part 1*, but Deighton quotes the Ju 87 B-1 radius as only 150 miles, thus suggesting this aircraft could reach nowhere near as far as the Wash. Presumably he meant the Ju 87 B-2 with a more powerful engine and heavier bomb load that may have resulted in a more limited range than the B-1.

76. TNA ADM 199/65 1486/39, "Air Attacks against Ships, 1939," Minute from R. M. Ellis for DNAD to Director of Trades Division, dated 14 December 1939.

77. Hezlet, *Aircraft and Sea Power*, p. 145.

78. TNA ADM 199/64, From Admiral Drax to the Admiralty, dated 3 August 1940; "Suggestions by Rear Admiral Fraser (F.O.I.C. Harwich No.Q.102.A/40 of 26 July, 1940)."

79. TNA ADM 199/64, From Rear Admiral Fraser to Flag Officer Harwich, dated 26 July 1940, "Interception of Enemy Aircraft Attacking the Coast and Shipping off the Coast."

80. TNA ADM 1/9920 1546368, T. S. D. 295/39/G, "Air Attacks on Home Fleet, 26 September 1939 (8)."

81. Prime Minister to Secretary of State for Air, 23 September 1940, as quoted in Allen, *Who Won the Battle of Britain?*, p. 139.

82. Aerial photograph of Dunkirk, in "Why the Invasion Armada Never Sailed," in *Bomber Command: The Air Ministry Account of Bomber Command's Offensive against the Axis, September 1939–July 1941* (HMSO, 1941), p. 67.

83. Hezlet, *Aircraft and Sea Power*, p. 172.

84. Griehl, *Junkers Ju 87 Stuka*, p. 201.

85. Data relating to RN resources at time of Crete in Hezlet, *Aircraft and Sea Power*, pp. 172–73. It cannot be assumed that all of these 130 aircraft would have been manned or even that the numbers of naval fighters were exactly the same in September 1940 as they were in May 1941. Churchill indicated that fifty-five pilots were transferred from the Royal Navy to the RAF and took part in the Battle of Britain; see Churchill, *The Second World War*, vol. 2, *Their Finest Hour*, p. 144.

CHAPTER 4: WHO WON THE BATTLE OF BRITAIN?

1. Allen, *Who Won the Battle of Britain?*, p. 191.

2. TNA ADM 1/10556, From Forbes to Admiralty, 4 June 1940.

3. W. S. Churchill, "Their Finest Hour," speech to Parliament at Westminster, 18 June 1940, The Churchill Centre and Museum at Cabinet War Rooms, London, http://winstonchurchill.org/learn/speeches-of-winston-churchill/1940-finest-hour/122-their-finest-hour(accessed 3 March 2010).

4. F. K. Mason, "Well, who did?—and who didn't?" *RUSI Journal of the United Service Institute for Defence Studies* 119, no.4 (1974): 84–85.

5. H. Montgomery Hyde, *British Air Policy between the Wars, 1918–1939* (Heinemann Ltd., 1976), pp. 503–5.

6. Allen, *Who Won the Battle of Britain?*, p. 182.

7. For example, German historian Dr. Karl Klee wrote that "the invasion and subjugation of Britain was made to depend on victory in that battle and its outcome therefore materially influenced both the further course and the fate of the war as a whole." K. Klee in Jacobsen and Rohwer, *Decisive Battles of World War II*, p. 91. Also see Luftwaffe General Werner Kreipe's statement that it was a strategic failure contributing "to our ultimate defeat." Kreipe also described the decision to fight the Battle of Britain as a "turning point" and asserted that the "German Air Force . . . was bled almost to death," as quoted in Terraine, *The Right of the Line*, p. 219.

8. Conversation between Galland and Ben Fisz in 1967 as reported in Mosley, *Battle of Britain*, p. 35.

9. Mosley, *Battle of Britain*, pp. 196–97.

10. Table II, "Monthly Totals of Shipping Losses, British, Allied, and Neutral, May 1940 to December 1940," as quoted in Churchill, *The Second World War*, vol. 2, *Their Finest Hour*, p. 639. Figures quoted represent British losses for the period June to September 1940 inclusive.

11. Churchill to Roosevelt, 8 December 1940, in Churchill, *The Second World War*, vol. 2, *Their Finest Hour*, pp. 499, 529.

12. Ibid., p. 529.

13. Churchill's daughter-in-law Pamela Harriman, speaking on the television documentary *Churchill*, UKTV History, broadcast 26 October 2004.

14. Prime Minister to Secretary of State for Air, in Churchill, *The Second World War*, vol. 2, *Their Finest Hour*, p. 561.

15. TNA AIR 16/677, Dowding to Air Ministry, "Strength of Fighter Squadrons Necessary for the Defence of Great Britain," 16 September 1939.

16. R. Wright, *Dowding and the Battle of Britain* (MacDonald, 1969), pp. 103–9.

17. TNA AIR 10/5556, "The Employment of the Bomber Force in the Event of Invasion of Holland and/or Belgium, Note by the Chief of the Air Staff," 9 May 1940.

18. TNA AIR 2/7068, Dowding to Air Ministry, 16 May 1940.

19. Wright, *Dowding*, pp. 102–7, 111–17.

20. TNA AIR 10/5556, Loose draft, "Fighter Strength," dated "about 24 May 1940."

21. L. McKinstry, "How the Spitfire Nearly Missed Its Finest Hour," *BBC History Magazine* 8, no. 11 (2007): 17–20.

22. TNA CAB 27/648, "Appendix. Air Ministry Programme. CP. 218(38). Minute by the Chancellor of the Exchequer."

23. C. Ponting, *1940: Myth & Reality* (Hamish Hamilton Ltd., 1990), pp. 30–32.

24. TNA CAB 27/648 CP 247 (38), Minute by the Chancellor of the Exchequer.

25. N. Gibbs, *Grand Strategy*, vol. 1, *Rearmament Policy* (HMSO, 1976), pp. 38–39.

26. LH 11/1943/27, "The Battle of Britain," Extract from a Letter from Air Marshall Sir Hugh Dowding, 9 May 1943.

27. Deighton, *Fighter*, p. 68.

28. TNA AIR 6/60, Air Council, "Increase of Output of Pilots," Note by AMT and AMSO, 6 August 1940.

29. TNA AIR 41/15, *The Air Historical Branch Narrative*, pp. 395–97. Also see Churchill, *The Second World War*, vol. 2, *Their Finest Hour*, pp. 291–92.

30. TNA AIR 16/609, Table: "Casualties to Personnel of Fighter Command, 10 July–31 October 1940—Killed on Operations."

31. TNA AIR 41/15, *Narrative*, p. 396.

32. Ibid., pp. 395–97.

33. T. Hamilton, *The Life and Times of Pilot Officer Prune* (HMSO, 1991), p. 39.

34. Peter Brothers, interview by Nigel Lewis, "The Fewer," *BBC History Magazine* 1, no. 2 (2000): 16.

35. TNA AIR 16/636, "Minutes of Conference on Training held at Headquarters, Fighter Command at 11.00 Hours on 23.10.1940."

36. TNA AIR 41/15, "Dowding to S of S, 15 November 1940," *Narrative*, p. 400.

37. AIR 19/488, Minute to DCAS, 23 November 1940, minute to S of S dated 25 November 1940, and undated minute signed "AHMS."

38. Allen, *Who Won the Battle of Britain?*, p. 186.

39. Lucas, *Flying Colours*, p. 95.

40. TNA AIR 2/7355, Park to Dowding, "German Air Attacks on England 8 Aug–10 Sept," 12 September 1940, par. 18.

41. J. E. Johnson and P. B. Lucas, *Glorious Summer* (Stanley Paul & Co., Ltd., 1990), p. 3.

42. P. Townsend, *Time and Chance* (Book Club Associates, 1978), p. 111, as quoted in Bishop, *Fighter Boys: Saving Britain 1940* (Harper Perennial, 2003), p. 314.

43. IWM, Ref. no. 10478, as quoted in Bishop, *Fighter Boys*, p. 315.

44. IWM, Archie Winskill no. 11537, as quoted in Bishop, *Fighter Boys*, p. 315.

45. Bishop, *Fighter Boys*, pp. 92–93.

46. IWM HTT 226, Tizard papers, Letter from Dowding to Tizard, 25 November 1939.

47. Another factor likely to compound this error would have come from the literature the pilots read as boys during the inter-war years. Some may have read Manfred von Richthofen's *Der Rote Kampfflieger* (The Red Battle Flyer), in which the use of short bursts was advocated. Only inexperienced pilots fired long bursts.

48. IWM HTT 226, Tizard papers, Letter from Dowding to Tizard, 25 November 1939. Deighton also mentions an incident during the Battle of Britain when six Spitfires

of 74 Squadron failed to bring down a Dornier Do 17 despite firing seven thousand bullets; see Deighton, *Fighter*, p. 107.

49. Allen, *Who Won the Battle of Britain?*, p. 79.

50. TNA AIR 33/10, "Report No. 11. Visit to Sutton Bridge on 3 May 1940. Notes by the Inspector General," dated 14 May 1940, signed Ludlow Hewitt, Air Chief Marshal, Inspector General.

51. TNA AIR16/659, Letter from RAF Staff College to Dowding, 3 October 1940.

52. Angelucci and Matricardi, *World Aircraft World War II, Part 1*, p. 57.

53. McKinstry, "How the Spitfire Nearly Missed Its Finest Hour," pp. 18–20.

54. Table in Allen, *Who Won the Battle of Britain?*, p. 80.

55. Mason, "Well, who did?—and who didn't?" p. 85.

56. Deighton, *Fighter*, Table 2, p. 106. This gives a gun weight of twenty-two pounds for the Browning and advises that each gun carried three hundred rounds. Table does not include details of the Colt.

57. Letter from the Imperial War Museum to A. J. Cumming dated 21 September 2000, quoting R. Wallace Clarke, *British Aircraft Armament*, vol. 2, *RAF Guns and Gunsights from 1914 to the Present Day* (Sparkford Stephens, 1993).

58. Note by the Controller of Research and Development (Air Marshal Sir R. Sorley) in Appendix VI, "Factors Involved in the Conception of the 8-Gun Fighter," in M. Postan et al., *History of the Second World War: Design and Development of Weapons: Studies on Government and Industrial Organisation* (HMSO, 1964), pp. 538–39.

59. Ibid.

60. Postan et al., *Design and Development of Weapons*, p. 103. Also see Deighton, *Fighter*, p. 102. The gull-wing prototype flew in 1933, but the redesigned prototype with curved wings and Rolls Royce engine flew in 1936.

61. R. Wallace Clark, "Main Aircraft Guns Used by the Major Powers in the Second World War," in P. Jarrett, ed., *Aircraft of the Second World War* (Putnam Aeronautical Books, 1997), p. 199.

62. Mason, "Well, who did?—and who didn't?" p. 85. Also see Sorley, Appendix VI in Postan, *Design and Development of Weapons*, p. 538.

63. Letter from Imperial War Museum as quoted in Allen, *Who Won the Battle of Britain?*, pp. 78–79.

64. Postan, *Design and Development of Weapons*, p. 108.

65. Ibid., p. 109.

66. IWM HTT 226, Letter from Tizard to Dowding, 24 November 1939. Though a civilian scientist in World War I, Tizard had learned to fly at his own expense. On one occasion, while flying a Sopwith Camel he unsuccessfully attacked a German Gotha bomber, breaking off when his guns jammed. Wallace Clark (in Jarrett, *Aircraft*, p. 199) indicated the Browning .50 and Colt Browning Mk II were separate guns but with almost identical specifications.

67. IWM HTT 226, Dowding to Tizard, dated 25 November 1939.

68. Allen, *Who Won the Battle of Britain?*, p. 80.

69. Allen, *Who Won the Battle of Britain?*, p. 79.

70. TNA AIR 20/5202, "Dowding's Despatch," par. 14–19 (iii).

71. Deighton, *Fighter*, p. 107.

72. IWM HTT 113, Letter from Dowding to Air Vice Marshal W. S. Sholto Douglas, dated 6 July 1938.

73. Postan, *Design and Development of Weapons*, p. 53.

74. Bishop, *Fighter Boys*, p. 92.

75. TNA AIR 16/636, "Notes on the Conference Held at Headquarters, Fighter Command, on 5 December 1941 to Discuss Raising the Standard of Training at Fighter Command OTUs."

76. IWM HTT 226, Dowding to Tizard, 25 November 1939.

77. Deighton, *Fighter*, pp. 172–73.

78. R. Hough and D. Richards, *The Battle of Britain: The Jubilee History* (Hodder and Stoughton, 1989), p. 95.

79. Bishop, *Fighter Boys*, p. 305.

80. TNA AIR 2/3146, From Fighter Command HQ to Air Ministry, "Fighter Tactics," 30 June 1940.

81. IWM HTT 226, Memorandum from Dowding to Group AOC, 25 October 1939, "Lessons from the First Air Combats in the Fighter Command."

82. TNA AIR 2/3146, Minute from DSD to ACAS, dated 7 November 1939.

83. Hough and Richards, *The Battle of Britain*, p. 206.

84. Deighton, *Fighter*, p. 77.

85. Hough and Richards, *The Battle of Britain*, p. 156.

86. TNA AIR 41/15, Signal C.82, Dowding—Group Commanders, *Narrative*, p. 351.

87. A. Price, "Myth and Legend," *Aeroplane Monthly* 25, no.10, iss. 294 (1997): 23.

88. TNA AIR 2/5196, Minute from DCAS to VCAS dated 29 July 1940, and "Extract from the Minutes of the Meeting of the Expansion and Re-Equipment Policy Committee Held on 3 August 1940."

89. Allen, *Who Won the Battle of Britain?*, pp. 191–95. Analysis based on unofficial score lists.

90. Squadron Leader Blackwood, "No. 310 (Czechoslovak) Squadron," http://www.geocities.com/Pentagon/4143/310.html (accessed 10 January 2001).

91. A. Zamoyski, *The Forgotten Few: The Polish Air Force in the Second World War* (John Murray, 1995), p. 91.

92. Allen, *Who Won the Battle of Britain?*, pp. 194–95.

93. Bishop, *Fighter Boys*, p. 322.

94. Jenkins, *Churchill,* p. 632. However, Luftwaffe General Deichmann was "adamant" that this decision was based on military considerations but with the political implication of preparing Britain for peace negotiations. See TNA AIR 2/781, as quoted in Ray, *The Battle of Britain*, pp. 92–93.

95. P. Craig and T. Clayton, "Bravery in the Blitz: Our Finest Hour," *Daily Mail Weekend*, 28 November 1999, p. 18.

96. Bishop, *Fighter Boys*, p. 322.
97. TNA AIR 41/16, Appendix 37, "German Views on the Battle of Britain," *Narrative*, p. 4.
98. LH 11/1943/27, Dowding to Liddell Hart, 9 May 1943.
99. Air Marshal Sir Keith Park's statement on 16 September 1940 at Fighter Command HQ as quoted by the Battle of Britain Historical Society in "The Battle is Won," http://www.battleofbritain1940.net/0052.html (accessed 3 October 2005).
100. TNA PREM 4/3/9 and AIR 20/502, par. 106, "Dowding's Despatch on the Battle of Britain."
101. TNA AIR 2/7355, Park to Dowding, "German Air Attacks on England, 6 Aug–10 Sept," par. 36.
102. Ibid., par. 38.
103. Ibid., par. 39.
104. bid., par. 41.
105. Ibid.
106. TNA AIR 2/7396, Sholto Douglas to Air Ministry, "Pilot Strength in Fighter Command," 7 January 1941.

CHAPTER 5: MY SYSTEM MAY NOT BE PERFECT

1. Wright, *Dowding*, p. 280. "Stuffy" was Dowding's nickname on account of his dour personality.
2. Salmond Papers, B2638, as quoted in Ray, *The Battle of Britain*, p. 139.
3. A. J. P. Taylor, Letters to the Editor, "The Dowding Dismissal: A Key Document Now Revealed," *Times* (London), 22 January 1970, p. 11.
4. LH 1/145, "The Leader of the Few," *Guardian* (London), 16 February 1970, p. 65.
5. Times (London), 16 February 1970, p. 10, as quoted in Ray, *The Battle of Britain*, p. 18.
6. P. Craig, "The Tactical Genius Who Ensured So Much Was Owed to So Few by So Many," *Daily Express* (London), 14 August 2000, pp. 22–23.
7. *Fighting the Blue: The Battle of Britain*, DVD (Espresso TV Ltd., 2005).
8. 1st Viscount Hugh Trenchard (1873–1956). Trenchard was known as "Boom" because of an exceptionally loud voice and abrasive manner. He led the Royal Flying Corps as a major general in World War I and was criticized for sending crews in inadequate aircraft over enemy lines, in conditions of enemy air superiority for little operational gain, during the Fokker Scourge of 1915–16. Trenchard was an important influence on the merging of the Royal Flying Corps and the Royal Naval Air Service into the Royal Air Force in 1918. Chief of Air Staff, 1919–29, and commissioner of the Metropolitan Police, 1931–35, he was recognized as a forceful and effective advocate of strategic bombing and offensive action.
9. Mason, "Well, who did?—and who didn't?" p. 85. Confirmation that Britain was developing more advanced types than France, Italy, and Poland can be found in Angelucci and Matricardi, *World Aircraft: World War II, Part 1*, pp. 9–11, 183–85, 243.
10. Wright, *Dowding*, p. 53.
11. Allen, *Who Won the Battle of Britain?*, pp. 43–45. Also see J. D. Scott, *Vickers: A History* (Weidenfeld & Nicolson, 1962), pp. 201–2. It is not unheard of for manu-

facturers to anticipate and influence design trends in this way. At the time of writing Devonport Management Ltd., based at Devonport, Plymouth, gave publicity to one of their warship designs they claimed will never be built because it does not adhere to British MoD specifications. Even so, they must be hoping that the MoD will alter their future specifications to fit their design.

12. F. Mason, *Battle over Britain* (McWhirter Twins, 1964), p. 86.

13. McKinstry, "How the Spitfire Nearly Missed Its Finest Hour," pp. 17–20.

14. D. Zimmerman, *Britain's Shield: Radar and the Defeat of the Luftwaffe* (Sutton Publishing Ltd., 2001), p. 226.

15. Ibid., pp. 1–10.

16. R. Higham, "Entry for Ashmore, Edward Bailey (1872–1953)," *Oxford Dictionary of National Biography*, cited at http://www.oxforddnb.com/articles/72/72028-article.html (accessed 12 March 2007).

17. Zimmerman, *Britain's Shield*, p. 16.

18. TNA ADM 199/64, "Notes on the Air Defence of Great Britain."

19. TNA ADM 199/64, Appendix B to "Notes on the Air Defence of Great Britain."

20. Allen, *Who Won the Battle of Britain?*, p. 58.

21. Ibid., p. 136.

22. Angelucci and Matricardi, *World Aircraft: World War II, Part I*, pp. 115, 17. Entries for the Dornier Do 17 and Heinkel He III bombers suggest that even without a bomb load, typical speeds would have been closer to 250 mph. It is impossible to be precise about this aspect because of the impact of bomb loads and headwinds. Also see Robinson, *Invasion 1940*, pp. 192–93. Robinson advises that on 15 September 1940, the bombers flew into 90 mph headwinds that cut their speeds by half.

23. TNA AIR 10/5556, *Narrative*, p. 37.

24. Air Chief Marshal Sir Philip Joubert de la Ferté, KCB, CMG, DSO, assistant chief of Air Staff in 1940. Joubert was sufficiently closely associated with Churchill during 1940–43 to be asked to write a contribution on him for C. Eade, ed., *Churchill by His Contemporaries* (The Reprint Society, 1955).

25. Zimmerman, *Britain's Shield*, p. 178.

26. TNA AIR 2/5056, Dowding to Air Ministry, "RDF Policy," 17 January 1940.

27. TNA AVIA 7/183, Unsigned and undated note, headed "Part I. Present Filtering Organisation."

28. TNA AIR 2/5056, Dowding to Air Ministry, 31 January 1940.

29. TNA AIR 19/476, Churchill to Sinclair, 12 October 1940.

30. TNA AIR 19/476, Draft Reply to Prime Minister, undated but probably October/November 1940.

31. TNA AIR 19/476, Churchill to Sinclair, 27 October 1940; Joubert to Assistant Private Secretary and Chief of Air Staff, 30 October 1940; Draft of letter to Prime Minister, 9 November 1940; Assistant Private Secretary to Vice Chief of Air Staff, 9 November 1940; Private Secretary to Vice Chief of Air Staff to Private Secretary of the Secretary of State, 10 November 1940, as quoted in Zimmerman, *Britain's Shield*, p. 210.

32. Zimmerman, *Britain's Shield*, p. 210.

33. TNA AIR 16/677, Dowding to Churchill, 24 October 1940. With regard to Dowding's RDF scenarios, it is plausible that two of 12 Group's RDF stations south of Norwich were well placed to track raids moving toward the Thames estuary, an area within 11 Group. Duxford and Castle Camps fighter stations were also within a few miles of each other on different sides of the boundary, all of which suggests potential for confusion. Dowding's diagram would have clarified the matter but this could not be found at the TNA.

34. J. Colville, *The Fringes of Power: Downing Street Diaries, 1939–45* (Hodder & Stoughton, 1985), p. 246.

35. Zimmermann, *Britain's Shield*, p. 212.

36. TNA AVIA 7/183, unsigned and undated note, headed "Part I. Present Filtering Organisation."

37. TNA AVIA 7/410, J. A. J. Tester to Air Ministry, dated 9 October 1939.

38. TNA AVIA 7/410, E. C. Williams to Sigs 1, Air Ministry, dated 6 August 1940.

39. Hyde, *British Air Policy*, p. 505.

40. TNA AIR 20/2268, From R. Watson-Watt to S of S, Air Ministry, 21 December 1940.

41. TNA AIR 8/577, loose minute sheet from Joubert, 14 January 1941.

42. Zimmerman, *Britain's Shield*, p. 193.

43. TNA AIR 10/5556, *Narrative*, p. 37.

44. Zimmerman, *Britain's Shield*, p. 189.

45. TNA AVIA 7/183, E. C. Williams, "Height Measurement by RDF," 3 June 1940.

46. R. Watson-Watt, *Three Steps to Victory* (Odhams Press, 1957), p. 245.

47. TNA AIR 16/877, "Minutes of a Meeting Held at Air Ministry on 19 October 1940 to Discuss the Calibration of R.D.F. Stations."

48. Zimmerman, *Britain's Shield*, p. 228. This device would revolutionize RDF technology by emitting more radio waves than other short-wave valves, and advanced models were one hundred times more powerful than the original prototype that by itself was twice as powerful as anything the Americans or anyone else possessed.

49. LH 11/1943/27, Dowding to Liddell Hart, 9 May 1943.

50. Lucas, *Flying Colours*, p. 129; Hough and Richards, *Battle of Britain*, p. 321; Ray, *The Battle of Britain*, p. 103.

51. Telegram from Chief-of-Staff, Army, referring to Order Nr. Ic. 5834-1op, 23 June 1917, as quoted in B. Robertson, ed., *Von Richthofen and the Flying Circus* (Harleyford Publications, Ltd., 1964), p. 65. The term "circus" was applied by the Royal Flying Corps because of the garish colors on the aircraft and perhaps because the units were shuttled around the front by train. The Imperial German Air Force, in order to overcome its deteriorating position from mid-1917, began concentrating its best pilots and machines into elite units of four squadrons that could be switched from one area of the front to another, in order to gain local air superiority for an offensive or to be a "fire-brigade" when emergencies arose. It rarely meant very

large formations going aloft. Because there was no radio communication between the aircraft, it was difficult to handle the large formations of forty to fifty aircraft, which sometimes appeared in early evenings, only in good weather, and usually on the German side of the lines.

52. Deighton, *Fighter*, p. 217. Also see A. Price, "Battle of Britain Day," *Royal Air Force Historical Society, no. 29* (2003): 15, as quoted in Robinson, *Invasion 1940*, pp. 192–95.

53. Lucas, *Flying Colours*, pp. 135–36.

54. Deighton, *Fighter*, pp. 271–72.

55. Wright, *Dowding*, p. 221.

56. J. Johnson, *Full Circle: The Story of Air Fighting* (Chatto and Windus, 1964); Johnson and Lucas, *Glorious Summer*.

57. Allen, *Who Won the Battle of Britain?*, pp. 117–18.

58. Lucas, *Flying Colours*, pp. 135–36.

59. Price, "Battle of Britain Day," as quoted in Robinson, *Invasion 1940*, p. 191.

60. Allen, *Who Won the Battle of Britain?*, p. 119.

61. Johnson, *Full Circle*, pp. 236–37.

62. Terraine, *The Right of the Line*, p. 200.

63. TNA 20/5202, Dowding's Despatch, par. 198–204.

64. Allen, *Who Won the Battle of Britain?*, p. 120.

65. TNA AIR 16/281, From Park to AOC Debden; North Weald; Hornchurch; Northolt; Tangmere; Biggin Hill; and Kenley.

66. Galland, *The First and the Last*, p. 100.

67. Allen, *Who Won the Battle of Britain?*, p. 137; A. Price, *A Pictorial History of the Luftwaffe* (Ian Allan, 1970), p. 58.

68. Wright, *Dowding*, p. 126.

69. TNA AIR 10/5556, "The Employment of the Bomber Force in the Event of Invasion of Holland and/or Belgium, Note by the Chief of the Air Staff," 9 May 1940.

70. Price, "Myth and Legend," pp. 22–23.

71. Allen, *Who Won the Battle of Britain?*, p. 137.

72. TNA AIR 2/7355, Park to Dowding, "German Air Attacks on England—8 Aug–10 Sept," par. 31.

73. TNA AIR 2/7355, Dowding to Air Ministry, dated 22 September 1940, par. 4.

74. S. Cox, "The RAF's Response," in P. Addison and J. Crang, *The Burning Blue* (Pimlico, 2000), p. 60.

75. Ray, *The Battle of Britain*, pp. 160–67.

76. TNA AIR 75/63, From Morris Wilson to Ministry of Aircraft Production, BRINY 1763, 4 December 1940. Text includes message from Sir John Slessor to CAS, 2 December 1940.

77. TNA AIR 19/258, Churchill to Sinclair, dated 3 April 1941; APS to S of S, 5 April 1941; "Air Ministry sells Threepenny Thriller," *Daily Herald* (London), 28 March 1941, p. 3. TNA STAT 14/226, From J. M. Parrish, MoI, to C. Plumbley, HMSO,

dated 28 March 1941, indicated that thousands of copies of the illustrated edition were being printed in a wide variety of languages.

78. Posting from John Marquis, "Meeting with the Germans," BBC, 19 November 2003, http://www.bbc.co.uk/dna/ww2/A2061875 (accessed 3 April 2010).

79. TNA AIR 19/258, APS to S of S, dated 5 April 1941. Despite official disapproval, British newspapers did publicize the exploits of outstanding British airmen. Albert Ball, VC, is one of Nottingham's local heroes, and the smashed windscreen of his aircraft was in the Castle Museum when A. J. Cumming saw it in the 1960s.

80. LH 1/245/1, From Liddell Hart to Jerrold, dated 20 February 1942.

81. Lucas, *Flying Colours*, pp. 164–65; Allen, *Who Won the Battle of Britain?*, p. 48. This photograph is widely published and appears in Terraine, *The Right of the Line*, p. 430. Dowding appears uncomfortable, in a bowler hat and carrying an umbrella, amid a group of laughing and relaxed pilots.

82. L. Hudson, *Contrary Imaginations* (Penguin, 1966), as quoted in R. Barry, "History Shakers," *Times Educational Supplement*, 10 January 1998, p. 10.

CHAPTER 6: WRONG-WAY CHARLIE'S NAVY

1. S. Roskill, *Churchill and the Admirals* (Collins, 1977), p. 120.

2. "Our No. 1 Sailor," *Sunday Post* (London), 21 April 1940, p. 18. Furthermore, despite detailed front-page coverage of the Norway campaign on 9 and 25 April 1940 in the *New York Post*, there is no mention of any British commander by name.

3. Strictly speaking, this period begins with the final defeat of Napoleon at Waterloo in 1815, which is the date ascribed to it in P. Kennedy, *The Rise and Fall of British Naval Mastery* (Penguin Books, 2001), p. 150.

4. Lord Montagu of Beaulieu, "Aircraft for Victory: Lord Montagu on Lessons of Jutland Bank," *Times* (London), 17 July 1916, p. 10. The article claimed: "In the future more than half of the work of the Navy would be done in the air. . . . An airship was the equal of at least three cruisers from the scouting point of view and even more destroyers." Montagu claimed the results of Jutland were "not all that could be wished" because there was only one seaplane and no scouts.

5. P. Groves, *Behind the Smoke Screen* (Faber and Faber, 1934). Groves was a noted British airpower theorist during the inter-war period.

6. "Admiralty Reply to Criticism," *Times* (London), 8 November 1940, p. 9. This lengthy article focused on attacks by members of parliament Mr. Stokes and Commander Bower, referring to the culture of secrecy surrounding the loss of the aircraft carrier *Glorious* and other events to protect officers in senior positions. Bower was complaining about being "victimized" because of his efforts to "discuss" the conduct of operations with the First Lord. Much criticism was aimed at the First Sea Lord, who was strongly defended by Mr. Alexander, the First Lord.

7. Hough, *Bless Our Ship*, p. 188.

8. "Master of the Med," *Daily Mirror* (London), 10 February 1941, p. 1. Cunningham was certainly a well-known personality during the war. A blow-up of his photograph appeared on the front page of the *Daily Mirror* following the naval assault on the

Italian naval base at Genoa on 9 February 1941. A random sweep of newspaper front pages in the early phases of the war rarely mentions the names of military commanders. This changed as the war progressed.

9. Churchill, *The Second World War*, vol. 1, *The Gathering Storm* (Penguin, 2005), p. 386.

10. S. Roskill, *The War at Sea, 1939–45* (HMSO, 1954), pp. 267–68.

11. M. Stephen, *The Fighting Admirals: British Admirals of the Second World War* (Leo Cooper, 1991), pp. 44–47.

12. C. Barnett, *Engage the Enemy More Closely: The Royal Navy in the Second World War* (Hodder & Stoughton, 1991), p. 34.

13. D. van der Vat, *The Atlantic Campaign* (Birlinn Ltd., 2001), pp. 227–28.

14. R. Brodhurst, *Churchill's Anchor* (Leo Cooper, 2000), pp. 167, 129. This event is dealt with in detail in G. S. Snyder, *The Royal Oak Disaster* (William Kimber, 1976).

15. J. Levy, "Lost Leader: Admiral of the Fleet Sir Charles Forbes," *The Mariner's Mirror* 88, no. 2 (2002): pp. 186–93.

16. T. A. Heathcote, *The British Admirals of the Fleet, 1734–1995: A Biographical Dictionary* (Leo Cooper, 2002), pp. 84–86.

17. Barnett, *Engage the Enemy*, p. 44.

18. "FP Notes," *The Dollar Magazine*, 1931, pp. 217–18; "Vice-Admiral C. M. Forbes, DSO, CB," *The Dollar Magazine*, 1933; Letter to A. J. Cumming from Janet Carolan, Dollar archivist, 29 January 2005.

19. Bacon, *Britain's Glorious Navy*, pp. 63–64. According to this excellent wartime book on the working of the Royal Navy, each cadet sat an entrance exam conducted by the Civil Service Commissioners. Gunnery training was then conducted for one term at HMS *Excellent*, followed by sea-going training at HMS *Vindictive* for two terms to prepare for an examination in seamanship. Now rated as an acting sub-lieutenant, he would have joined the RN College at Greenwich and taken gunnery, torpedo, and navigation courses at Portsmouth. He would therefore have taken five examinations rated one, two, and three, the results of which determined the date of seniority as sub-lieutenant.

20. "Naval Honours: The Jutland Bank Battle: Sir John Jellicoe's Despatch: Supplement to the London Gazette," *Times* (London), 16 September 1916, p. 3. Jellicoe placed Forbes' name on the list of officers recommended for service in the Battle of Jutland: "My Flag Commander who has always allowed me great assistance. This officer was Executive Officer of HMS *Queen Elizabeth* during the whole period the ship was employed at the Dardanelles."

21. BL, The Jellicoe Papers, Add. 52565 f.117, Letter from Forbes to Jellicoe. The letter also indicated he had been a guest at Jellicoe's home and wanted to be remembered to his children.

22. R. H. S. Bacon, "The Command of the Navy and Its Ships," in Bacon, *Britain's Glorious Navy*, p. 66. The C-in-C normally had, as a personal aide-de-camp, a flag lieutenant responsible for the signaling of the fleet. The flag captain is usually the flagship's captain

but also has the responsibility of organizing the domestic routines of all the ships as well as his own. Bacon described this as a responsible and onerous position.

23. TNA ADM 196/90, "Captain's Confidential Reports," reports by Chatfield on Forbes, July 1925–July 1928 and 6 December 1931.

24. C. Caslon, "Forbes, Sir Charles Morton (1880–1960)," in E. Williams and H. Palmer, eds., *Dictionary of National Biography*, 1951–1960 (Oxford University Press, 1981), pp. 369–71.

25. Bacon, *Britain's Glorious Navy*, pp. 49–66. The Second Sea Lord and chief of Naval Personnel dealt with manning and training issues. The First Sea Lord and chief of Naval Staff were responsible for dealing with larger issues of policy and maritime warfare, and were assisted by the vice chief of the Naval Staff and numerous assistant chiefs of naval staff. The First Lord is, of course, a politician and member of the cabinet.

26. "Obituaries: Sir Charles M. Forbes," *Times* (London), 30 August 1960, p. 15.

27. TNA ADM 1/10225, "Morale in the Home Fleet," Minute dated 13 December 1939 from Director of Personal Services. This has been dealt with in detail in chapter 3, and the problems seem to have been resolved by the beginning of 1940.

28. ROSK 4/50, From Sir Godfrey Style to Roskill, dated 10 March 1979. This can only be a reference to Forbes' chief of staff, Admiral E. L. S. King.

29. IWM 95/5/1, Papers of Commander J. A. J. Dennis, RN, p. 40.

30. Ron Babb, interview by A. J. Cumming, Bishopsteignton, Devon, on 7 April 2004. Mr. Babb was in his nineties but remained a clear and coherent witness. Later in the war, Mr. Babb was made an officer and put in charge of the engine room of a Hunt-class destroyer. Also see ROSK 4/17, Letter from Tovey to Roskill, dated 1 January 1962. The allegation that Forbes may not have visited his ships enough was made tentatively to Roskill by Forbes' successor as C-in-C Home Fleet.

31. Hough, *Bless Our Ship*, p. 96.

32. "Obituaries: Sir Charles M. Forbes," *Times* (London), p. 15.

33. G. D. Franklin, "A Breakdown in Communication: Britain's Over-estimation of Asdic's Capabilities in the 1930s," *The Mariner's Mirror* 84, no. 2 (1988): 202–14. Also see G. D. Franklin, *Britain's Anti-Submarine Capability*, 1919–1939 (Frank Cass & Co., 2003), p. 190.

34. G. Till, *Air Power and the Royal Navy*, 1914–1945 (Jane's, 1979), pp. 179–80.

35. TNA ADM 186/338, *C.B. 3001/36—Progress in Naval Gunnery—Part VII: Gunnery in Foreign Navies* (1936), p. 96. This mentions the Japanese practicing at very long range; 28,000 meters were mentioned in this connection.

36. A. Raven and J. Roberts, *British Battleships of World War II* (Arms and Armour Press, London, 1976), pp. 276–77, as quoted in J. T. Sumida, "The Best Laid Plans: The Development of British Battle-Fleet Tactics, 1919–1942," *International History Review* 14, no. 4 (1992): pp. 681–700.

37. Sumida, "The Best Laid Plans," p. 689.

38. TNA ADM 196/90, "Captain's Confidential Reports," Report by Admiral de Robeck on Forbes, June 1923–August 1924.

39. Great Britain, Admiralty, Naval Staff, Tactical Division, P[rogress in] T[actics], 1935, October 1935, pp. 66–68, as quoted in Sumida, "The Best Laid Plans," p. 690.

40. Till, *Air Power and the Royal Navy*, 1914–45, pp. 144–45, as quoted in Sumida, "The Best Laid Plans," p. 691.

41. LH1/245/32, Sir H. Dowding, "The Great Lesson of This War: Sea-Air Power Is the Key to Victory," *Sunday Chronicle* (London), 29 November 1942.

42. R. H. S. Bacon, "Fleet Battle Tactics," in Bacon, *Britain's Glorious Navy*, p. 252.

43. Brownrigg, "Gunnery in the Royal Navy," in Bacon, *Britain's Glorious Navy*, pp. 221–22.

44. ROSK 6/30, From Forbes to Roskill, 22 February 1950. The German torpedo dropped from the air was fragile and made the bomber vulnerable to AA fire as a result of the slow approach speeds required. Consequently torpedoes were almost exclusively used against merchant ships.

45. Captain E. Altham, RN, "A Discussion: Speed and Gun Power in Warships (Adm. Sir C. Forbes in the Chair)," on Wednesday, 16 March 1938, *RUSI Journal of the United Service Institute for Defence Studies* 83 (1938): 271–90.

46. Levy, "Lost Leader," p. 188.

47. TNA ADM 239/261, "Section L-Factors Affecting Naval Operations," *The Fighting Instructions*, 1939, signed by Forbes and Pound.

48. A. J. Marder, *From the Dardanelles to Oran: Studies of the Royal Navy in War and Peace, 1915–1940* (Oxford University Press, 1974), pp. 53–54, as quoted in Sumida, "The Best Laid Plans," p. 695. Marder noted that he was relying on second-hand testimony and had not actually read *The Fighting Instructions* of 1939, which were not the same as the *Fleet Tactical Instructions*.

49. Naval historians are aware that *The Fighting Instructions* were originally designed in the seventeenth century as a code of conduct for the Royal Navy and intended to place the responsibility for operations on the commander of the fleet. They laid down certain procedures, the most important being the line of battle. They became mandatory in the eighteenth century, and in 1744 Admiral Mathews was court-martialed and cashiered for ignoring them, while in 1756 Admiral Byng missed a chance to save the base at Minorca from the French because he wished to avoid Mathews' fate. Sadly, Minorca was lost and Byng was executed on his own quarter-deck. From this point, sanity gradually re-established itself and by Trafalgar, Nelson was able to keep to the spirit if not the letter of these instructions.

50. TNA ADM 239/261, "The Battlefleet Action," *The Fighting Instructions*, par. 226, pp. 49–50. Also see Marder, *From the Dardanelles to Oran*, pp. 53–54, as quoted in Sumida, "The Best Laid Plans," p. 695.

51. The Pacific war was not an exclusive carrier campaign either. See Till, *Air Power*, p. 180.

52. Ranson, *British Defence Policy*, p. 31.

53. R. V. Brockman, "Dudley Pound," in L. G. Wickam Legg and E. T. Williams, eds., *Dictionary of National Biography, 1941–1950* (Oxford University Press, 1971), pp. 689–92.

54. BL 52565, The Cunningham Papers, Letter from Forbes to Pound, 22 August 1939.

55. TNA ADM 239/261, *The Fighting Instructions*, 1939, p. 10.

56. BL 52565, The Cunningham Papers, Pencilled notation in Forbes' handwriting on letter from Forbes to Pound, 22 August 1939.

57. R. Bennett, *Behind the Battle: Intelligence in the War with Germany*, 1939–45 (Pimlico, 1999), p. 176.

58. Barnett, *Engage the Enemy*, p. 135.

59. F. H. Hinsley, *British Intelligence in the Second World War, vol. 1, Its Influence on Strategy and Operations* (HMSO, 1979), p. 103.

60. ADM 1/10715, From Forbes to Admiralty, "Intelligence on Whereabouts of Main German Forces (Home Fleet Submission No. 49/H.F.991390 of 12 January 1940)," 12 January 1940.

61. Roskill, *The War at Sea*, pp. 82–83. As an armed merchant cruiser, *Rawalpindi* stood no chance against *Scharnhorst* but fought for fourteen minutes, scoring only one hit on the German battle cruiser. It is worth noting that *Scharnhorst* was a battle cruiser armed with nine 11-inch guns, while *Deutschland* was a pocket battleship with six 11-inch guns but was nevertheless generally classified as a battle cruiser.

62. Bennett, *Behind the Battle*, pp. 39–40. Unfortunately this book is badly referenced in that footnote numbers do not appear within the text despite the existence of a footnote section in the back. It has not been possible to say exactly where Bennett got this from.

63. Levy, "Lost Leader," p. 191. The two naval battles at Narvik were notable successes for the Royal Navy. Despite heavy opposition, Captain Warburton-Lee's destroyers sank two German destroyers and damaged "fairly severely" another five on 10 April. Approximately six German-controlled merchant ships were also sunk. A second attack on 12 April by Admiral Whitworth resulted in the loss of eight large German destroyers and one U-boat. See Roskill, *The War at Sea*, pp. 175, 177–78.

64. Churchill, *The Second World War*, vol. 1, *The Gathering Storm*, Appendix R.

65. Raeder, *My Life*, p. 311.

66. Letter from Forbes to Admiralty, 15 June 1940, as quoted in Roskill, *The War at Sea*, p. 198.

67. "Admiralty Reply," *Times* (London), 8 November 1940, p. 9. Aircraft statistics from Levy, "Lost Leader," p. 190.

68. Roskill, *The War at Sea*, p. 198.

69. Ibid., p. 195.

70. TNA ADM 1/113, Appreciation from Director of Plans to First Sea Lord, 13 January 1941.

71. ROSK 6/30, Letter from Forbes to Roskill, 28 January 1950.

72. W. M. Stoneman, "Oslo Falls to Germans: Sea, Air Battles Raging," *New York Post*, 9 April 1940, p. 1.

73. ROSK 4/42, Letter from Captain Bonatz to Roskill, 12 February 1975.

74. ROSK 4/49, Letter from Hamilton on HMS *Aurora* to Forbes, 27 May 1940.

75. Roskill, *The War at Sea*, p. 202.

76. Churchill, *The Second World War*, vol. 1, *The Gathering Storm*, p. 339.

77. ROSK 4/75, From Mr. E. A. Seal, Ministry of Works, to Vice Admiral Sir Ralph Edwards, "Draft minute to the Prime Minister."

78. A. Danchev and D. Todman, eds., *War Diaries, 1939–1945: The Diaries of Field Marshal Lord Alanbrooke* (Weidenfeld and Nicolson, 2001), pp. 318, 401, 409–10, 444–46, 450–51, 456, 458–59, 472, 483, 515, 528, 532, and 568. Churchill's C-in-C Home Forces and later CIGS made many scathing references to Churchill's inability to grasp details, to relate one front to another, or to think in the strategic long-term.

79. Ismay, *The Memoirs of Lord Ismay*, p. 218.

80. ROSK 5/124, Letter from Controller of the Navy Ralph Edwards to Roskill, 28 July 1954. Also see "Admiralty Reply," *Times* (London), 8 November 1940, p. 9. Edwards may have been among the group of younger naval officers on the operations staff said to have approached Commander Bower, MP, about the conditions of excessive secrecy surrounding the evacuation of Norway and expressing "grave disquiet" regarding the "whole conduct of naval operations" by senior officers.

81. ROSK 4/17, Letter from Sir John Tovey to Roskill commenting on draft chapter, dated 1 January 1962. Phillips commanded the naval task force comprising the *Prince of Wales* and *Repulse* sent to the Far East in 1941. Japanese land-based aircraft sank both ships and Phillips, who went down with the ship, has been castigated for stubbornly pressing on without an air umbrella.

82. BL 525565, Letter from Pound to Forbes enclosing letter from Pound to Vian.

83. TNA ADM 1/10556, From Forbes to Admiralty, 4 June 1940.

84. TNA ADM 1/10556, Minute from DOD (H), June 1940.

85. TNA ADM 1/10556, Minute from ACNS (H), 4 June 1940; Minute of D of P, 15 June 1940; DOD (H), June 1940; and D of P, 17 June 1940.

86. G. Till, "Naval Power," in R. Holmes, ed., *The Oxford Companion to Military History* (Oxford University Press, 2001), p. 633. Raiding hardly represented a policy of unqualified success. The Walcheren raid of 1809 was one of the worst disasters in British military history, with the loss of 23,000 men to disease. The Dieppe raid of 1942 cost 3,367 casualties, 106 aircraft, several landing craft, and a destroyer.

87. Churchill, *The Second World War*, vol. 2, *Their Finest Hour*, p. 275. The bodies are generally believed to have been the result of a disastrous German embarkation exercise where the landing craft capsized as a result of bad weather.

88. TNA ADM 1/10566, "Notes of Conference held in First Sea Lord's Room at 15.30, Friday 7 June 1940."

89. TNA ADM 1/10556, Minute of ACNS (H), 18 June 1940; messages to C-in-C Home Fleet from First Sea Lord, 23 and 24 June 1940; and minute from S. H. Phillips, 26 June 1940.

90. R. McLeod and D. Kelly, eds., *The Ironside Diaries, 1937–40* (Constable, 1962), pp. 188–89.

91. Erskine Childers, *The Riddle of the Sands* (Dent, 1979; first published by Smith, Elder & Co., 1903).

92. "We Never Surrender," *Daily Mirror* (London), 5 June 1940, p. 1; and "We Shall Fight On Unconquerable," *Daily Sketch* (London), 18 June 1940, p. 1.

93. "Leadership, Give Us Leadership," *Daily Mirror* (London), 18 June 1940, p. 1.

94. Churchill, *The Second World War*, vol. 2, *Their Finest Hour*, p. 255. Minute from Fuehrer's Headquarters, 16 August, 1940, *Fuehrer Conferences*, p. 128, suggests that ten thousand troops were to be landed the first day of the invasion. Perhaps ten thousand airborne troops could be added to this, making up to 20,000 troops landing on the first day.

95. Colville, *The Fringes of Power*, p. 192, entry for 12 July 1940.

96. Brodhurst, *Churchill's Anchor*, p. 167.

97. Alanbrooke, *War Diaries*, p. 108. The entry of the C-in-C Home Forces for 15 September 1940 does not show much confidence in the army's ability to defeat an invasion, even though Brooke later denied this was a true representation of what he really thought at the time. Also see T. Ben-Moshe, *Churchill: Strategy and History* (Harvester-Wheatsheaf, 1992), p. 274. Ben-Moshe believes the history of the later D-day planning suggests the British were still wary of another large-scale confrontation with the Wehrmacht. If it had been left to the British, there would not have been a D-day in 1944.

98. Roskill, *The War at Sea*, p. 17.

99. TNA CAB 120/438, From Churchill to General Ironside and others, 10 July 1940.

100. From Churchill to Pound and others, 9 November 1939, as quoted in Churchill, *The Second World War*, vol. 1, *The Gathering Storm*, Appendix II, p. 668.

101. Minute from Churchill to S of S for War, 7 July 1940; further concern is noted in a minute to Pound, 27 July 1940, as quoted in Churchill, *The Second World War*, vol. 2, *Their Finest Hour*, pp. 237–38.

102. Minute from Churchill to Pound, dated 4 August 1940, as quoted in Churchill, *The Second World War*, vol. 2, *Their Finest Hour*, p. 531.

103. Ibid., p. 639.

104. Ibid., p. 489. As indicated in a previous chapter, the radar installed in the heavy ships for the purpose of giving early warning against air attack was ineffective in the fjords, making AA defense even less effective than usual.

105. Roskill, *The War at Sea*, p. 257.

106. Ibid., p. 257.

107. Winterbotham, *The Ultra Secret*, p. 59.

108. BL 52565, Letter from Pound to Cunningham, 20 September 1940.

109. Levy, "Lost Leader," p. 193.

110. J. Levy, "Holding the Line: The Royal Navy's Home Fleet in the Second World War" (PhD thesis, University of Swansea, 2001), pp. 118–25.

111. Hough, *Bless Our Ship*, p. 104; also see the chronological table, p. 193. Kelly was heavily damaged on six occasions, two of which resulted from collisions with other British ships. She was finally sunk by dive-bombers at the Battle of Crete.

112. Churchill, *The Second World War*, vol. 1, *The Gathering Storm*, p. 339.

113. ROSK 4/49, Letter from Forbes to Godfrey Style, 6 February 1947.

114. ROSK 4/17, Tovey to Roskill, dated 1 January 1962.

115. "The Navy's Task Greatest Ever Faced: Help for Greece," *Times* (London), 30 October 1940, p. 2.

116. "Admiralty Reply to Criticism," *Times* (London), 8 November 1940, p. 9.

117. Leland Stowe, "Britain Sent 1,500 Raw Troops without Artillery or Planes to Norway . . . and Slaughter," *New York Post,* 25 April 1940, p. 1.

118. Bennett, *Behind the Battle,* pp. 67–69. Bennett suggests that the *Bismarck* was sunk in May 1941 because a variety of intelligence sources came together, including "the newest source of all, high-grade Sigint, [which] came to the rescue in the nick of time."

CHAPTER 7: WHY WE FIGHT? THE BATTLE OF BRITAIN

1. Press release from Ministry of Information Films Division in Imperial War Museum, as quoted in A. Calder, *The Myth of the Blitz* (Pimlico, 1997), p. 248.

2. Ben-Moshe, *Churchill: Strategy and History,* p. 125. Ben-Moshe described this as "a supreme strategic objective." He also pointed out that it was Roosevelt who approached Chamberlain, Halifax, and Churchill in 1939, but the only Briton to show real interest in "institutionalizing personal contact was Churchill, who had always attached importance to U.S. involvement in Europe and to Anglo-American cooperation."

3. TNA CAB 65/13, confidential annexes, WM (40) 139/1, 140, 141/1, 142, 145/1, as quoted in D. Reynolds, *In Command of History: Churchill Fighting and Writing the Second World War* (Allen Lane, 2004), p. 169; Churchill, *The Second World War,* vol. 2, *Their Finest Hour,* p. 157. Churchill claimed that the question of fighting on was never "on the War Cabinet agenda," and said they were "too busy to waste time upon such unreal academic issues." See also C. Ponting, *1940: Myth and Reality* (Hamish Hamilton Ltd., 1990), pp. 103–18. Ponting deals cynically with Churchill's version of events, and uses Chamberlain's diary entry of 26 May 1940 as evidence that Churchill was prepared to make peace by sacrificing Malta, Gibraltar, and some African colonies if we could "get out of this jam." Churchill vetoed an apparent peace initiative made by Lord Halifax and R. A. B. Butler behind his back at a cabinet meeting on 19 June 1940. Churchill dominated the cabinet from the time of the attack on the French fleet at Oran on 2 July 1940, and later that month he quashed peace feelers put out by the British ambassador to the United States, Lord Lothian. Also see J. Charmley, *Churchill: The End of Glory* (Hodder & Stoughton, 1993), p. 405. Charmley points out that having to consider the idea of a negotiated peace did not make Churchill less resolute, but to keep Lord Halifax in the cabinet he needed to indicate the possibility of a compromise peace if the circumstances were right.

4. R. P. Post, "Britain Told Not to Count on Heavy U.S. Aid Till 1942," *Washington Post,* 27 December 1942, p. 2.

5. J. P. Kennedy, unpublished diplomatic memoir, quoted in Michael Beschloss, *Kennedy and Roosevelt: The Uneasy Alliance* (Norton, 1980), pp. 198–200, as quoted in D. Stafford, *Roosevelt & Churchill: Men of Secrets* (Abacus, 1999), pp. xvi–xvii.

6. D. Stafford, *Churchill & Secret Service* (Abacus, 2001), pp. 85–88.

7. First World War Debt (Hansard, 23 October 2002), "Written Answer to Lord Laird," http://hansard.millbanksystems.com/written_answers/2002/oct/23/first-world-war-debt (accessed 15 May 2009).

8. J. G. Utley, "Franklin Roosevelt and Naval Strategy, 1933–41," as quoted in E. J. Marolda, *FDR and the American Navy* (Macmillan Press, 1998), p. 51. Utley described FDR as a man who believed that "American prosperity and security depended on access to the raw materials and markets of the world" (p. 49). J. R. Leutze, *Bargaining for Supremacy: Anglo-American Naval Collaboration, 1937–41* (University of North Carolina Press, 1997), p. 7. Leutze believes that FDR's desire for collaboration on naval issues was rooted in Japanese renunciation of all naval treaty limits in 1936.

9. C. Whitham, "Seeing the Wood for the Trees: The British Foreign Office and the Anglo American Trade Agreement of 1938," *Twentieth Century British History* 16, no. 1 (2005): 29–51, http://tcbh.oupjournals.org/cgi/content/abstract/16/1/29 (accessed 25 April 2005).

10. Leutze, *Bargaining for Supremacy*, p. 5.

11. D. Hobson, *The National Wealth: Who Gets What in Britain* (Harper Collins, 1999), pp. 842–44, 869.

12. "The Press: Britain's Newspapers," *Time*, 29 April 1940, http://www.time.com/time/magazine/article/0,9171,794999,00.html (accessed 22 May 2009).

13. An impressionistic survey of the December 1940 issues of the *San Francisco Chronicle* at the National Newspaper Library, microfilm reference MA191, seems to confirm this. Even a year before Pearl Harbor, the comic strip "Tracey and the Pirates" showed Japanese soldiers as the villains of their stories.

14. The Washington Post Company, http://www.washpostco.com/history-history-history-1925.htm (accessed 8 June 2005).

15. Colville, *The Fringes of Power*, p. 732.

16. Hobson, *The National Wealth*, pp. 842, 844.

17. D. Woodruff, "Bracken, Brendan Rendall Viscount Bracken (1901–1958)," in E. T. Williams and H. M. Palmer, eds., *Dictionary of National Biography, 1951–60* (Oxford University Press, 1971), pp. 135–37. A former director of publishers Eyre & Spottiswoode, Bracken ran several newspapers and was editor of the *Banker*. His biographer declared it difficult to estimate the value of his influence but acknowledged his role in the prompting of appointments and patronage. It was also claimed "he was in his element at the centre of power . . . one of the two or three men closest to Churchill." Bracken became First Lord of the Admiralty toward the end of the war.

18. Calder, *The Myth of the Blitz*, p. 247.

19. D. C. Stephenson, "Excerpts from Our Letters: Unfair Applause," *Washington Post*, 28 July 1940, p. 6.

20. Dr. G. Gallup, "The Gallup Poll: 60% Favor Greater Aid to England," *Washington Post,* 29 December 1940, p. 11.

21. J. C. Schneider, *Should America Go to War?* (University of North Carolina Press, 1989), p. xviii.

22. Interview with LeSueur, BBC WAC R34/472/1, Stewart (MoI) to Controllers of Programmes and Home Service, BBC, 2 January 1941, as quoted in N. J. Cull, *Selling War: The British Propaganda Campaign against American "Neutrality" in World War II* (Oxford University Press, 1995), p. 114. The MoI decided at the end of 1940 that the line had outlived its usefulness and asked the BBC to discourage its use in broadcasts.

23. "Rise of Aid-to-Britain Sentiment," *Washington Post*, 29 December 1940, p. 11. This graph is imprecisely drawn but a figure of 88 percent seems reasonable.

24. Gallup, "The Gallup Poll: 60% Favor Greater Aid to England," p.11.

25. Professor Stanley Schultz, "'Dr. New Deal' Becomes 'Dr. Win-the-War,'" lecture 20 in American History 102: Civil War to the Present, http://us.history.wisc.edu/hist102/lectures/lecture20.html, University of Wisconsin (accessed 1 May 2002).

26. Post, "Britain Told Not to Count on Heavy U.S. Aid Till 1942," p. 2.

27. PA BBK/D/496, From Rothermere to Beaverbrook, 16 July 1940.

28. "Sectional Vote on U.S. Entering War, Giving Greater Aid to Britain," *Washington Post*, 29 December 1940, p. 11.

29. TNA INF1/435, "Annex 1 to the Minutes of the 20th Meeting of the Inter-Allied Information Committee, June 3rd—Modifications in the Inter-Allied Information Service."

30. L. Harper, *Chicago Defender*, 1940, as quoted in Schneider, *Should America Go to War?*, pp. xvii, 44.

31. Gallup, "The Gallup Poll: Voters Prefer Roosevelt if British Lose," *Washington Post*, 4 September 1940, p. 1.

32. E. K. Lindley, "Our Best Defense: Bolstering of British Morale," *Washington Post*, 20 December 1940, p. 17.

33. J. Harris and M. J. Trow, Hess: *The British Conspiracy* (André Deutsch Ltd., 1999). This is a central premise of conspiracy thrillers on this topic.

34. Churchill to Roosevelt, dated 8 December 1940, as quoted in Churchill, *The Second World War,* vol. 2, Their Finest Hour, pp. 494–501.

35. Churchill to Roosevelt, 20 May 1940, ibid., pp. 50–51; S. Conn and B. Fairchild, *The Framework of Hemisphere Defence*, pp. 34–35, as quoted in Leutze, *Bargaining for Supremacy*, p. 75.

36. Dr. G. Gallup, "U.S. Public Favors Occupation of Islands in Caribbean if Hitler Wins, Poll Shows: 87% Would Take Over Foreign Holdings near Canal," *Washington Post*, 21 July 1940, p. 2.

37. "'Act of Havana Text': How Americas Will Act in Emergency," *Washington Post*, 30 July 1940, p. 7.

38. Memorandum of conversation between Cordell Hull and Lord Lothian, 24 June 1940, Franklin D. Roosevelt Library, New York, Box 7, Roosevelt Papers, as quoted in Leutze, *Bargaining for Supremacy*, p. 104.

39. TNA FO A 3297/2961/45, Letter from Poynton to Balfour, 14 July 1940, as quoted in Leutze, *Bargaining for Supremacy*, p. 105.

40. Spartacus, "Walter Lippmann," http://www.spartacus.schoolnet.co.uk/USAlippmann. htm (accessed 8 June 2005).

41. W. Lippmann, "Today and Tomorrow: Havana and the Battle of Britain," Washington Post, 30 July 1940, p. 7. Lippman was once a "darling" of the "liberal intelligentsia" and a critic of the British Empire. See Stafford, *Roosevelt & Churchill*, pp. 147, 180.

42. TNA FO 371, "Address by the British Ambassador to the United States, The Most Hon. the Marquess of Lothian, at Yale University Alumni Luncheon on Wednesday, June 19th, 1940."

43. H. Brogan, *The Penguin History of the United States of America* (Penguin Books, 1990), p. 571. Cordell Hull, Roosevelt's secretary of state, was known for his inclination to lecture "unreceptive ears . . . on the glories of free trade."

44. J. G. Norris, "Bill Now Goes to Conference; Would Register 24,000,000 Men, Delay Service Pending Drive to Recruit Army," *Washington Post,* 7 September 1940, p. 1. The Burke-Wadsworth Bill went before Congress in September, calling for the immediate registration of 24 million men between 21 and 44 years old. This article suggests a degree of presidential caution insofar as it allowed a sixty-day trial of voluntary enlistment for 400,000 volunteers. Only if this failed would the president draft enough men to make up the difference. Critics claimed the figure was unattainable and the trial was a ploy to delay the draft issue until after the November election. Also see Brogan, *The Penguin History of the United States of America*, p. 540.

45. Stafford, *Roosevelt & Churchill*, p. 75.

46. "Goering Speaks to America: Honeyed Words and Boasts," *Times* (London), 31 July 1940, p. 3. Karl H. von Wiegand was one of William Randolph Hearst's best-known correspondents. Wiegand was billed as the "personal acquaintance of Chancellor Adolf Hitler for more than 17 years [who] has had more interviews with the German Chancellor than any other American"; see "The Press: Report from Madrid," *Time,* http://www.time.com/time/magazine/article/0,9171,792053,00. html (accessed 5 April 2010).

47. "U.S. Acts Swiftly to Start Bases; Britons Hail America as Ally; Leaders of Congress Favor Deal," and "British Pledge Never to Sink or Surrender Fleet," *Washington Post*, 4 September 1940, pp. 1, 4.

48. Leutze, *Bargaining for Supremacy,* pp. 126–27.

49. E. T. Folliard, "Churchill Put Spirit in Britain," *Washington Post*, 2 December 1940, p. 7.

50. "Europe's War in Review: A Year of Triumph for Adolf Hitler: Can the British Take All the Germans Have to Give?," *Washington Post*, 1 September 1940, pp. 1, 3.

51. An International News Service Correspondent, "Pilots Have What It Takes: RAF Oblivious to Odds, Small Force Takes on 200 Nazis," *Washington Post*, 3 September 1940, pp. 1–2.

52. "British Say They're Winning Control of the Air from Nazis," *Washington Post*, 2 September 1940, pp. 1, 5.

53. F. R. Kelly, "Cup of Tea Saves RAF Pilot as Nazis Attack for Revenge," *Washington Post*, 2 September 1940, p. 5.

54. "British down 175 Raiders," *Daily Mirror* (New York), 16 September 1940, p. 1.

55. J. G. Norris, "New Weapons, Tactics Marked Warfare in 1940," *Washington Post*, 29 December 1940, p. 6.

56. TNA AIR 75/63, From Morris Wilson to Ministry of Aircraft Production, BRINY 1763, 4 December 1940. Text includes message from Sir John Slessor to CAS, dated 2 December 1940.

57. The Associated Press, "British Claim Toll of 1,967 Nazi Raiders: Review of War's First Year Says RAF Has Proved Superiority," *Washington Post*, 3 September 1940, p. 5.

58. C. Webster and N. Frankland, *The Strategic Air Offensive against Germany, 1939–45* (HMSO, 1961)., p. 58.

59. J. MacDonald, "Berlin Shakes under Terrific RAF Blasting," *Washington Post*, 1 September 1940, p. 2.

60. "German Forests Blasted," *Washington Post*, 5 September 1940, p. 5.

61. "Four-Motored Nazi Planes Blast London," *Washington Post*, 3 September 1940, p. 5.

62. PA BBK/D/496, From Rothermere to Beaverbrook, 19 July 1940.

63. International News Service, "Knox Sees Britain Surviving Attack," *Washington Post*, 8 September 1940, p. 8.

64. Notes given by Admiral Richardson to Secretary Knox, 12 September 1940, as quoted in Leutze, *Bargaining for Supremacy*, p. 181.

65. "Britain Will Not Lose War, U.S. Air Corps Observer Asserts after Return," *Washington Post*, 4 December 1940, p. 1.

66. PA BBK/D/414, Minute from Beaverbrook to the Prime Minister, 26 December 1940. Churchill described Purvis as "highly competent and devoted," in Churchill, *The Second World War*, vol. 2, *Their Finest Hour*, p. 23.

67. PA BBK/D/414, Précis for Prime Minister. 27 June 1940.

68. Leutze, *Bargaining for Supremacy*, p. 79.

69. R. C. Albright, "British Need Cash, Morgenthau Says," *Washington Post*, 18 December 1940, p. 2.

70. "From Our Own Correspondent, Help from America: Colonel Knox's Warning: U.S. and Axis Navies Compared," *Times* (London), 18 January 1941, p. 4.

71. TNA FO 954/29A, Telegram from Lothian to Churchill, 29 November 1940.

72. "Roosevelt Proposes to Lease U.S. Arms," *Washington Post*, 18 December 1940, pp. 1–2.

73. "Propagandists for Britain: Tributes to USA Correspondents," *Times* (London), 23 July 1941, p. 2.

74. TNA PREM 1/439, Letter from W. Will to Sir J. Reith, 1 April 1940.

75. TNA INF 1/849, MoI Policy Committee Minutes, 31 July 1940.

76. From Our Diplomatic Correspondent, "American Complaints of the Censorship: Grievances of Correspondents in London," *Times* (London), 28 November 1940, p. 5.

77. A. Aldgate and J. Richards, *Britain Can Take It* (Basil Blackwell, 1986), p. 4. Nevertheless, the official situation was confusing. At one point the MoI was held to have no responsibility for the "communication of news to the press or for press censorship." Probably as a result of a complaint from the Newspaper and Periodical Emergency Council in April 1940 deploring the censorship chaos, procedures were strengthened to improve departmental liaison.

78. M. Balfour, *Propaganda and War* (Routledge & Kegan Paul, 1979), p. 64. The remark is attributed to Alfred Duff Cooper.

79. P. Knightley, *The First Casualty Is Truth: The War Correspondent as Hero and Myth-Maker from the Crimea to Kosovo* (Prion Books, 2001), p. 244.

80. "The Country Is against Stricter Press Control," *News Chronicle* (London), 26 August 1940, p. 1. This article reflected underlying cynicism about "official" news. One unidentified British newspaper was said to have published Gallup evidence on public opinion to back up their argument that the public distrusted official control over the news.

81. TNA INF 1/849, Minutes of MoI Policy Committee, 22 July 1940.

82. TNA FO 954/29A, Letter from R. C. Lindsay, Washington, to Anthony Eden, 7 February 1938.

83. Knightley, *The First Casualty*, p. 244.

84. E. Sevareid, *Not So Wild a Dream* (Athenaeum, 1978), pp. 165–69.

85. Ibid., pp. 177–78.

86. Stafford, *Churchill & Roosevelt*, pp. 49, 123.

87. Edward R. Murrow, CBS broadcast, 1 October 1940, as quoted in Knightley, *The First Casualty*, p. 263.

88. "Mr. Quentin Reynolds," *Times* (London), 18 March 1965, p. 14.

89. PA BBK/D/404, Letter from Beaverbrook to Reynolds, 10 November 1940.

90. Cull, *Selling War,* p. 182.

91. PA BBK/D/404, Telegram from Reynolds to Winchell, 9 August 1940. Winchell was a controversial figure credited with inventing the gossip column. Despite dying in disgrace, Winchell was once a popular figure in America with a syndicated column appearing in more than two thousand daily newspapers and a weekly radio show. His career went into decline with the rise of television and his public support for Senator McCarthy's communist witch-hunt in the 1950s.

92. Cull, *Selling War*, pp. 80, 132. Cull says that Winchell was one of several American reporters fed rumors by British intelligence agencies regarding Nazi oppression in occupied countries.

93. Spartacus, "Heywood Broun," http://www.spartacus.schoolnet.co.uk/USAbrounH.htm (accessed 8 June 2005).

94. TNA FO 371/24231, A3961/26/45, Hopkinson to MoI, 17 August 1940, as quoted in Cull, *Selling War*, p. 89.

95. Cull, *Selling War*, p. 90.

96. Charles A. Lindbergh in Stephen Ives, producer/director, *The American Experience*: *Lindbergh* (Insignia Films, 1990), Des Moines Speech, available at http://www.pbs.org/wgbh/amex/lindbergh/filmmore/reference/primary/desmoinesspeech.html (accessed 5 April 2010).

97. TNA FO 371/24321, A3799/26/45, Halifax to Sinclair, 19 August 1940, as quoted in Cull, *Selling War*, p. 90.

98. Interview with Barry Cornwell, as quoted in P. Knightley, *The First Casualty*, p.258.

99. E. F. Heyn, "The American Aces," in Bruce Robertson, ed., *Air Aces of the 1914–18 War* (Harleyford Publications, 1959), pp. 96–97.

100. C. Cook, "The Myth of the Aviator and the Flight to Fascism," *History Today* 53, no. 12 (2003): 41.

101. Cull, *Selling War,* p. 47.

102. Hough, *Bless Our Ship*, pp. 31, 188.

103. Cull, *Selling War*, p. 113.

104. PA BBK/H/298, Letter from M. Milder of Warner Bros., London, to Beaverbrook, 29 July 1940.

105. As quoted by P. M. Taylor, "Propaganda in International Politics, 1919–1939," in K. R. M. Short, ed., *Film and Radio Propaganda in World War II* (Croom Helm, 1983), p. 35.

106. Cull, *Selling War*, p. 90.

107. Charles A. Lindbergh in Stephen Ives, producer/director, *The American Experience: Lindbergh* (Insignia Films, 1990), Des Moines Speech, available at http://www.pbs.org/wgbh/amex/lindbergh/filmmore/reference/primary/desmoinesspeech.html (accessed 5 April 2010).

108. Cull, *Selling War*, p. 51.

109. PA BBK/H/298, Letter from Jarratt to Beaverbrook, 23 June 1941.

110. F. Capra, *The Name above the Title* (W. H. Allen, 1972), p. 326.

111. Cull, *Selling War*, p. 329–36.

112. Capra, *The Name above the Title*, p. 353–56.

113. Imperial War Museum, Film and Video Archive, ADM 10, *The Battle of Britain.*

114. Ben-Moshe, *Churchill: Strategy and History*, p. 308. Ben-Moshe suggests other reasons for failing to produce war aims. First, he mentions the "memories of the misunderstandings supposedly produced by Wilson's Fourteen Points" always being on the minds of Churchill and Roosevelt. Second, the joint formulation of war aims would have been time consuming and had the potential to damage Anglo-American relations.

115. TNA STAT 14/226, From J. M. Parrish, MoI, to C. Plumbley, HMSO, 28 March 1941.

116. *The Battle of Britain: 8 August–31 October 1940* (HMSO, 1941), p. 7. The pamphlet attempted to describe in detail "the method of defence" but apologetically

stated it was not easy to do this without giving away "state secrets." There was no mention of RDF and it merely remarked: "Information regarding the approach of the enemy is obtained by a variety of methods." Bearing in mind the Germans already had a detailed knowledge of RDF and in 1941 would have their own very effective radar chain in operation, the security aspects seem somewhat exaggerated, but the secrecy probably reflected a fundamental British distrust of the perceived inability of Americans to keep secrets.

117. TNA INF 1/849, Report of Planning Committee on a Home Morale Campaign, 21 June 1940. Not that it should be assumed the British press was totally cowed by official control—the effect of "approved" articles such as a commentary on the failure of Napoleon to invade England in the *Evening Standard*, 19 June 1940, was said to have been "offset by articles from precisely the wrong point of view (e.g., recent leading articles in the *Daily Mail*), or by an alarmist presentation of the news (e.g., air raids). No directive, however full, can prevent this."

118. R. Overy, "The Few Versus the Very Few," *BBC History Magazine* 1, no. 2 (2000): 18.

CHAPTER 8: CONCLUSION

1. R. Holmes, "The Man Who Made His Own History," *BBC History Magazine* 6, no. 4 (2005): 36–40.

2. J. Ellis, *The World War II Databook: The Essential Facts and Figures for All the Combatants* (Aurum Press, 1993), Table 74. This source gives 5,553 Merchant Navy crewmen casualties in British registered ships in 1940. I have divided this by 366 days to reach a daily figure of 151.72 and multiplied this by the 114 days of the Battle of Britain to reach the total of 1,730.

3. Single-engined Fighter Pilot Strength, RAF and German Air Force: Tables 1 & 2, in R. Overy, *The Battle of Britain: The Myth and the Reality* (Penguin, 2000), p. 162. For example, on 1 August 1940, the Germans had 869 operational pilots, and on 17 August 1940 the RAF had 1,379. Even on 1 September the Germans had only 735 as against the RAF's 1,492 for 31 August 1940.

4. C. Meyer, "Farewell to a Mortgage from Hell," *Sunday Times* (London), 31 December 2006, quoted in City Commentators, *The Week*, 6 January 2007, p. 32; A. Cumming, "We'll get by with a little help from our friends: The Battle of Britain and the Pilot in Anglo-American Relations, 1940–45," *European Journal of American Culture* 26, no. 1 (2007): pp. 11–26.

5. Reynolds, *In Command of History*, p. 186.

6. LH1/245/32, Sir H. Dowding, "The Great Lesson of this War: Sea-Air Power is the Key to Victory," *Sunday Chronicle* (London), 29 November 1942.

Index

About the Author

Anthony J. Cumming was born in Sussex, England, in 1953. He entered higher education after a career in local government and the British civil service and gained his MA in naval history at the University of Exeter. He obtained his PhD at the University of Plymouth in 2006, where he is now an honorary research fellow. That year, he also won the University of London's prestigious Julian Corbett Prize for Research in Modern Naval History for his essay on the ability of the wartime Royal Navy to withstand air attacks. Cumming is interested in all aspects of modern military history and has published scholarly articles in several academic journals. *The Royal Navy and the Battle of Britain* is his first book. He is married and lives in Devon, England.